PROTECTED

by Joshua Hale

Protected

Trilogy Christian Publishers

A Wholly Owned Subsidiary of Trinity Broadcasting Network

2442 Michelle Drive, Tustin, CA 92780

Copyright © 2024 by Joshua Hale

Scripture quotations marked ESV are taken from the ESV® Bible (The Holy Bible, English Standard Version®), copyright © 2001 by Crossway Bibles, a publishing ministry of Good News Publishers. Used by permission. All rights reserved.

All rights reserved, including the right to reproduce this book or portions thereof in any form whatsoever.

For information, address Trilogy Christian Publishing

Rights Department, 2442 Michelle Drive, Tustin, Ca 92780.

Trilogy Christian Publishing/ TBN and colophon are trademarks of Trinity Broadcasting Network.

For information about special discounts for bulk purchases, please contact Trilogy Christian Publishing.

Trilogy Disclaimer: The views and content expressed in this book are those of the author and may not necessarily reflect the views and doctrine of Trilogy Christian Publishing or the Trinity Broadcasting Network.

10 9 8 7 6 5 4 3 2 1

Library of Congress Cataloging-in-Publication Data is available.

ISBN 979-8-89041-788-6

ISBN 979-8-89041-789-3 (e-book)

TABLE OF CONTENTS

A Subconscious Mission I Gave Myself..................................7

Be Protected...9

Protect Yourself..15

Protect Your Faith..17

Should I Have Left This Part out of the Book?........................19

Keep Going..23

With Eyes That Look Toward Heaven
    And One Wing in the Fire...25

The Inevitable Changes Within...27

This Is Reality...29

This Is Me..43

Just a Kid and His Treehouse..55

The Symphony of Young Life..61

You Don't Have to Change Your Accent..................................79

The Mayor, the Man, the Chief, and a Pall-Mall Cigarette:
    How I Got Hired As a Police Officer..............................83

Double Down on My Decision..87

Know When to Get Up From the Table....................................89

Don't Insult Your Host..93

Another Side of Human Life..95

Noche de Muertos en Michoacán...I Gained Respect for
    Religious Freedom...111

I Hate Water Polo: The Kentucky Police Corps Edition.................117

Night Terrors...121

Jesus, Superheroes, and People Just Trying to
    Do the Right Thing.................................139

Just People Trying to Do the Right Thing.......143

Trains and Railroads.................................147

Real World Danger....................................149

The Serious Side of the Tracks....................151

The Aftermath Memories.............................153

The Unmistakable Sound of the Thunder Stick
    That Can Go Boom................................155

Is That a Monkey?....................................161

The Great Masquerade................................167

Chasing Demons.......................................187

Unexpected Answers When I Didn't Ask the Question.....193

Healing from Unexpected Places....................195

The Good Ole Days of Policing.....................199

"Have You Ever Killed Anyone?"....................205

Silent Machines and Life-Changing Surprises.....213

Love Notes to My Girls..............................221

    To My Wife.......................................222

    To My Daughters..................................223

A Prized Possession..................................225

More than Child's Play..............................227

Hunting the Predators...............................239

A Real Issue...245

Letters from Prison..249

Officer Down..253

Welcome to Supervision...273

Crazy Supervisor Moments..279

The Baby on a Doorstep..281

"Merry Christmas to All," Said the Grinch....................................283

There Is So Much More to Say...287

"Talk to Me": Stories from a Police Negotiator............................289

Operation: Save Bambi..297

Working During the COVID-19 Pandemic.....................................299

Bodies All Around Us..305

The Day God Made Me Lay Down...309

Vacation Brought Motivation...321

Return to Work..323

A Lot to Be Thankful For, and People
      Who Have Gotten Me There...325

A List Incomplete..327

The First Great Ride: The Comeback...329

Learning When to Keep Your Mouth Shut....................................331

When One Door Closes...Retirement...333

You Will Never Find That Perfect Bottle of
      Root Beer Again: Don't Stop Looking.......................................339

The Healing Waters...341

Epilogue..347

———————∞———————

A Subconscious Mission I Gave Myself

There are a lot of people I should say "I am sorry" to. There are a lot of people who should say they are sorry to me, but I will never get that apology. In writing this book, I have done a lot of reflecting on my life and what has led me to where I am today. I might as well get over expecting an apology from people. I have given my heart over to Jesus and tried to let Him replace my insecurities, but that doesn't mean it is easy. Since I was a child, I have always felt like I have had something to prove.

If you tell me I can't do something, in my mind, I take that as a challenge, and I will do everything I can to step up and make it happen anyway. Call it defiance. Call it a need to feel approval when I didn't get it in my life. Call it what you want, but one thing is certain. When I was told I was not going to be able to do something, I set out to prove people wrong, whoever it was.

I have been told I couldn't be a cop. I have been told I couldn't be a leader. I have been told I would never be good at music. I have been told I couldn't do well in marriage. I was even told I couldn't write a book or my writing wasn't good enough. Maybe not, but here we are. I have been told I shouldn't do this or I shouldn't do that.

I have learned to live by the philosophy that Jesus will take the broken and turn them into something put back together and use the formerly broken to help other people. I gave myself a mission a long time ago, long before policing. I wanted to help people. I wanted to bless people.

If God has called me for a purpose, why should it matter what anyone else in the world thinks about me and what I do? My mission is not finished. My mission is still in the works.

Be Protected

This book has been written for several reasons. The first reason being that I have always wanted to write and publish a book. The second and third reasons are that I want to interact and educate the general public and law enforcement on my experiences so that we may be able to bridge that gap that divides us into separate cultures. Although it may not seem that there is a cultural difference, just observe the next Police Officer you may see and watch his or her mannerisms and behaviors. There are things that we do in our lives to keep ourselves and our families safe every day.

Watch when you go into a restaurant and see an Officer sitting there who will probably have his back against a wall or a booth and will probably be facing the door to the restaurant. Watch when you see us standing on the street. We are always on guard. It's not that Officers are trying to be rude to you. It's just that we have to think differently in order to keep ourselves, those we love, and the general public safe.

For those of my brothers and sisters in blue, brown, green, gray, or other color out there reading this, these next few pages are directed straight at you. Remember the oath that you were sworn to when you first became a Police Officer. I know in every department or agency across the United States and the world the oath Officers take will be different, but I bet every single one of them has something to do with honesty, integrity, and honor.

Remember this. God has placed you in a position of authority to protect others and maybe even sacrifice yourself to save someone else. If you don't believe in God like I do, then you have the option of having your own faith or beliefs, but if you are in this calling just to try to look good in a uniform, then you are in it for the wrong reason. This is real life, and real people get hurt, including yourself, if you are not careful.

Stay true to yourself and your values and don't take life too seriously. Life is hard enough as it is. As for your family, protect them from the rest of the world. I don't mean locking them in a room in your home like a kidnapper, but I do mean that you need to shelter them from that evil that you fight every day. It will be a spiritual and emotional struggle sometimes for you to separate the two worlds. One of my biggest difficulties is knowing how to shut down the Police Officer and remain the loving dad and husband I need to be.

There are days when you will want to be left alone and won't want to deal with anything. You cannot take out your aggression from your job on your family. They don't deserve your wrath. I am speaking from experience, so I understand that there is always room for improvement in me, as well. When you come home from whatever crazy schedule you work, spend time with your kids. They get over the idea that Daddy or Mommy is a Police Officer. They just need you to be a loving parent. With the dangers our kids face today, they need all the love we can give them. As a man of faith, I have always been raised with the understanding that God will hold me doubly accountable for the protection and spiritual upbringing of my wife and my children.

Keep your marriage and your family sacred. If you can't stay faithful to your family or your spouse, just don't get married. Remember, whether we like it or not, we are judged just as much in our private lives as we are in uniform. Don't think for one second that just because you take off your uniform, you can hide out as a civilian in your plain clothes. People will still recognize you even when you are not wearing the blues. Keep your integrity and remember that you swore an oath. And not only that, you are supposed to be holding yourself to a higher standard. Somewhere along the line, our society has decided that it is okay to do things and go back on our word or make promises we never intend to keep. It is that kind of thinking that got our world into trouble in the first place. If you don't believe me, look at how messed up the so-called justice system we have in this country is. Lawyers can say anything and everything in court to spin it as the truth. This does not make it so. So, just be the best you can be publicly and privately.

And more about your marriage and relationships. Cops have had a notorious reputation for having failed marriages as a culture. It seems that it comes with the job. That is most definitely not a requirement. You and your significant other have to work at it. It is going to be hard in marriage and even harder for you and your spouse than many others. You can't un-see all the things we see in our careers, and you must have an outlet other than your marriage.

Even more so, if your spouse or significant other is also in a high-stress job, this can not only be dangerous on the streets for you but also at home.

So, don't talk about work all the time (or ever, if you can help it). This will be nearly impossible because you will want to tell about all the stuff that was going on during your shifts. Just keep in mind that you will never truly relax if you continue living in your job constantly. This is called hypervigilance. It will be that constant scanning for the threat and that exaggerated intensity of behaviors all the time. This type of behavior all the time will leave you utterly exhausted.

I'm going to be very honest with you here: I will many times not even discuss my work day or what has happened when I walk in the door of my house. However, it is crucial that you take the time to decompress from the craziness the world has thrown at you during the day. For me, I have had the opportunity to often pick up my children and take them home. When I got home, I had to send them in for a snack or to go play for a few minutes together so Daddy could take off the uniform and just wind down. They knew that this is time that Daddy needs to go from Police Mode to Daddy Mode. This will also give me time to go into Husband Mode. This, for me, is a critical step that I must take on a daily basis in order to have a good evening or rest of the day.

Take the time to play with your kids and be a big kid with them. It is healthy. They don't understand what the bad guys do or what you have had to face in your job. What they do understand is when Mommy or Daddy is too busy working or too tired from work to play with them or spend time with them. You only have your children's attention for a few short-lived years that you cannot get back once they grow up. Cherish them. The time will go by in what seems to be a blink of an eye when you look back on it.

My wife and I have raised one of our girls already to adulthood, and I already miss those moments I cannot get back. She is going to do great things in this world and has a sweet heart. I want to continue to grow closer to my children, even as they grow older. I want to spend time with them, even though I am physically, spiritually, and emotionally exhausted very often. It does not matter.

This is my responsibility as a father. This is also a responsibility as a husband. It is my job to work toward a greater relationship with my wife, as well. She has dealt with a lot in my career. She deserves my best, too. When I go home every day, they don't need to know about the amount of people I had to argue with about the law or how many disgruntled employees I had. They don't need to know about how many people's problems we had to solve when we had no business being in the situation, to begin with, as the police. They need to know I am present for them in my home as a husband and father. And if I don't give them attention, there are plenty in the world who would, and not in a good way.

As a leader in my home, I also understand that I control the spiritual temperature in my household. I also understand the devil likes to put the family and marriages under spiritual attack. One of my favorite moments each day is when my children and I have had the chance to take my girls to school and when we say our prayers at night. It gives us the opportunity to talk about God in a way that is uninterrupted since they are, of course, a captive audience at that point. This is one of the most important parts of my day. Proverbs 20:7 says, "*The righteous who walks in his integrity-blessed are his children after him!*" So, of all the things that my children and I do together, none is more important than their spiritual growth. I have not always been the best shepherd to them, and I have failed. I am thankful they continue to love me as I continue to grow as a person. The last segment of Joshua 24:15 says, "*But as for me and my house, we will serve the Lord.*" Men, you especially are held accountable by God for how you treat your family and how you shepherd them.

Now for the marriage. Take the time to take your spouse or significant other on dates. And don't just be lazy and go to dinner and a movie all the time. Mix it up and go somewhere different and somewhere that you won't be interrupted and recognized by twenty people when you are trying to focus on the important person in your life. This was really difficult for me. I know a lot of people, and I am an extrovert. My wife is an introvert. You need to meet your spouse wherever they are and as *whoever* they are and forget what anyone else thinks about your marriage. They don't get to participate as a spectator in your relationship.

I mean, really try to *date* them. There was a time when you first met each other that you felt like you could spend every moment listening to them and what they had to say. If you are a significant other to a cop, you feel like you could let them tell their stories the entire time you were with them when you first met. Now, it may be that you can't stand listening to the cop stories because you know that is what seems the only life a cop knows how to live.

In part, that is true. Since I've been honest with you this whole time throughout the book, it should be once again noted that I have struggled with this, too. What I mean by this is that Police Officers really struggle to shut down that hypervigilant stage that we live in. If we tell stories all the time, we get to stay in that moment. It could also be a coping mechanism for us to deal with all the trauma we see on a daily basis. That goes for all first responders. If you have a spouse who wants to talk to you, take the time to listen. Put down your cell phone or the TV remote and just listen, even if it is just for the respect of it all.

For a spouse or significant other, this may be a good time to bond with your mate in a loving way you didn't think you would be able to. This could be that gentle nudge from you or a smile to affirm that you support them in what they do. Proverbs 7:7 says, *"Do not forsake her, and she will keep you; love her, and she will guard you."*

This might also be a time that it is necessary for you to reel them back in a bit before they go out into the ocean of police stories that they live on. My wife can give me *that* look, and I just know that it is time to shut up about cop stories because wherever we are and whomever the audience is at the time, it is not the time or place to be telling my wild stories of life on the beat. She has never embarrassed me about it, but I know when it is time to stop. And cops love to tell war stories! This really does become a delicate balance for you and your spouse, and you will just have to work through it one step at a time. All I can say is, just don't give up on each other and don't let the rest of the world and the dangers we face be the doom of your family or your marriage.

Be faithful always to your family and your spouse. You took an oath to live a life of honor, and if you are married, you made vows before your spouse and God. Be an example that others will want to aspire to, not shun away from. The best thing you can do for your children is be good to your spouse. I am not here to beat you over the head with a Bible, and I realize people make mistakes, but if you allow yourself to be put in that situation, that is when the devil will intervene. And he will use anyone or anything he can to destroy your marriage.

What you may or may not realize is that your children, especially, are watching how you treat your spouse and, in return, will grow up and treat their spouse the same way or will be treated how they see someone being treated. You need to love your spouse. And no, do not love them how *you* need love. Love them how *they* need love. If you don't, there are plenty of outside threats to your marriage out there and about 8 billion people in the world. It was no accident. God brought my wife and me together, and it is no accident for you and your significant other. It is your responsibility to nurture that relationship and protect your marriage. Do not be arrogant and think you do not need to better yourself and stop dating your spouse just because you got married to them. This is the biggest mistake men can make other than letting the world take them away from Jesus.

I highly recommend these two books: *The Five Love Languages* by Gary Chapman and *The Road Back to You: An Enneagram Journey to Self-Discovery* by Ian Morgan Cron. Both of these books will help you to discover both who you are and who your significant other or spouse is. If you are not married, read them anyway. They will help you to know what your personal love languages are, as well as what personality you have. There are probably thousands of other books, but these have been impactful in my walk with God.

Spoiler alert and warning! Be ready when you read these books to take a really good look in the mirror spiritually and begin a process of healing. These books are so well-written I felt like I was looking at myself in the pages as I turned them, flaws and triumphs alike. There are some parts of these books that will be difficult to read. Suck it up, Buttercup! We have to grow and learn if we will ever become what Christ would have us to become for His kingdom.

Protect Yourself

Along with making sure that your family is provided for and that you spend the time with them that is needed, it is equally important that Officers take the time for themselves. In this tough job, you need time to get away from everything that goes on at work. And, as experts will tell you, having a family is stressful, too. It is not a bad stress usually, but it can be difficult to toe that line sometimes, depending on the family dynamics. For this reason, it is extremely important for you to go and find a hobby or play a sport or exercise. Not only will these improve your physical health, but also your mental, spiritual, and emotional health. And when planning what to do, be sure it does not revolve around a bar or drinking. Plan something that will be beneficial to you, not detrimental to your health. This may prove to be more difficult than you think.

When it is time for your shift, *suit up*. This is one of the most important steps to keeping yourself safe out there. Just like decompressing at the end of the shift, it is equally important for you to mentally prepare yourself for the dangers you face every day. This job is for real, and real people get hurt or worse, including cops. Do *not* take for granted that you will come home at the end of your shift. I hope that is the case, and that should always be your ultimate goal, but remember that you are a sheepdog protecting the sheep amongst the wolves.

Wear your protective gear. You are given gear for a reason. Vest, boots, belt, extra magazines, the whole works. I know it is uncomfortable to wear that vest for what seems like an eternity, and I know that it has been known to cause back problems. Quit making excuses and just do it. We already have enough dangers out there without the danger of not wearing the gear provided. I have seen Officers out there with a ridiculous amount of cool gear and gadgets, and there is no way they actually use it all. If you have it issued to you or given to you, use it.

Wear your seat belt. As silly as this sounds, how many Police Officers (and citizens, too) die needlessly and would have been saved if they had just worn their seatbelt? This is a rhetorical question...The answer is thousands of people would be saved.

You need to be brave. As an Officer, if I told you that I had never been scared, I would be lying to you, and I will say that to any Officer telling me they have never been afraid. We are human, and if you are an Officer, you need to accept that. The facts are, though, that this career and calling does not leave much room for constant fear. You must be brave to the fullest extent that you can be and learn not to react to knee-jerk emotions. You must be brave because someone out there needs you to be because they cannot. Above all, have faith that what you do out there is seen from God above. My all-time favorite verse in the Bible is Isaiah 41:10. It says, *"Fear Not, for I am with you; be not dismayed, for I am your God; I will strengthen you, I will help you, I will uphold you with my righteous right hand."* Isaiah 41:13 says, *"For I, the Lord your God, hold your right hand; it is I who say to you, 'Fear not, I am the one who helps you."*

To me, this is not just another verse, and it has helped me on many occasions when I wanted to give up. It is not just a verse. This is a command. The verses themselves give me strength just by viewing them. It is most important for each of us to have an escape of some kind and a way to build ourselves back up when we are down. Hopefully, these things I discussed will help you in your life, as well.

PROTECT YOUR FAITH

The many things in this world we see in our jobs and otherwise can cause us to falter from our faith in God. It took me a long time to learn that, each day, God allows someone to come across your path in some way that will either help you to grow, help them to grow, or help others. Try to use these experiences and the terrible things we see to grow spiritually and to learn that God has put you out there for a reason. Learn to count your blessings every single day and know that nothing on this earth is permanent. Life is so precious and precarious.

If you talk to a police cadet in the academy, nearly every one of them will answer in the same manner. They became a cop to help people. What most (including me at the time) do not understand is just how much what we do really does affect people's lives. We truly have the authority given under law to make someone's life go in one direction or another. Even more, we have been given the power to take a person's life. There have been situations where we, as the police, have really screwed it up. The world doesn't turn a blind eye anymore. In fact, the world knows about it because of social media and will be your judge, jury, and executioner before all the facts even get released.

That being said, many times, we underestimate just what kind of situation people have in their life at the time, and we often fail to see the big picture. Cops are great at getting the details of the incident, but many times, we fail to investigate what led up to the incident or even go back to do a follow-up to see what transpired after our initial encounter. It's on to the next call. No time for all that. If I saw that there was a flaw in the mannerisms of Police Officers sometimes, it would be this. As Officers in the world today, we are expected to be the police, parenting experts, social workers, medical experts, animal control officers, lifesavers, problem solvers, teachers, legal advisers, blah, blah, blah. The list of responsibilities the police are called for goes on and on. It's no wonder the stress is astronomical in our lives and we become so depressed or angry at life.

It seems that the older we get in our careers, the less sympathetic or even empathetic we are to the needs of others. The world seems so cold anymore and has turned on itself. Oh sure, we get the job done, and we play the part of whatever situation we are needed in, but often, we become jaded because of the constant negativity we face. Let's face it: cops are constantly in the spotlight and scrutinized by the media, and we always have the Monday Morning Quarterback situation when we are given split seconds to make a decision that could change someone's life forever. And do not even get me started on any section of the mainstream media and their brainwashing of society as we know it today. I heard a politician I knew say once that "the police are a necessary evil." She said it with disdain and disrespect that made me wonder if she knew who it was that protected her at all, and she was the Mayor of the city who hired me. What kind of recruitment does that do for the future of law enforcement?

Should I Have Left This Part out of the Book?

This portion was hard to decide on whether or not I would put it in the book. Thanks to those in political and ideological interest groups and with sections of the national media, our nation has been a powder keg of raw emotions based on little to no facts other than those spread by social media and the parties listed above. Examples of officer-involved shootings or deaths have been plastered all over every major outlet possible and spread like wildfires through a dry season. Again, many of the cities burned and looted (in my own state, as well) have not been based on facts but assumptions and those who would use it as an excuse to commit crimes. Little to no prosecution occurred against criminals who burned and rioted in cities because it was part of "freedom of speech." I would love to see where in the Constitution of the United States of America it shows that freedom of speech includes destroying other people's property and possessions, throwing temper tantrums when you don't get what you want, or choosing to occupy a street or property you don't pay for.

Now, you must understand my tone in this part of the book. This is raw emotion put onto paper or screen (whatever you are reading this on). I have anger, frustration, sadness, and many other emotions. I am angry that I cannot speak out and say what I want because Police Officers are supposed to protect all people's freedom of speech, even those who despise us. Even those who would spit on us and would still call us when they needed us, we have to protect. I often do not agree with someone's *agenda* or ideology, but that doesn't mean I don't have a job to do. I don't get to have an opinion most of the time when I put on this uniform. If two organizations show up at the same place to protest, I may disagree with both of them, but I have a duty to protect all of the people at the protest. This duty changes when people resort to rioting and committing criminal offenses.

I am frustrated because the public overall is good, but when police mess up (and we do mess up), we are not given the grace many are given. Police are not Jesus, we are not saints, we are not angels, we are human. We are imperfect beings who make mistakes. But most of us out here want to do the right thing and just signed on to save lives and make a difference. And we want to get rid of bad cops more than the general public does because it gives the rest of us a bad name.

I have had people who are supposed to be close to me jump on the bandwagon all over social media with posts about *defund the police* and not call me one time to talk to me or discuss my perspective on what it is like to walk a day in our boots. Defund the police! Take away their weapons! Do you have any idea how much that hurts? These are the people who are supposed to love you the most and be the proudest to support you the most, not blasting propaganda on social media against it. And for the record, even if it is not my city, the ripples are felt all over the world. It is a crack in the breaking down of society at its core. I have had people rip me apart on social media just for being the police.

This world needs Jesus.

Let me know again how well it is working out with criminals following the law in the United States since America is one of the most violent countries in the world and has one of, if not *the* highest, addiction rates to drugs. I'm pretty sure there are over several billion cell phones in the world to contact people, and social media seems to work to contact people these days if anyone wants to discuss it. I am open to ideas. I welcome the conversation. I welcome the input on how we could improve and the ideas people have on making us successful. After all, the police are a representation of society, whether people choose to admit it or not.

I will not apologize for the life I (and my family) have given to the service of others. And I will not apologize for a career in which people are privileged to have the freedoms in this country our military (and first responders) have fought and died to protect. I have had my friends' caskets covered from their sacrifice given to serve others. What a ridiculous notion it is to believe there should be complete anarchy with no law and order. I was there when the flags draped over the caskets were then folded and handed to the loved ones.

Finally, I am sad our justice system is in the shambles that it is in. I am open to reform. I welcome new ideas and ways to help others find their ways (most of the time) back to society, and I want people to have a fair and impartial system where every race, religion, and creed is represented and not persecuted. Sadly, it is run by imperfect people. We can only do the best we can to find honest people.

Keep Going

It is important as an Officer for you to obtain that mental toughness and be able to walk in the places few people want to talk about in conversation and no one wants to go. You have to be that one who sometimes has to write a ticket to someone that costs them money for committing a traffic offense even though you know you might not be able to pay your own bills on time because the salary we live on is so minimal sometimes. You need to understand that there will be people out there who don't respect the police, and sometimes even they don't understand why, and yet they will direct all their anger and hatred at you when they don't even know you. Romans 8:28 says, "*And we know that for those who love God all things work together for good, for those who are called according to His purpose.*" You are called for His purpose. Nobody ever said this job would be easy. If it was easy, anyone could be a Police Officer. I promise you, those who criticize you rarely have the courage to suit up and fight back the darkness. We have a lot of social media giants and keyboard warriors, but rarely those with the courage to stand up publicly and do what is right. That goes for celebrities, politicians, and anyone who would criticize others without the knowledge or courage to make a change.

When you are out there on the streets, remember what the Bible says about our calling. Philippians 2:14–15 says, "*Do all things without grumbling or questioning, that you may be blameless and innocent, children of God without blemish in the midst of a crooked and twisted generation.*" What that means in simple cop terms is: *This ain't gonna be easy. Suck it up and roll on. You will get through this.*

Spend time in prayer and in church. Get into a Bible study. Above all, take the time that is needed to protect your faith and your beliefs. No one can fight this battle for you. This is not just worldly battles you fight. Remember what Ephesians 6:12 says. It says, "*For we do not wrestle against flesh and blood, but against the rulers, against the authorities, against the cosmic powers over this present darkness, against the spiritual forces of evil in the heavenly places.*" These are places we cannot see, but make no mistake, my fellow warriors, you will have an impact on the spiritual world with your actions. Stand strong in your faith. You owe it to your spouse, your children, your family, and yourself.

Be protected.

With Eyes That Look Toward Heaven...
And One Wing in the Fire

I believe I have always been the type of person to at least try my best to do the right thing. I would think that anyone who knows me would say the same thing. At least, I hope this is the case. I should make it a point to say that my life has been turned upside down, sideways, and the right side up again more times than I can count, just like everyone else.

I have learned my lessons, and I have loved, and I have lost many things and people in my life who were very important in shaping the man I am today. It is not easy to one day wake up and realize many of the people you thought were your friends now either don't want to talk to you because you are a Police Officer or only call you when they need something or want to get out of a ticket. It is difficult not to have a cold iciness come over your heart and keep the warmth that you have known all your life. Family members, so-called friends—it is really all the same.

It is difficult to want to be a good person to someone who spits in your face or tries to physically hurt you. To tell you the truth, I really don't know which one is worse, having to find out who your *real* friends are or having someone spit in your face. I heard an expression once that always makes me laugh. "A true friend stabs you in the front." Anyone reading this who knows me or has spent significant time working with me knows I say it in jest all the time. What other expression could be so blunt and yet so true and comical at the same time?

Since becoming a Police Officer, I have seen many scenes of life and death that you could only imagine or watch in a movie. Today's society glorifies this type of thing in shows and movies like ancient Rome glorified death in the Coliseum. I had battled with depression, the early stages of alcoholism, and not knowing where to turn when I needed help. People lied to me every day in my job on patrol, and we always deal with people in the maddest, saddest, most emotional, most distraught times of their lives. I have even often found myself asking the questions: "Who am I to help these people when I still struggle with my own insecurities every single day?" "Why am I doing this job anyway?" "Does it ever really do any good?" "God, why am I doing this?" "What is my purpose?"

Everyone in Christianity especially talks the talk and says, *"Here am I, Lord, send Me."* And yet, when push comes to shove, not everyone will want to do what needs to be done. I have never lived a perfect life as much as I have wanted to, but I have tried to keep my eyes toward heaven. I have lived a little left of living right sometimes. When I think of Jesus, I remember the picture in my grandfather's church with Jesus and His perfect hair, as if He had gotten ready for the Olan Mills photo.

The Jesus I have come to encounter over the years has been the one who rescued me when I was in danger and the one who was with me on the dark streets and when I was scared in the woods, a man was going to pop up over a hill while an entire SWAT Team (ours was called the Emergency Response Unit) and a bunch of State Troopers were approaching an open field and he had a rifle. My Jesus is the one who rescued me from alcoholism and has chased after me time and time again when I went astray. My Jesus is the Jesus who was telling the parable of the ninety-nine sheep while He was looking for me, the lost one, to complete the hundred.

Law enforcement is a career where we have to deal with unimaginable circumstances for the generally ungrateful while making sure we are doing it right by the law created by man so we don't get judged for being the ones who did the unthinkable in a matter of seconds. And we are held accountable for the rest of our lives. Society does not *really* want to know what we have to deal with. They just want it done.

So, in closing this short chapter of the book, thank your local law enforcement. Take care of them because they take care of you. Reach out to their families who are fighting the fight with them, even if only emotionally. Don't leave them on an island to themselves.

Go home safe. You are doing what God has called you to do, whether you believe or know that or not. To my brothers and sisters out there in blue, brown, gray, and every other color of the uniform, keep fighting the good fight, go home safe. Keep your eyes on Jesus and the good of heaven as you have one wing in fire.

The Inevitable Changes Within

When I was hired as a Police Officer, I was young, didn't care how much I got paid and was as green a rookie as the grass in the summertime. Throughout the course of my twenty years in law enforcement, I have served under seven different Chiefs of Police, numerous Assistant Chiefs, lots of Majors, two Lieutenants earlier in my career, lots of Sergeants and Corporals, and worked with many, many different Officers. I have seen over 275 people leave our agency in that twenty-year span (I counted) and have seen many, many changes.

When I first started, we were still in the dark ages of policing, in my opinion. We had a long way to go. Now, and my opinion is a little biased, we are one of the premier agencies in the Commonwealth of Kentucky, and we are recruiting people from all over the country. We still have a long way to go, but there are some pieces in place to make some more valuable changes for our community and our Officers.

It was always going to happen. There is only so long you can live in the old styles of policing. The social influences of the culture and times will always have an influence on how things occur. A police department is its own culture. It is a sociologist's dream (or nightmare), depending on the way it is viewed. The changes from within a police organization are inevitable. The question is, will an agency adapt to the changes or fail?

Many of the ways I have written about in this book are either antiquated now or will be in the future. We can't stop that. Maybe this will be a glimpse into the world as I saw it then and the world as I see it now. In some ways, we have made vast improvements. In some ways, like anything else, we still have a long way to go as a society.

THIS IS REALITY

"Present...Arms!"

I heard a voice echo through the crowd of people and slowly obeyed the command. Hundreds of arms slowly lifted in unison. The silence could have been cut with a knife. We stood there at attention, without moving, and with what felt like barely breathing.

It really was a sight to see all of this. Rows and rows of people gathered outside a little small-town high school nestled in the mountains of Eastern Kentucky. It was an occasion most people had never seen before and probably would never see again. I have seen four now. It is the most noble occasion I have ever had the privilege to be a part of. It really doesn't matter how many you see, though. You are never really prepared for it when it happens again. You just do your duty and show up for support.

The silence was finally broken with the airy sound of bagpipes that began their eerie tune with somewhat of a lulled mixture of humming and honking that exploded into a high-pitched and melancholy song. The sounds echoed off the walls of the red brick building as we stood there, unmoving. This was only the first of many times I would hear this sound today shatter the silence and mourning.

After what seemed like a short eternity of sorrow in the songs of the bagpipes, the sounds faded away and eventually gave in to the silence once again. We stood there, never moving a muscle. Moments turned into forever until the silence was finally broken again.

I found myself amazed and in somewhat of a state of shock as I listened to what followed. From far down the line, I could see the family gathering around as Honor Guard members slowly and carefully loaded the caskets into two separate vehicles. The sobbing and crying accompanied them, and in the air, there was a feeling of sadness that loomed around, just like the gray clouds that blocked the sun that day. The Honor Guard Commander gave short, crisp commands to his Guard Members that were all but at a whisper in the afternoon weather. It was misty and cool outside as we all stood there, arms still raised in salute.

"Order...Arms!!"

All the arms that had been raised in salute slowly and methodically lowered at the same time after that simple two-word order that was separated briefly by a pause. We were dismissed for the time, shortly after this, to return to our vehicles and prepare for the rest of the day, which would continue to be emotionally tiring.

I remembered that there were a large number of police cruisers and emergency vehicles when we arrived. We were directed into a certain position by young cadets from an agency that had come to assist. It seemed, though, that the number of vehicles had at least doubled, if not tripled, since I had walked into the doors for the ceremony. However difficult it may have been because many of the vehicles looked the same, we found our white patrol car and got in.

After sitting there for a few minutes and again playing the hurry-up-and-wait game, one by one, each officer driving a vehicle illuminated the emergency lights. Light bars, strobes, grill lights, caution lights, and every other emergency light, it seemed, was lit up like it was Christmas time. That was only the beginning. It was so much more amazing than that. In fact, it is somewhat difficult for me to even put into words and describe everything that my eyes had beheld. I let my mind slip away, and I allowed my thoughts to stray briefly to the ceremony that happened just a few minutes ago.

It was hot and stuffy in that medium-sized gymnasium. Looking at the walls and the decor, I wondered how many basketball games had been played in that gym. How many games went down to the last few seconds with fans on their feet, hoping that their team would be victorious? How many cheers went on by young cheerleaders cheering on their players or possibly their high school sweetheart? One thing was certain: there was no cheering on this day.

As each and every person filed into the gym slowly and quietly, I watched as Honor Guard members ushered and directed us to our seats. I remember having to sit sideways in the seat because the duty belt would not allow me to sit properly. So, rather than sitting *in* the seat, I actually sat *on* the corner of the seat. I was so uncomfortable. I felt bad for even thinking that due to the reason that I was here. I was not there for a basketball game.

Just like it would happen a few moments, I remember the ceremony started with a local Minister and Chaplain for the police department singing "Go Rest High On That Mountain," made famous by the country singer Vince Gill. Immediately following that song, he sang "I Can Only Imagine" by the Christian group Mercy Me. Both of these songs really hit home for me, and I could not help but find myself with watery eyes trying to fight back full tears.

Both those songs held significance in my life since I heard "Go Rest High On That Mountain" at several friends' funerals and also my uncle's, and I myself sang "I Can Only Imagine" at my grandmother's funeral on Mother's Day with my cousins and my sister. Needless to say, the songs brought back memories. I listened intently as the man singing hit every note with a beautiful voice that truly was a blessing to the ceremony. The songs were accompanied by the occasional sniffle from someone in the audience. More times than not, it was from someone sitting close to me wearing the same type of clothing I was.

I remember he stood behind a podium on a small stage that was behind two caskets, both open. One casket displayed a young Police Officer in uniform silently resting with grace and peace. The other casket, a canine that served as that Police Officer's partner.

These two lost their lives when a car full of teenagers collided with the police vehicle, attempting to stop them from going any further in the vehicle pursuit, within which they were already engaged with other Officers. Let me be clear. That Officer and his K-9 were killed by the acts of someone being reckless!

I could feel my temper flaring as I sat there in the fold-down seat of the gym and listened to the gentleman tell the story about what had happened. I looked at the hundreds of faces of many others dressed in the same type of uniform as me and saw the looks of shock and denial...and anger.

I had never met the man who was being laid to rest. I had never petted his dog or backed him on a call. Except for the picture and later walking by the caskets for the final respects, I could not have even told you what the man looked like. Did that matter? *Absolutely not!*

Bottom line: He was a Police Officer, so I knew him. It was an unspoken bond that I cannot even explain.

I was reminded while I was sitting there during the ceremony of an expression I once heard while I was in college. It had not really registered in my mind until that day. It was very simple and yet so powerful. *From the outside looking in, you can never understand. From the inside looking out, you can never explain.*

I have no idea to this day who said that, but it is one of the most profound sayings and thoughts that I have ever heard in my entire life. I could not get it out of my head. It just kept repeating itself over and over, and I cannot explain why. I tried to focus again on what was being said by the Minister.

The portion of the service that he spoke on that stuck in my mind was what he said about the dog. I feel like it was quite possibly the most simple and one of the best sermons I have ever heard. He talked about the life of a dog and how simple it was. It's true. The life of a dog is so simple that the only thing the dog lives for is to please the master. He went on to talk about how the K-9 was a drug dog that found drugs in houses and cars. The Minister talked about how none of that mattered. The dog didn't know it was a good dog finding drugs and getting them off the streets. The only thing he knew was that he was pleasing his master and doing what he was supposed to do. That is what made the dog happy.

I sat there numb to the haunting analogy that he intertwined with the way we should live our lives as Christians and good people. I grew up in church and have been surrounded by it my whole life, and I had never heard something so simple that had such a sharp edge to it. The words penetrated my very soul and woke my spirit again. I don't know if I will ever forget the words that old country preacher said in that hot and crowded gymnasium.

My mind now back in the vehicle, I found my eyes wandering again as I sat there and made small talk with the other Officer who was driving the car. We had both worked third shift the night before, and we both had to work that night. It seems like it always worked out like that. I was mentally, physically, and emotionally exhausted, but I would not have missed this for anything. I felt like I *needed* to be there. This was only the most recent of the several that I have been to since becoming a Police Officer in 2003.

It was nearly an hour-long ride to the small hillside that would be the final resting place of these two souls. It was not even so much a cemetery; it was just a hillside next to a family's home. The ride there was probably one of the most amazing things that a Police Officer can see in his career, no matter how long you have been on the street.

I said earlier that all the Officers had illuminated their emergency lights, and this was the reason. In one long and seemingly never-ending parade, police vehicles and ambulances crept along the little mountain roads of Eastern Kentucky, with fire trucks blocking roads and cross-streets. Hundreds of cars with lights moved with only the sounds of various engines at a lull humming as they followed, one after another, to the grave site. There were no sirens or horns, just the lights moving with cars in near silence down the curvy roads.

Most people have never seen anything like it. *Most* people will never see anything like it after this one. Again, this is my fourth. This was my fourth funeral for an Officer in a five-year timeframe. As we moved slowly along the roadways, my mind again began to flash back to those others before finally being brought back to the present by my friend who was driving. It never gets any easier. It doesn't matter how many you go to or how many you see.

All the way there, I saw people standing on the roadside. Men, women, children stood there. Grandparents, sons, daughters stood there and looked on as we all passed by. People got out of their cars in the middle of the highway to stop and look and pay their final respects to the fallen. Some people stopped and prayed with their eyes closed and heads bowed. Some, mostly the children, waved as they saw car after car of Police Officers drive by them. Veterans held their hands and hats over their hearts. Some saluted us. Hundreds of people watched us. I was as amazed as they were. It truly was something to see.

Even those who were just stuck in the traffic at least nodded their heads politely as we rolled by. It is, of course, customary to stop for funerals, but not all pay their respects. Some just get caught in the wrong place at the wrong time in their eyes. No one ever *likes* to sit in traffic for an hour, no matter what the occasion or reason. Surprisingly, though, everyone seemed to take the time to show respect and give some sort of acknowledgment to us all as we moved past them. All those we saw seemed to have a look of concern or remorse on their face as if they knew the Officer.

No doubt everyone had at least heard the news about what had happened. We were in a small area in the mountains, and word always travels to find if it is of any importance or value. Actually, after coming from a fairly small community myself and knowing what it is like, I think it would be safe to say that even *un*-important news and gossip travels fast. Nevertheless, there were people there all along the way, and they were respectful and proper no matter how they might have found out. It was this way the entire trip until we got to the damp hillside deep in the mountains.

We all slowly parked our vehicles in the wet grass in the middle of a big field. I was at first a little worried that we might get stuck. Our car was about midway to the front of the group and surrounded on all sides by other police vehicles. So, our exact location on the grass had been driven over so many times now that it was not really grass anymore. I was now a mixture of matted-down greenery and a slush of mud. Oh well, if we were going to get stuck, so were a bunch of other people in the exact same field and place we were.

I got out of the car, immediately looking down to see where my shiny shoes were stepping. I could at least attempt to not get them muddy. I grabbed my hat from the back seat of the cruiser and placed it on my head before walking away from the car. I glanced at the windows and saw my reflection to make sure the hat was seated straight. The day was not nearly over, and I should still try to look presentable. My feet squished on the damp ground as I began walking toward wherever it was that were going. I didn't know, but someone did because there were huge amounts of Officers moving in that direction.

I remember thinking to myself amusingly that we were all moving and herding like a bunch of sheep or cattle, and I was just hoping that *someone* really did know where they were going and that we, as a group, were not just being macho and stubborn. No doubt, though, as organized as these things went, it really didn't matter how many Officers didn't have a clue what was going on. Someone would. It never takes long for us to catch on after that. We are only human, though.

There were so many cars that we had to park a good distance from where we were going. I think we must have walked about a hundred yards or so before we finally got ready to stand at attention again. As we were walking up the hill, I made small talk with some of the other Officers from other departments about where they were from and how work was going. Nothing out of the ordinary and definitely a conversation about something that could be ended abruptly if the moment or occasion arose for it. Although it was nice to meet new people and faces, we were all there for a reason, and we tried to show the reverence it deserved.

Our conversations were interrupted by the sounds that I had not heard since we were leaving high school. The rumble of, I think, two dozen or so Harley-Davidson motorcycles thundered and echoed through the mountains as they arrived at the tail of the processional. With the occasional sputter from the engine from the cold and several revs of engines as they slowed to a stop, most just idled until each one could take its place for the halt of the endless caravan of vehicles. Then, their drivers joined us at the grave site on the hill.

As we walked up the damp hillside, I finally got to see the large number of other police K-9s and their handlers scattered about the terrain. Some of the dogs just lay there or sat obediently next to their masters. Some howled and barked at the other dogs around them. I could not help but smile slightly at all of them barking profusely at one another. Still, others of them jumped about and paced around the Officers who held their leads and were quickly scolded in some other language and put in their place. It was as if those dogs were paying final respects just like we were, although not quite as silently.

We were placed in rows very similar to the ones at the high school. We were given brief instructions in a hushed fashion as we all lined up accordingly. Most of us immediately went to parade rest as the stragglers continued to walk up the hillside to where we stood. I watched as Officers around me checked their uniforms to make sure they were squared away and in the proper appearance.

Covers on heads with close-cut styles and high and tights, boots and shoes shined, shiny buttons and pins, and ties up to the neckline were what most wore. Some wore white gloves. Most were bare-skinned below the wrist line.

Shiny leather gear, mostly with some basket weave and nylon styles thrown into the mix, was what held duty gear and weapons secured in holsters. We were all there, ready for the ceremony to begin. A few moments later, I heard it, but just barely even as quiet as it was here.

"Detail...Attention!" I heard the Honor Guard Commander grunt in a low voice. It was enough, though. Like toy soldiers, we all popped to attention, bodies erect and eyes forward. No movement. Back to the same position as before we returned, shoulders back and everyone still. For what always seems an eternity when you are at attention, we stood there.

A breeze had risen through these hills, and it whistled softly through the trees around us. An almost unrecognizable mist lightly brushed over us as my face glistened softly with nearly microscopic raindrops as they rose and fell with the gentle winds. The mist continued to lightly show its presence as we stood there in silence. After standing there for some time, I felt a drop of water that had formed from the mist slowly falling down my left cheek. I stood still, trying not to think about the nuisance it was when I was unable to move to wipe it away. It would not be the first drop of water to drag its way down the skin on my face.

I was quickly brought back to the reality of where I was when I heard the same sound that I had heard previously that day. This time, from far off in the distance, I heard the sad and eery sounds of the bagpipes and drums.

I listened intently to try and decipher the tune that moved across and crept through the mountains like a ghost in the wind. It was, at first, difficult to determine where exactly the sound was coming from. I could tell it was somewhere below us, but I could not tell from which direction. The sounds of the pipes and drums bounced off hillsides far off in the distance and distorted the sound and song with a softer echo that faded away. I could not keep my mind from focusing on the song and trying to catch it with the echo before it disappeared.

As I stood there and listened, I was quickly reminded of where I was yet again when the songs of the bagpipes faded away and left nothing but a snare drum, keeping the rhythm and the march.

Brrrratt...Brrrratt...Brrratt. Silence again. I waited. *Brrratt...Brrratt... Brrratt.*

The snare drum kept time for the entire Honor Guard as I began to see each one of them coming from up the hill. They had been behind me and below me at the bottom of the hill, which is why I had been unable to find the location of the processional. I soon was able to see each and every member of the Honor Guard as they climbed the hill and came into view.

The bagpipes soon began their sad songs again, and I watched from the corner of my eye as not one but two caskets were slowly brought up the hill. The guard members slowly passed by all the rows and rows and rows of Police Officers standing at attention. I watched as, with methodic and robot-like movements, the guard members moved their arms and feet in unison.

Police Officers on horseback had arrived and joined the ranks. One lone horse stood without a rider, signifying the fallen soldier or fallen rider. It seemed as if even the horses could tell the sadness of the occasion and barely even made a sound. I could only but barely see the horses without turning my head. Had I not listened to the sound of their hooves striking the ground softly, I would have never realized they were even there. However, when finally able to look at the magnificence of those horses shortly after this time as they were leaving, I was able to develop the appreciation and respect that even the animals had shown. It truly was amazing in so many ways.

They were about twenty yards from me now. As slowly as they had marched there, they finally came to a crisp, quiet stop. The guard members switched the positioning of their hands and then lowered the caskets to the ground. They straightened their bodies back to attention and then shifted to one side and stepped away from that which they had just carried up the hill.

Nothing for several moments. No movement, no sound except the wind whistling lightly throughout the trees. From my location on the hill, I could then only faintly hear the Minister giving the burial ceremony as he spoke quietly. Then, once again, silence. I could still feel the mist on my face as I listened intently and waited for something...anything. I waited to again hear more sounds of sadness.

The silence was broken by the crackle of a voice from an intercom, I daresay, a loudspeaker of some sort. I could not even begin to describe my emotions as I listened intently to the loud voice that boomed through the mountainside. The loud voice took on the role of a dispatcher calling for the unit number of the Officer who was now being laid to rest.

No answer.

The voice again called the unit number of the Officer who had not responded when called upon the first time. Again, there was no answer. Another moment or two of silence followed after there was no answer for the second time.

Then, as if to answer the radio again, the loudspeaker came alive for one final time and announced that the Unit number being called for was now 10-7. 10-7 is the code used for being out of service. Immediately following this statement was announced the name of this valiant officer and his police K-9 and that they had served their community well. "May God have mercy on them henceforth." Those were the words that still echo in my mind even today. And even still now, I am haunted by the words, ideas, and the notion that it is possible that it could be me lying there or being the reason that all these people had come together for one common cause.

"Present...Arms!"

Slowly and again, in unison, every Officer raised a salute for one final time for the day. I knew what was next in the ceremony, and I hated the fact that I did. I knew what happened at the last funeral like this that I went to, but it still never gets easier.

My mind wandered again to those thoughts that had just been cut short from the loudspeaker as it finished. I stared straight ahead at the Officers in the row in front of me. My peripheral vision to my left and right caught sight of the Officers who stood on either side of me. Any one of us could have lost our lives at any time. It made me wonder why I signed up for this job and took on this career to begin with. I suppose it is only a natural feeling that someone might have doubts in a situation like that. One would only wonder why, after having those thoughts, we continue to do what we do.

My attention was refocused by the sound of a trumpet that slowly winded its way through the hillside and amongst the ranks and files and rows of Police Officers standing without movement. An eerie tune that most everyone knows, but no one really wants to hear. Even those who have never been to a funeral like this know the song. As a musician myself, I remember it being one of the first songs that I learned because of the scale structure of the song.

Of all the songs from the bugle or trumpet and those utilized in the military or police fields, none is so easily recognized or will pull at the heartstrings so much as this song. Twenty-four notes in the song, no more. TAPS.

It was made famous by the United States Military during the time of the Civil War. Interestingly enough, a different version of it was used as the signal for Extinguishing Lights in the camps or "Lights Out." It was not until Union General Daniel Adams Butterfield thought it inappropriate and too formal to use a bugler to signify the day's end that the version we know today was re-written and adapted to fit his brigade in July of 1862. The song that was played for the fallen soldiers eventually spread throughout the entire Union and later the Confederacy, as well. Eventually, the song TAPS was made an official bugler's call after the completion of the American Civil War.

I trust without a doubt that the same sadness that had befallen us on this day was of the same sorrow that loomed in the air nearly 150 years ago. I would suspect that those men felt the same way I did, with a heavy heart and an angry stirring in my spirit toward the people who had caused this to happen.

I felt as if I were wrong for feeling that way, but I could not stop the expansive flow of emotions that eventually led to the tears that ran down my cheeks. Why shouldn't I be upset? Why shouldn't I be mad at the real reason we were there? It pains me to think that people can act this way towards each other.

The sound of the trumpet crawling throughout the hillside was not the only sound I heard anymore. I could now very clearly hear the sobbing and crying of the family and friends from even the distance that I was away from them. I heard from within the ranks of Officers the same sounds of sniffles and crying, though there was no bodily movement still from them as they stood at attention. I looked at the Honor Guard members as they stood close by the caskets and the family. I watched as their faces leaked the emotions that they really felt, no matter how professional and sharp they appeared. Tears streamed down the faces of those Honor Guard members as their faces hung heavily with the feeling of remorse.

Though it didn't quite register what had been said by the Honor Guard Commander when he gave his commands, I very quickly realized that command that had been given. I heard the last of the words he had said, and it was immediately followed by gunfire. The twenty-one gun salute cut through the ranks and the mountainside like a set of knives. It startles you when they first go off. Seven Honor Guard Members in a perfect row give three shots, the shots that seem to go on forever. Then, nothing.

For several more moments of eternity, there was no sound. All of a sudden, it seemed like the hills were coming to life from beneath. There was a thundering sound that shook the ground below my feet. As the sound got louder, the vibrations in my feet slowed and eventually stopped as I heard a group of Blackhawk Helicopters fly over in formation. I was only slightly able to see them before they dropped back out of sight beyond the top of the hill upon which we stood.

Shortly after this, we were all dismissed, and the ceremony was over. There was no joking and not much talking, as is so typical of Police Officers. I glanced back at the caskets and the family still remaining on the hillside as a reminder to myself never to forget. It seemed unlikely that I would ever forget such a day. There was so much that had happened and so much that we had all been a part of. I wondered if any of the other Police Officers on the hillside that day had been feeling in any way the same manner that I had felt.

We must never forget those who have paid the ultimate price. Theirs is the story worth telling. They are the true heroes. In the New Testament of the Holy Bible, there is a scripture that I had heard many times throughout my life up until that day. This day, however, that scripture rang out in my head like the giant bell of a clock tower. I could not get it out of my head. John 15:13 says, "*Greater love has no man than this, that he lay down his life for his friends.*" Words cannot express how much this verse fits the occasion. It doesn't matter if you believe in God or the words and scriptures of the Bible or not. This scripture is one that speaks for itself. How much love and compassion could be shown to people from just the acts of one man and his dog who were working their assigned shift? And yet, how often are those people taken for granted, whether we realize it or not?

I will not lie about it one bit. On that day, I questioned myself and whether or not I should continue in the endeavor upon which I had begun when I became a Police Officer. Although several years had gone by since I first stood proud in my uniform, I wondered if it was all worth the price that might someday have to be paid.

There was, no doubt, a spiritual struggle within me that day. I battled my own demons that day as I fought with carnal knowledge that, someday, that might have to be me with a flag draped over my casket. I wondered if anyone would come to my funeral if it was me. Would there be such an amazing display of valor and courage as exemplified there that day? Would I be the one who was remembered as a hero?

As I fought my own mental battle in the car ride home that day and then had to go to work that night, I realized something. I realized that day that I had become a Police Officer for a reason and that my task was not yet completed in the line of work we call First Responders. I still had a purpose, and although it may not have been completely clear, I knew it was not time to stop what I had started just yet.

So, how is it that a man decides what path he should take? How is it that someone must choose what side they want to fight for? Is there ever really a choice, or are we just thrown into the lives and the crossfire that consumes everyone else around us? I would personally like to think that each person on this Earth can choose to be a good person or not to be a good person. It is how we perceive those decisions to do so in our daily lives that shape the people we are to become. Is every decision or path that we take going to be right all the time? Of course not, but it is in those moments of life that we define who we really are. It is then that we discover what we are really all about. This is the path that I have taken.

This Is Me

We live in a society where mediocrity is often rewarded. I was never raised this way. I was raised to work hard, pay my dues, and God will keep His plan in my life and will order and guide my steps. I have not always been successful in my attempts at things, and the learning came from the hard lessons and failures I had along the way. Some of those lessons are on full display in this book. I had to become very vulnerable in order to even remotely believe I would be able to procure a good product of a book, and it might still only be mediocre to those who might see my opinions as different than their own. That is okay in my eyes. This was about doing something for myself, about completing an accomplishment in my life, about crossing something off the bucket list, if you will. This was about me telling a few stories of my own and maybe, just maybe, making a difference in the life of someone who needs it. This is me.

My name is Joshua Ian Hale.

I am married to a wonderful woman who keeps me on my toes, and we have two beautiful daughters whom I will talk about throughout this whole book. They get their own sections, so I don't want to spoil too much about them too much yet.

Now for the meaning:

Joshua comes from the Hebrew name *Yehoshua* and means "Jehovah saves" or "God is deliverance."

Ian is of Scottish Gaelic origin and the Celtic version of the name "John."

Hale is of European bloodline. Although I don't know quite where it begins, I know England is a part of it. In addition to all that, I have Cherokee Native American blood coursing through my veins and married a fiery woman with Cherokee Native American bloodlines coursing through her veins, so I think I'm doing okay. Our children have a little fire to them, as well. That's good because this world is going to be tough, and I want them to be strong. To top all that off, Ian is the first name of one of my favorite authors, the author of one of my favorite characters. Ian Fleming wrote all of the James Bond novels. I think I'll take it.

I grew up in a small town called Campbellsville, Kentucky. I didn't have a whole lot of "friends," but I had a few really good ones. I had a lot of great acquaintances over the years, though. I learned, over the years, that there is a big difference between the two. I wasn't the most popular kid in school, nor did my family have a ton of money.

I was born in San Antonio, Texas, at Brooks Army Medical Center in Fort Sam Houston in December of 1979 around 10:00 p.m. during a Monday night football game. My dad was stationed there at Fort Sam Houston during his days in the Army. He was a Surgical Assistant and did Fencing, like Zorro, or so I thought as a kid. He taught me a little bit about it, and I might remember enough to get myself stabbed in a real sword fight now.

Once he got out of the military, we moved to that little town of Campbellsville where I grew up because my grandfather pastored a church there. I was raised in the church, and I was raised to be a good person. When I was acting up, which happened a lot, I was corrected by anyone in my family who happened to be close. Whatever weapon of opportunity was available for discipline was used. A switch, a wooden spoon, a hymnal swatting me on the butt, whatever it took. I was somewhat wild. I had two nicknames from my family: "Savage" from my dad and "Jabber-Jaws" from my grandmother. That is still true to this day. Discipline was delivered, however, and I gained respect for adults in my life, and I have it to this day. I feel like this is where much of society is failing today. We don't teach "old school" anymore. My great-grandmother even said I was her little preacher, although I had no idea why at that age.

My life growing up was a good life, and although we were never rich, I don't remember needing anything. I know my mom did a great job hiding it from us if we did need something. I was often disappointed when I couldn't get expensive shoes or clothing like the other kids when I was younger, but in hindsight, it taught me a valuable lesson, and I realized that I don't really need all that stuff. Sometimes, we went to Goodwill or the thrift shops to get clothes instead of the big-name brand stores. I don't fault my family for that. I actually respect them. I have done the same thing for my kids. However, it also taught me to go after something if you want it. This created the drive and the hunger at a young age, even though I did not realize it at the time. God was planting a seed.

The thing about a seed is it could sit on the windowsill for decades and never do what it was intended to do. It is not until it is planted in a dark place that it truly begins to show what its purpose is. Many times, I wanted to skip the necessary steps in the process and get to the good parts. But let's be real about it: there were many not-so-great parts, too.

My parents got divorced when I was almost middle school age. Before that, I had played baseball and basketball as a young kid, something I am still passionate about today. My dad would be my coach, and my mom was the number one fan. I don't recall her ever missing a game or any performance I ever did. My dad would say things like "Keep your eye on the ball" when I was playing baseball and would throw with me over and over and over. He would hit grounders straight at me and tell me to get the glove in front of my face. There were some subtle life lessons built in here: *If you don't watch the ball or keep your focus, you will get hit in the face.* My love for sports comes from my dad. Life lessons began at a young age.

As I said, my mom was always the number one fan growing up and still is that way to this day, though now she has to share the title with my wife. She was supportive in many ways for this book being written. My mom has always found a way to make things work and be a support system in my life. I got my gentleness from her and learned forgiveness from her. She is a woman who supports her family in all ways she knows how, and if she doesn't, she finds a way somehow. She loves Jesus, and she has been an inspiration to me my whole life and someone I could turn to for anything at any time.

One day, they had to cancel baseball due to a storm. I can't remember if it was a game or practice, but I am pretty sure it was a practice. It was raining really hard to the point where we could barely see the roadway in my dad's little yellow truck. We had another kid in the truck with us we were taking home that day. My dad was driving; he was on the passenger side, and I was in the middle. There wasn't a seat belt, I remember. If there was, it was only a lap belt. With what happened next, a lap belt wouldn't have done anything to stop me from coming out of it.

A vehicle hydroplaned into our lane, and there was just enough time for my dad to turn the vehicle to angle it somewhat inward toward his side. The impact was a collision of crunching metal, shattering glass, and screeching tires in split seconds of time. I felt an impact like a cinder block on my chest. Then, everything went black.

I woke to the sounds of sirens and pain, my vision blurring just a little as I heard people talking to me. I was crying, of course, scared of what was going on. I was only in the fourth or fifth grade at the time. They asked me questions like "Are you okay?" and "Can you feel this?" while telling me not to move. I heard my dad still nearby talking. I started to open my eyes. They told me not to open my eyes. "Keep them closed tight and don't look." I didn't. Looking back now, sometimes I wish I had.

We were taken to the local hospital, but my dad was hurt really bad. He had to be taken by medivac helicopter to a better hospital for multiple internal injuries, broken bones, fractures, and there would be surgeries to follow. I didn't even get to see him that night. The other boy had a broken leg, I think.

Me? I had maybe a scratch or two from the glass, but I was hurting like I had been punched repeatedly, and I was bruising on my left side. I later found out I had a concussion from it, and Mom had to wake me up every two hours that whole night. I wasn't even admitted to the hospital, and my dad was stuck in one while I got to go home. I felt horrible. When I got home, I had to immediately take a shower. I remember the glass raining off of my head and plinking on the shower floor with the water.

That might not have been the first moment God intervened in my life, but it was definitely a moment He protected me. By all accounts, in that accident, if you saw the truck, you would understand that there should be no way I should not have been ejected from the vehicle or, at the very least, crushed under the dashboard. My dad had thrown his arm in front of me in that split second to protect me and hold me in, to save me. He had to have had divine help.

I have worked on enough accidents as a Police Officer and know enough about physics and the way collisions occur to know about objects and people in vehicles when there is an impact. Something else pinned me back into that seat with a force I cannot completely describe. The concrete block was just the closest I could come to it. My dad's arm is *not* a concrete cinder block.

That was me being protected.

When I went back to school after the accident, that was the most attention I have ever gotten while being in school. I chuckle about it now because, for a brief moment as a kid, I was popular. Popularity faded quickly again soon, and it was back to the usual. Oh well. Popularity is nothing in the grand scheme of life.

My dad's recovery was a rough road, but he was able to pull through, thankfully. The next few years would be hard for me as a kid, though. I don't think it is being selfish as a kid if you don't understand what adults have going on in their lives. You just want to keep everything as you know it. I believe I grew up or was made to believe the family could be perfect or *should be* perfect.

I have no idea where this fantasy in my mind came from. Maybe I created it for myself for my own comfort and healing over the years. I think we have a tendency to do that in our lives. Either way, we all know family is not perfect, nor will it ever be. People are just people, flaws and all. We just never really want to admit it to ourselves. It just is what it is sometimes. Sometimes, the most difficult people in life to deal with are family. I wish it was more like my fantasy. It would be simple. It would be like my naïve childhood, but then again, children are not supposed to know what adults deal with. Sometimes, I wish adults would grow up. It took twenty years of policing and dealing with other people's family drama to realize how much I don't want to tolerate it in my own family. The expression "silence is golden" is often great when conflict needs to be avoided. But silence can also be wasted time you can never get back when tragedy strikes and you wish you had done things differently. We only get one shot at life.

When my parents did get divorced, it was very difficult for me. My sister and I became very close for a time. My grandfather (my dad's father) had taken a church in Florida by this time, and we would go there to see them and spend time with my dad, too. It was fun, just different. Our summers were spent chasing lizards in the yard and going to Disney World and SeaWorld with the church kids. I think I went to Disney World about twenty-five times that summer. Then, my sister and I had to go back home to Kentucky because we had school. It was hard leaving my dad that summer. I also missed my mom back home.

My grandmother is a homemaker and a preacher's wife. She can cook and sew, and she would make us outfits that matched as little kids so she could recognize us if one of us went astray from the pack in public. She made beautiful quilts for the beds, and I had one of them on my bed through most of my childhood, and I still have it today. Grandma would work just as hard as anyone else in the church with no pay or recognition, just the acts of service and love for Jesus and her husband, my grandfather. I could write another whole book about lessons learned from all my grandparents over the years. Maybe someday.

I remember us going to the Florida springs and how cold but crystal clear the water was. It was paradise. I just never knew it. Then, they moved a few other times. I remember a house in Cincinnati, them taking a church in Portland, Tennessee; at some point, they moved back to Campbellsville while I was growing up and still in college and then finally back to Portland. Grandpa passed away on February 2, 2022. It was the day after Grandma's birthday. His last act was to sign her birthday card.

I was very blessed as a child, though I didn't realize it at the time. God began teaching me and molding me into something at a very young age through the experiences life would have us go through. Grandma and I often have long talks about life now, and we talk as grown-ups, a totally different experience from when I was a child.

My paternal great-grandmother was a grandparent who was around for all of my childhood and into my adulthood. I was the oldest grandchild on my dad's side of the family, and I remember her telling me as a child to tell me to "just call me Grandma Three since I am your third grandma." It stuck. We all started calling her that. She lived to be ninety-nine years old, and she was a firecracker! She would make us biscuits with chocolate gravy (and it was delicious), and we would work puzzles together. She was as sharp as a tack, almost up until when she passed away.

At her ninety-ninth birthday party, I remember asking her, "Grandma, you have lived almost a century. What advice can you give a young man like myself?" Not sure what kind of day Grandma was having with her responses when she said to me, "Eat lots of hot peppers, pickles, and onions."

I looked at her confused and said, "Grandma, I asked you for advice on life, and you tell me to eat lots of hot peppers, pickles, and onions?"

Without missing a beat, she glared at me and then smiled wryly and said, "I'm still here, aren't I?"

"Yes, ma'am." What else was I going to say? We both got a laugh out of it, and I hugged her and wished her a happy birthday again, telling her I loved her.

My grandpa was a man for Jesus as long as he was alive. He was saved at a very young age and led a lot of people to Jesus. He was a man who not only made a ripple on the pond for people's lives. He truly made waves and an impact. He was a great role model for me, and he was born in 1933. That is a far stretch from my age. Learning from him about how to grow a garden, how to hunt, how to trap, how to fish, how to survive were some of the most important life lessons I ever learned. Looking back, though, it was never about those things with him. It was about spending time with his grandchildren. There are so many stories that could be told about my childhood, as with every grandchild or grandparent. I miss fishing with him, and I long for his advice sometimes.

My grandmother on my mom's side was a woman who I loved spending time with when we got to see her. She was an expert Rook and Bridge card player, and her hobby was crocheting and sewing. She would tell us stories of the card games while she was sewing and looking through one of those giant magnifying glass lights so she could see the stitch better. You know, the kind on the swivel. She told me about attention to detail (even though I didn't listen much) and could make a beautiful afghan quilt. Now, I don't have enough patience to go get one out of the closet sometimes. She loved elephants and Yahtzee, and I could always, always make her laugh. She loved Jesus and loved to hear all four of her daughters (my mom and aunts) sing. It didn't happen often, but when it did, it was awesome! The harmonies from the four sisters were outstanding, and even if they hadn't sung together in years, it's like they just picked up where they left off. She loved Barbershop Quartets, and she especially loved it when they sang the song "Mister Moon."

I loved to see that smile on her face and to watch her clap her hands when they did. If it wasn't that, it was watching musicals like "White Christmas," "The Wizard of Oz," or "The Music Man" over and over, and to her, they never got old.

I never got to meet my grandfather on my mom's side. He passed away when I was a baby. I am told he was a great businessman who was also a Barbershop Quartet Judge. Nicknamed "Doc" because he was a pre-med student at Purdue University. When he was almost finished with that program, he decided to drop it and pick up an Engineering degree instead. He was incredibly intelligent. After college, he started his own business. He started out in the Varsity Four barbershop quartet out of Purdue University, where he and my grandmother went to college. He was then the Director of West Towns Chorus in Chicago, Illinois. Then, when they moved to Glasgow, Kentucky, he coached the winning quartet called the Four Renegades and the Imposters. That is where my mom and dad met in high school. "Doc" eventually became an International Barbershop Quartet Judge, usually judging vocal expression. He was later inducted into the Barbershop Hall of Fame. So, I guess it is safe to say I can see why my grandmother and my mom and aunts love the Barbershop Quartets and musicals. It might even be where I get the basis and love for jazz and blues bands I have. Who knows? I sure do wish I could have met him. Maybe one day. We sure would have a lot to talk... sing about. Or maybe, just maybe, I would just sit and listen.

Music was instilled in me at a *very* young age. I think nearly everyone in my family on both sides of the family could either sing or play an instrument, or both. And some of them at the same time. It was embedded into my very being.

Both my parents remarried, and I got a lot of life lessons from my stepparents, even if I didn't grow up with both of them. They are good people. My stepmother is a Respiratory Therapist, and she and my dad live in Western Kentucky now. I even have step-siblings who I consider siblings. I think it is just a title. Family is family. Does it really matter what the title is at the family dinner table? It should be the one place we have peace, yet often in life, it is the one place we expect a war. It doesn't have to be this way. I hate it, and I dread it more than anything when it is like that.

My stepfather is a former Marine, so the military was still in the family, just like Dad had been in the Army. He dealt with me when I was a jerk teenager, and I began to learn discipline about work ethic and how to support my family in the future. I know I was hard to deal with at that age. I learned how to work hard, and when I got a smart mouth, he had ingenious and, dare I say, devious ways to make me understand his point and make me learn a lesson. I still know them to this day. He never raised a hand to me or hit me once. In my mind, I suffered from manual labor.

My wife's family has always been wonderful to me, and I have been so loved and accepted by them for our entire marriage. All of my in-laws are good to me, and they are there if I ever call or need anything for the girls or me. I try my best to be the best man for my wife and the girls I know how to be. That is how I want our family to work. They have supported my career and our family through it all, and they take care of my girls. For that, I am so thankful *to* and, more importantly, *for* all of you.

In getting back to me, I have always been a die-hard Denver Broncos fan, no matter how good or bad the teams have been over the years. That's my team. My dad was a Broncos fan, and I was raised a Broncos fan. I was raised on University of Kentucky Basketball, and it is hard to accept mediocrity from basketball when you are a UK fan. I love the Pittsburgh Penguins hockey team, and I have always been an Atlanta Braves fan, although the Cincinnati Reds are now my closest home team. So, I am all over the map (literally) when it comes to sports teams. It really has no rhyme or reason. I can't explain it, so I don't try.

As much as I love sports, though, there are certain requirements, such as height, weight, and talent. The talent part I was okay at in baseball, but in other sports, such as football and basketball, I was literally not built for it. I am five feet eight even as a man now, and that wasn't going to cut it as a sports player. Couple that with the lack of talent in those areas, I am now just a fan who screams at the television to my team like they are going to hear me on the other end. I know there are lots of people out there like me.

My favorite movies as a kid were "Top Gun," the "Indiana Jones" movies, and "The Goonies." I remember recording them when they came on television with our VCR. Some of you reading this may not know what the heck that even is. Google it. I wanted to be a fighter pilot like Maverick when I was a kid. It was my goal to join the military and fly jets. I scored well on the ASVAB in high school, and the Navy Recruiter was promising me everything in the world. My whole family was against it, and then I was told by someone I was too short to fly, and that was probably true at the time.

If that didn't work out, I was going to be an archaeologist because I love adventure and I love history, but then I realized many archaeologists struggle financially, and it might have been a difficult career to navigate with a family. It was at this point in my life I was trying to plan for the future, even though it would be completely different from anything I ever thought about as a kid.

I decided those were not what I was called to do. I didn't know what I was going to do. Here's a big part, though, so pay attention. I do remember when I decided I wanted to be a Police Officer. I don't remember talking about it, dreaming about becoming one, or even thinking about it before this time. I decided to become a Police Officer when I saw a show on television that came out in 1996. The show was called "Pacific Blue," and it was about bicycle cops! I wanted to be a bike cop. It was a show about beach cops. I, even later in life, applied at Ocean City, Maryland Police Department. It just never worked out. But as a kid, I just started watching "Cops" as much as I could, and it was on from there!

When I graduated high school, I spread my wings and flew the coop and went to Eastern Kentucky University. It was directly next to the Department of Criminal Justice Training and was the top law enforcement training facility in the United States. I immediately declared my major in Police Administration and my minor in Music. I even got a partial scholarship for music.

I mentioned the music aspect of my life. When I was growing up, I was singing at a very young age in church and began playing instruments in the sixth grade. I talk more about it later in another chapter, but I had a fantastic band director who expected nothing but greatness out of us. I learned much of the discipline and attention to detail from him. He was an intense person when we were in practice because he expected the best. He was hard on us, but it taught me not to quit, no matter what.

I played and sang music even into college on a scholarship for instrument and voice. Throughout high school and some of college, I did marching band

and orchestra, and then I even picked up choir in high school and performed musicals. Music was my life at the time. It was there I learned much discipline. I had to hear it from football players who would make fun of the band and talk about how it was not a sport and we were just there to entertain. That's right. We were there to entertain, but if you have doubts about it, try playing an instrument from music you have memorized, marching to a formation, keeping count in your head, not running over someone in the process, and making your instrument blend with all the other instruments with good sound. This is done in all types of weather. To my music teachers throughout middle school, high school, and college, I am grateful for the lessons both in music and in life.

Later on, though, in my sophomore year of college, I was in a crisis mode regarding my schedule. I was a Police Administration major, and the building was on the furthest side of campus across a major bypass road. I was also a Music minor (which might as well be a major), and that building was on the complete opposite side of campus. I had fifteen minutes between classes and had to ride a bicycle because I could never find parking in time for class. I was working two jobs, and I was in a fraternity. My life was very overwhelming at that time. I could not dedicate the time I needed to police studies because the minor in music took up most of my time because of marching band, orchestra, choir, private lessons, ensembles, and the list goes on. If you are a music minor, you might as well be a music major in college. I was thankful for all the opportunities, and I was on a partial scholarship, but something had to change.

I made the excruciating decision after much deliberation in my sophomore year to take a step back from music, drop my scholarship, and work on my Police classes. I picked up another minor in Psychology to balance it all out. I was devastated for a while. My tuition went up, and I still think about it to this day. But it was during this time God intervened, and I found out about the Kentucky Police Corps program, which I talk about in this book. The music didn't stop, though.

During this time, I started a DJ-ing company and started working at parties and weddings. I started with CDs at parties and rented equipment, working my way up to buying equipment. Then, finally went digital. I have done huge festivals, weddings, parties, and even charity events. I love it. Contrary to the Don McLean song "American Pie," with this Kentucky boy, there won't be a day the music died.

The stories could go on and on about my life, as I am sure with anyone. My entire life had been about what I was or did. It was God who intervened and taught me it is not what I do that defines who I am. All of the things in this book are not who I am. Policing, music, public speaking, writing a book, working with people. Those are not who I am. They are what I do. God is going to find His purpose for me no matter what role I play as long as I am seeking His favor.

I hope you enjoy this peek behind the curtain and see there is no great Wizard of Oz, just a guy who pushes a bunch of random crazy buttons and hopes to get it right. Oh, and the horses I talk about in this book don't turn colors. If you don't know what I am talking about, then hey, go watch the musical.

Just a Kid and His Treehouse

In life, it really is amazing the things our brains remember as core memories and how those memories shape us for our future. When I was a kid, growing up was different than it is today. We lived in a neighborhood, but it was out in the country. There were lots of houses in the neighborhood, but the neighborhood had woods surrounding it in one area and fields backed up to it in other areas. The neighborhood is called Wildwood Acres, and we lived on Wildwood Way. I loved growing up there. Everyone knew everyone, and kids could be safe playing in the neighborhood. That neighborhood was my world to explore.

My friends and I would go to the creek, cross the fields, and I even had a favorite tree that had been hollowed out next to the creek you could get inside. It was awesome! One of the best things I ever had as a kid, though, was my treehouse. Across the street from my house lived my second cousin, so it would have been my dad's first cousin. He was an adult, obviously, so I treated him as such. I was raised to respect adults as a kid. I think they still live there today. Well, this treehouse was in his yard close to the barn that backed up to the woods. As far as I was concerned, this was the doorway to my kingdom back then as a kid. We went everywhere!

Now, this treehouse became *the* place for me as a kid. I camped out in the treehouse. We hung out there after school, and I went there when I was mad or sad. My English Setter, named Boo-Boo, would sit with me for hours in that treehouse as I read books and drew in art pads. (Side note: She was one of the best dogs in the whole world a kid could ever ask for.)

My friends and I would trade baseball and football cards there, build stuff out of wood and scraps we found wherever we could. It was my place. I don't really remember how the treehouse got there or it being built. I just remember being told I was allowed to use it as *my* treehouse. This treehouse was just a platform with rails and a ladder, no roof. But to me, it was everything.

I tried to build a roof onto it once. It didn't end well. We found scraps of wood, nails, metal, and lots of other junk to build the roof. Somehow, either I or one of my friends found an old, rusted tin barrel. We jumped on it over and over and over to flatten it into submission to use it as a piece of the roofing materials. We did just that, sort of. We assembled the roof the best we knew how and had to check to see how sturdy it was. I stood on it in just the right place. It looked terrible but seemed to hold up well. In all actuality, it really would just provide shade and no shelter, nor was it sturdy and safe. That same day of building it, my sister came down to the treehouse. She climbed up the ladder, and I somehow talked her into climbing onto our roof because I told her it was sturdy and needed someone else to help me test it.

What happened next is still a story that scars her and a literal scar that does the same. As you might have guessed, the roof was not sturdy; she did not stand in a place that would hold up, and the roof collapsed. As she fell through the roof, which in all actuality was only about three feet from the deck of the treehouse, she fell through the part with the rusted tin barrel. We had stomped the thing so many times it was no longer round but semi-flat with lots of jagged edges. One of those jagged edges went deep into my sister's leg.

Immediately, the screams came from her mouth, and the crying commenced. I had to go into helpful big brother mode, help my sister, and do damage control on the situation. Her leg started bleeding profusely, and the metal had cut her probably a half inch deep or more. It was a straight-up gash, and blood was everywhere...at least in a kid mindset it was. We got her to my parents, and it got doctored up. And I got in *major* trouble. I got grounded and spanked. This was back when parents took punitive and corrective measures to direct the path of their children rather than the world we live in today, but I will digress on that part. When my sister reads this in the book, there will probably be some anger that may resurface, or at the very least, she will glance at the scar on her and think of that fateful day.

The treehouse was many things to me, as I told you before. I have many great memories there. I also have a few bad ones. One of these memories was one that would shape my future and the future of others based on one event. To give you a little backstory on this memory, I must tell you about the first time I really experienced bullying in my life. Now, before I go any further,

56   Protected

let me tell you this is a word thrown around a whole lot. It is used when it is convenient and not used when it is necessary.

We had a bully in our neighborhood. His initials are J.M. I know his name, but maybe he has turned his life around, and I haven't seen him since I was a kid. So, I will take the high road and not call him out for this particular incident. To be honest, though, there had been several incidents. This guy was a jerk. He was high school age at the time, while my friends and I *might* have been in early middle school, if not late elementary school age. In my hometown back then, sixth grade was still in elementary school. It was either fifth or sixth grade for me.

I was a smaller kid, still not a big man now. I am five feet eight, and that is what you get, other than my stellar personality. So when a kid who was much bigger than me started trouble, I did what every reasonable kid does at that age: avoid him at all costs. It worked for a while. I had seen him get thrown off the bus by our wonderful bus driver, Mr. Colvin. I had seen him get yelled at and forced to leave us alone on the bus. My friends and I didn't feel completely safe, but we didn't feel unsafe as long as Mr. Colvin was driving like he usually did. Two words on why I felt reasonably safe: *old school*.

The bully, J.M., would challenge Mr. Colvin on the bus, and every single time, he lost. We thought we were in the clear. And to be honest about it, I don't even remember what his problem was other than he was just a real jerk. He would take backpacks, smack things out of your hand, throw paper wads, smack us "accidentally" as he walked by, say mean things, that kind of stuff.

On one uneventful day, my friends and I were in my treehouse minding our own business. I have no idea what purpose we were serving or what we were doing that day. I just remember what happened next. The bully, J.M., came toward the treehouse and was yelling and running his mouth the whole way through the yard. The treehouse could be seen from the road, but it was way down in the yard. In order to get to it, you would be seriously trespassing on the property in legal terms if you were not supposed to be there. J.M. came down to the treehouse screaming and cussing at us, and he started to climb the ladder of the treehouse.

Now, the current me would have coached the kid me, and we probably would have made our stand like King Leonidas from 300 and the Battle of Thermopylae. I know Leonidas died during that battle, but this was my treehouse, and we had to defend it like Kevin McCallister would have in "Home Alone." What I *should have done* is Spartan kick J.M. back down the ladder and start hollering and screaming for help or lead my team of friends to fight back. I did not do that.

J.M. came up the ladder and was on the platform before I could do or say anything. He was berating us and spitting profanities like the bully from "A Christmas Story." Unlike Ralphie, though, I hadn't fought back at that time. I would have been pummeled and had no place to retreat. Next thing I know, I found myself being lifted over the railing of my treehouse and hung over that same railing upside down by my leg. I was upside down, looking at the ground and screaming because if he had dropped me from that height, I likely would have broken something. And, unless I had been able to flip myself back upright, it might have been my neck. I was enraged. I was embarrassed. I was terrified.

As the blood rushed to my head, I remember there was more shouting and screaming, but it was not only coming from the treehouse. I looked over toward the street where the new shouting was coming from and saw new figures (while I was hanging upside down). It was adults, several of them, and then more adults were coming toward us after them. J.M.'s playtime was over.

A tense but quick negotiation took place between J.M. and the sets of parents and adults who were now in attendance to the party. I remember being lifted back over the railing by J.M., and not a word was being spoken in the process. There were no "I'm sorry" or "We will finish this later" threats coming from his mouth. He just laid me on the deck floor of the treehouse and exited down the ladder very quickly. As he got down from the treehouse, he was met with several adults who literally dragged him off the property forcefully. I don't even know if he was resisting the dragging. I just know he was being forcefully removed and taking an earful from the adults. I am pretty sure none of them were his parents; some of them had been ours. Our neighbors directly across the street, my second cousin, who owned the property.

All I know is that was the last time we ever had a problem with J.M. We saw him on the bus shortly after that, but then summer arrived, and we didn't see him anymore. Maybe he moved, maybe he decided to turn his life around after that near-beating he took (I'm actually not convinced he didn't get it as he was getting dragged away).

So what does all this about the treehouse have to do with my life as a Police Officer? Honestly, I didn't even know at the time I wanted to be a Police Officer, nor that I would ever do some of the things I have had an opportunity to do. The treehouse and its impact from that day ended up leaving an imprint in my mind for what the basis was and my first experience with bullying. There would be more, but this was a core childhood memory that would eventually be the foundation to become the change agent in a world needing help because of bullies.

Some people learn what bullying is through their family. Some of the cruelest people I have ever seen have been family members I have dealt with throughout my career in policing. Those who are meant to support someone in their worst time end up being the suspect or the assailant. Some people experience bullying in the workplace. Let's face it: if you are a jerk kid when you are young, most of the time, if that is not corrected, you are a jerk adult. Call it like it is. The list goes on and on for where people experience bullying.

Hurt people *hurt* people.

I learned that at a young age. It created fear. It created disdain for a person whom I really didn't know on a personal level. I knew nothing about J.M. and his personal life, and I didn't want to. I learned about what to watch for and how I didn't like to be treated. I learned lots of life lessons from this whole ordeal. I learned all these things in two places:

I learned them on a school bus where we send our kids at least twice a day for five days a week to go to school. It is supposed to be a safe place. It is a place where we trust other people to take care of our most vulnerable part of society. It is also a place where they have to learn the world for themselves, and we cannot be with them during that time.

And finally, I learned these things in a place that I considered my safe place. It was a place where I had lots of other great memories, just like other kids would growing up. It was a place I never thought anything like that would happen, just like all other victims think. It had been my happy place before that, and after that incident, it all changed.

I learned about bullying in my treehouse.

JOSHUA HALE

The Symphony of Young Life

I sometimes look at my life in many different ways so it makes better sense to me. Let's face it: life is just hard sometimes, and you sometimes wonder what in the world you were thinking at the time or how it all fits together unless you take the time to look at the big picture. I have no doubt in my mind that God has a plan for me and that He has all the answers. Unfortunately for any of us here on earth, though, we don't.

For humans, it is usually a roller coaster of emotions we ride that gives us the ups, the downs, the speed, the thrill, the terror, the fear of the unknown, or even the sudden stop. Sometimes, I feel we are supposed to experience something so we are better prepared for the next big task. When that time finally comes, we experience the feeling of understanding and have the strength to go on. I sometimes get the "Oh, that makes sense" type of feeling about situations I come across.

I think once you look at the big picture of your life, you tend to understand what type of person you really are and how you have become the way you are, whether that be good or bad. The decisions we make in life are what get us to where we are today. There is no magic moment that comes along and says to us that we are going to have things a certain way. The things happening to us in our lives are usually and oftentimes a direct result of the decisions we have made in the past.

Let me explain. People don't automatically struggle financially or have huge amounts of debt just given to them. If someone is in debt, it is because they made the decision to be or because they made bad financial choices. If someone is hooked on drugs or alcohol, it is because they made the choice to take the first hit or to put the bottle to their lips. Too many people blame their problems on the rest of the world when all that they really need to do is take the time to look into a mirror.

When I say this, though, I am not saying that I have a "gloom and doom" type of attitude toward things. It is actually quite the opposite. I believe any person has the ability to change at any time in a moment's decision and can change the path upon which they tread their feet in the future. No one has to be a bad person. No one has to be a good person. The decision is up to them. The decisions we make throughout our lives are things that either could or could not come back to haunt us, but either way, these decisions become a part of us, and the experiences make up who we are.

I know that is a very difficult thing for some to grasp or understand about their own lives, so I like to put things into different perspectives to help me make sense of them. We all have different things in life that we relate to more than others. For me, especially before policing, I suppose my forte would be my understanding of music and some of the many different areas of it.

An analogy that I like to use about life is one of a symphony of music. I think each and every person could look at their lives in this way because each and every person has different pieces or parts that don't make any sense at all unless they are all put together and intertwined. All the little parts make up one big concept or creation. These include the good and the bad parts or even the decisions we have made. If one thing doesn't look right, it may be because we cannot see the entire sheet of music, so to speak.

I believe all our experiences come together to make us who we really are. Music, for me, is one thing in my life that has remained constant and something that I have always known or understood. I have, for as long as I can remember, played sports and done other activities, but music is something more to me. It is part of me. I have not always continued down the path of music, but it never left me.

I still play sports for recreation now in my adult life from time to time, but it is not the same as if I had grown up doing so. I didn't know what I wanted to do with myself and, for a while, didn't have any direction. I suppose because I was ten years old at the time I had a traumatic event happen, someone could say that I had plenty of time to recover from it and redirect my life, but ask a ten-year-old who has just had that happen to him and see what kind of response you get about life.

I was just a normal-ish kid growing up. I rode the bus to school every day and came home just to go outside and play. I collected baseball and basketball cards and traded them around to learn my first concepts of commerce.

I explored and hiked the immediate world around me. I built things, I destroyed things. I had my one or two close friends in the neighborhood, and together, we got into more mischief than we should have. I loved my mom and dad, feared getting into trouble (I always did), and it absolutely thrilled me to terrorize my little sister. I had a real attitude problem in the early stages of my teenage life. I was confrontational with a lot of people and even started getting into trouble at school. I didn't get into any serious trouble, but it was enough that I spent a lot of time in detention or stayed after class for something stupid I had done or said.

Yep, that was my life...free and easy living, or so I saw it. I had tons of imagination and a world to conquer. I was the type of little boy who enjoyed life in general and the type that I am sure my family sometimes wondered if I would make it to age twenty-five. I went cow-tipping, took people snipe hunting (if you don't know what that is, I will leave that to you to expand your knowledge and have someone take you), built forts and treehouses, rode my bicycle everywhere, and jumped over make-shift ramps make from crates and boards, and almost blew up a kitchen with a chemistry set. Everything was about what I could learn how to do next or how much fun I could have doing one thing or another. It was my mother's nightmare about what I was going to get into next or if I was going to hurt or kill myself doing something dumb.

Throughout those early years of my life, I did my best to have fun at anything I did. When Christmas rolled around every year, I always enjoyed my toys and such, but if I got a present that required a big box, I would take it and all the pillows and blankets just to build a fort or a hideout between the coffee table and the couch. I would use that to ambush my sister when she would walk by or take a flashlight and pretend I was exploring a cave. That was the type of imagination I had. The older we get, of course, the less imagination we tend to have as adults for the most part. That has not completely stopped me. Now, rather than just imagining the things I did as a child, I try to go to real places and explore them.

Mountain Biking, hiking, horseback riding, rock climbing, finding caves, snorkeling the oceans, and exploring new and exciting places are my favorite things to do. I love the adrenaline rush of those moments and how they make you feel alive. If you have never done so, I highly recommend stepping out of your comfort zone sometimes and trying something that will invigorate your soul. It will be an experience you will never forget.

Although I had a very vivid imagination and the abilities God gave me to be almost fearless about anything and everything, there was something missing with me as a child at that time. I just felt like I needed to apply myself to something other than being destructive and having fun.

Now don't get me wrong when I say this. If you are a parent and you have a son or daughter like this, the worst thing you can do is limit their imagination. I happen to believe this is the time in a child's life when they find out what their limits are and learn on their own to go beyond them and conquer their fears. Never limit this and do everything within your power to encourage them to chase after their dreams. The world is bad enough without us taking our fears and forcing them upon our kids early in life. Who says that they have to grow up exactly how we did or that they can't make it in life being anything that they want to be?

Some people succeed because they are destined to. Most people succeed because they are determined to.

At that time in my childhood, I found it difficult to focus, just like I do as a grown adult now. I was never diagnosed by a doctor, but I swear to you, I probably had ADHD before it was a thing. I was so hyper I had to be forced to sit still sometimes in school. The problem with that is that when you force a child to sit still, most of them do the next thing that comes naturally to them. They talk. I was no different for a hyper kid. I was on all eight cylinders like an engine the entire time that I was awake. I laugh now, but it was not funny at the time. I got a D in Conduct from my third-grade teacher. Now, *that* is bad behavior.

My mother, the gentle-spirited woman that she is, would always lovingly wake me up in the morning after I had thrown my alarm clock across the room to make it shut up. I hated that thing in the mornings. It was one of those big box kind of alarm clocks. Some of them today come on in the mornings to whatever radio station you have it on. That did not work for me. My alarm clock sustained multiple battle wounds and markings because it made a different sound. I was not awoken at first by the gentle sound of a sweet alarm. It didn't have my mother's voice in the clock that would sweetly

64   PROTECTED

say, "Josh, it is time to get up for school." Nope, that wasn't it at all. My alarm clock might as well have smacked me in the face or poured cold water on me when it went off. It went, "Buzzzzz!"

Shut up! If I needed to get out of bed, God would naturally wake me up when he thought it was time. I used to hate mornings. I suppose that explains why I have done so well staying up late in college and working third shifts. I mean, I literally had to put the alarm clock across the room and make myself get up and turn it off, unplug it, throw it, or whatever violent idea crossed my mind that early in the morning to go back to the silence. After I had disposed of the problem temporarily, I would crawl back into bed and go back into Dreamland.

Then, my mother would come into the room and sit on my bed to gently wake me up the first time. She would tell me again the second time with slightly more force. She would then come into the room, turn on the bedroom light to blind my eyes, and say, "*Joshua Ian*, I said it was time to get up!! You're going to be late for school, and I do *not* want to drive you! *Get up!*"

That was usually an every-morning occurrence. Eventually, you have to learn to get yourself out of bed on time. Professors at colleges and bosses at work do not generally enjoy it when you roll in a half hour or hour late.

Needless to say, I needed some direction and something to do that would help me at that age. I needed something else to direct my path and give me a purpose. I found it when I was in the sixth grade. It was actually something that I have had my entire life and just didn't know it. It was the one thing that I did that has remained constant throughout my years as both a child and as an adult. Music.

When I was at the end of my fifth grade school year, the band director for the Taylor County School systems came to our classroom and talked to us about music. He was a younger teacher, and he brought in a bunch of different instruments and talked about each one. He showed us the sounds they each made and how they fit into the band together. It was really neat to see how they were played and how sounds changed depending on how you played. It was nothing short of new and amazing to me. I remembered my family members and how they could play music. I thought maybe one day I could be good at music, too. I had never realized until then that I was destined to be part of that family legacy. That was all I needed to reassure myself that I could do it, too. I was hooked.

I had wanted to play saxophone for as long as I could remember. I waited impatiently, as any hyperactive child does, for their turn to try something new. I watched all the other kids as they slowly and one by one had the instrument that best fit them selected for them. It was almost my turn. Two or three more kids and I would be set. I was going to be a natural at it. I wouldn't need any practice. I was going to be great.

My mind drifted off somewhere else because that is what my mind did as I imagined the notion of playing in huge concert halls with thousands of people coming just to hear me play saxophone. I imagined the thunderous applause I would receive when I played that performance perfectly and effortlessly with a beautiful melody of notes.

"Josh! Pay attention! It's your turn."

I was quickly brought back to reality by my teacher and the snickers of my classmates as it was time for me to step up and see what I was made of. I listened intently as the man explained each instrument and how to hold each one. I tried each one of them as he helped me position my fingers properly over the keypads or valves of each respective instrument. I tried a tuba to see if that would work. Nope, too big for me to hold. I tried a clarinet and squeaked and honked my way right to a headache. Nope, not that one, either. I went down the line until I finally saw it.

It was a beautiful, shiny, brass-colored saxophone. This was it. This was my moment to shine and my chance to show the world who I was. I picked it up with the assistance of the band director and tried to play.

Honk! Squeak! Honk!

Laughter broke out in the class, and I gave a cheesy grin. Okay, so I would need a little bit of practice. No big deal. *I suppose we can't all be Mozart.* But then again, Wolfgang Amadeus Mozart didn't play the saxophone either that I know of because it wasn't invented yet while he was alive. He died fifty-five years too early to have ever heard one played. Then, just when I was looking up with a smile of satisfaction and congratulating myself mentally on a good decision, the man said, "Here, why don't you try this one."

In a moment's flash, he had gently taken the instrument from my hands, and I saw my dream vaporize right before my eyes. I was crushed. No, that was all wrong. I was destined to play the saxophone and be great at it. It was going to be me standing there when the crowd jumped to their feet and cheered. This was not the way it was supposed to happen.

Well, I got that part right. He handed me another instrument that I really didn't want at first, but I quickly dealt with the concept that maybe he knew what he was talking about. This one was shiny and reflective of the lights, too. It was a lot smaller and not nearly as heavy as the saxophone. I vaguely knew what it was from the looks of it. He told me, "This is the trumpet. It is a member of the brass family. I think this one will be good for you, and you will do well with it."

"Blah, blah, blah...You will do well with it," is all that I heard from the man's voice. I now had to deal with the idea that my dream had just been chosen for me. Once I got over that false reality, I came to realize that I would learn more from that man than any other teacher throughout my entire life. And so it was. I became what is commonly referred to as a *band geek*. I didn't care. Call me what you will.

That name was actually fine with me because of several reasons. It gave me an organization to belong to and helped to give me direction where I was lacking it before. I also made some of the best friends I ever had throughout school during the years that I was there. Plus, in all honesty, my real friends I was already close to didn't care what I did, and they liked me for who I was— the sign of true friendship.

Over the next year or so, I would work very hard and practice all the time to get better at the instrument. I drove my mother crazy practicing and was finally told that I had to practice right after school and before she got home from work. Not too long after this, my mother remarried, and the man who is still my stepfather came into my life...and he didn't like the noise either. I didn't get it. I mean, I thought they wanted me to excel in the things that I was doing in my life. Actually, I know that they did want me to excel. They just didn't want all the excess noise after they had worked long hours all day long.

Either way, I practiced a lot and got to the point where I could carry a tune and was able to keep up with any person my age playing the instrument. It was new and exciting, and it gave me something to be proud of again. Little did I know that my musical world was about to change again.

Around the middle of the seventh grade or so, my band director told me he needed me to stay after school one day and to let my mother know about it. Was I in trouble? That was not a far stretch of the imagination. I stayed after school, and we arranged for me to go to her work after that. At the time, she worked very close by, and I could just walk to her work a few blocks away. As the bell for the last class rang and all the students started filing outside and getting on the bus, I went over to the high school where the band room was located and went inside. Some of the high school kids were gathering their stuff and putting up their instruments, while still others practiced their craft by ripping up and down musical scales or playing individually.

I timidly stood there and watched them as they went about their business until it was noticed that I had entered the room by the band director. He smiled at me and told me to come into his office and sit down because he had something that he wanted to talk to me about. I slowly inched my way into the office while dragging my feet and wondered if this was not some ploy to discipline me for something that I had unknowingly done. When I sat down, he asked me how my day went and made a small conversation with me until he got to the real reason for the after-school meeting. I knew I couldn't have been in that much trouble because my mother would have had to be there, and she would have been partaking in the let's-yell-at-Josh-because-he-has-done-something-stupid speech.

Luckily for me, that was as far from the truth as it could be. The real reason I was there was because he wanted to talk to me about my playing. He spoke very highly of me at the time and told me how proud he was of me. That was nice to hear because I was still at a pretty fragile point in my life and really liked having the male role model and the praise. He proceeded to continue about how he wanted me to do great things. Finally, he began telling me why I had been called upon. He wanted me to change instruments.

I was at first in shock about why he would ask me to do so, but I soon realized that it was because he needed someone who was decent at playing. He told me about an instrument that had not been in the classroom when he came to visit us nearly two years earlier for the pick-your-instrument day. He told me that playing this instrument would take practice and time and that he would need me to take private lessons so that I could catch up to where the rest of the band was. I wasn't quite sure why he wanted me to take on the task, but I wasn't about to pass up the opportunity and the challenge. He was right about one thing, though: it would definitely be a challenge.

He went into the storage room where all the instruments were kept and told me that I would have a certain slot in a cabinet to keep my instrument and that he would periodically check it to make sure that I was taking care of it. I followed him like a shadow, curious as to what was going to happen next. He told me that I would have to pay about thirty dollars to rent it for the entire school year. What I didn't know was that he was handing me an instrument that cost around three thousand dollars.

He reached into the cabinet and pulled out a semi-large black case. It was an oddly shaped case that didn't look anything like the square shape of a trumpet, trombone, or saxophone case. He flipped the four latches on the outside of the case after laying it over on its side. When he opened it, the lights above us made the newly viewed silver instrument gleam and shine.

Wow! I thought. *That looks really cool, and I would be the only one to have one of these in the entire band.*

"This instrument is called the French horn. It originates from Europe when the hunters would use it on the fox hunts while they rode horses through the fields and woods," he said as he picked it up and gently handed it to me. "Be careful with it."

"Is it expensive?" I asked.

"This one you are holding was about $3,000.00 when it was new."

The color drained from my face a bit. It must have. It looked pretty new to me, even if it wasn't. I could tell that this was going to be slightly awkward until I got used to it and could learn to properly carry it and play it. All I knew was that I had a really pretty silver instrument that no one else had and that it was up to me to learn to play so that I could be good. He told me a few things about the horn and showed me how to properly hold it. Then, he gave me a few books and sheets of music to help me and guide my path when I went to my private lessons. He also had not wasted any time. He told me that there would be another teacher coming the next day who would help me and start my lessons with me, and he told me it would take a lot of work and discipline to be good at this instrument.

And so it was that I became a horn player. To some people who don't understand music or have little respect for it, I got made fun of sometimes for playing an instrument, but as far as I could see, they were just telling me that to make themselves feel better. My thoughts were that they could make fun all they wanted to, and it didn't matter. They couldn't do it.

Over the next several years throughout high school, I was very blessed to be able to learn to play very well. I became first in the All-District Bands for several years in a row, first in the All-State Concert Band the one year I tried out, and eventually would get a scholarship to the college I was attending for music performance. I am privileged to say that I was one of the blessed high school students who was able to perform a solo on the stage at The Kentucky Center For The Performing Arts during a concert. It is a place where all kinds of events take place, from performances by the Louisville Orchestra to Broadway musicals such as "The Phantom of the Opera," "The Lion King," and "Cats."

I feel so lucky that I can be one of the ones to say I have actually had my dream come true of performing on a large stage like that in a very famous place, with thousands of people watching. I never thought, when I was just a kid trying something new in the fifth grade, that I would ever have that happen a few years later. It was amazing.

So, needless to say, music has played a vital role in my life, and still does today. I still sing and even have performed in choirs throughout late high school and early college. It helped to shape my existence and give me the structure and ideals that I have even now. It also helped to make me a well-rounded person who has a great respect for most things, whether that be music, history, sports, the arts, or otherwise.

I suppose now you can see why I used the analogy of a symphony to depict my life. It is what I have known for years now, and it just seemed to fit with the way I wanted to describe things, each little part of your life coming together to make the whole. As important a role music has played throughout my life, though, there have been many other factors that have come into play. Whether that be growing up in church, moving away to college and joining a fraternity, or eventually leading to the cause of this whole book when I became a Police Officer, everything has helped to shape who I am. I have made my promises to myself just as much as I have made my mistakes. I think the key is to be able to look back on your life and have no regrets. The past is the past. If God can forgive us, maybe we should learn to just deal with things and move on.

When I graduated high school, I spent the entire summer getting ready and preparing for the next big step in my life: college. Then, in the fall of 1998, I gathered up all the things I thought I needed and headed off to Eastern Kentucky University. It was there that I would have some of the best and worst experiences in my entire life. I made the best acquaintances a man could ever ask for. I eventually joined a fraternity, held leadership positions on campus, and took part in organizations.

When I was in high school, I was always the nice guy that everyone knew and could trust. I suppose that I still am, but when I was younger, I was also intimidated by what other people thought of how I should live my life. My mother told me at a young age that I would never be able to please everyone, so the best thing that I could do was to live my life the way I was supposed to and always strive to be a better man. I still live by that creed today. At the entrance of college, though, the only thing I wanted to do was get out of my hometown, spread my wings, and see how far I could fly before I fell. It didn't take long for the bird to fall.

I remember Mom going up there with me to help me move in. I think all parents do that when their children go to college. I remember she cried and cried and told me how proud she was that her baby boy had grown up and was becoming a man. It made me sad, too. It was the first time that I had ever really been away from home, and it truly was time to start becoming the man who could eventually stand on his own. It was sad at the time, but not for long.

I missed home for the first few weeks but immediately made friends on my dormitory floor. It didn't take long for high school to be no more than memories and for the fun to begin. It is a wonder that I ever made it out of college alive, and at times, it was questionable as to whether or not I would. The things we did were stupid, reckless, and absolutely some of the coolest things that I have ever seen. Luckily, I never physically got hurt, didn't fail out of college, and, most importantly, didn't go to jail.

I wondered while I was moving in if I was going to like it at all. Then, when Mom and my sister left after helping me, I realized it was just me, my new roommate, and all the crazies that lived on the floor that I would call home. It didn't take long for me to become a vital part of the group.

I remember thinking that I was really lonely that first night. My roommate hadn't moved in yet, and I was there by myself that night. I was lying there looking out the window at the pond that was behind our dorm, which separated our dorm from the Law Enforcement Complex, where I would take most of my classes. I was starting to doze off when I heard the elevator doors open up and what sounded like an entire football team yelling and screaming out in the hallway.

I went and peeked out my door, curious to see if I was going to get jumped by some guy and have him take the last of the *real* food that I would have in my room for the rest of college before I replaced it with ramen noodles and nearly-spoiled sandwich meat. I slowly stuck my head out and saw two guys having a push-up contest while the others cheered them on. Some of them had beer cans and whiskey bottles and were truly making a sport out of this. It was the first time I had seen anything this crazy. I had been to a few parties when I was in high school, but nothing to this caliber.

The only parties that I went to while in high school that even remotely compared to this were a field party one night and a party in my senior year. That party my senior year was just a preview of the ridiculous antics that would follow me when I met all these guys. Although, that party was of particular fun to me because it was close to a lake and was a pool party. While everyone else drove their cars to the house, this was the first time that I did anything really fun and crazy. I went and rented a boat. It was an instant success, and between nearly sinking the boat and jumping off the roof into the pool, it was my first step just before college to become more confident with my life.

Anyway, back to that night in the dorm. On this night, these guys were just plain nuts. And I loved it. I especially loved it and knew that I was going to enjoy college when my RA (Resident Advisor) came out of the elevator after it dinged and was flapping his arms and stuffing bread in his mouth, screaming, "I'm a bird! I'm a bird! *Kukaw*! I'm a bird!"

I really didn't know what to make of all of this. I mean, wasn't this the guy who they told me was going to take care of me and watch the floor to keep it safe? This wasn't what I had in mind when my orientation leader told me and my mom how dorm life was going to be. Was there a sober one among them? The answer to that is *no*. Not a chance there was a sober one in the group, and that was usually the way it stayed with a lot of those guys throughout all of our college time in the dorms.

We got into more trouble as a group in those two years than I have ever seen another group do.

We lived in that dorm my first year and moved to another dorm building my sophomore year. It was nearly every guy on the floor that moved, from one sixth floor to another sixth floor! We played football in the hallway, had Nintendo 64 and PlayStation tournaments, skipped class, went to other people's classes, and went on spring break together. It was more fun than should ever be allowed by any group of guys, and it is a wonder that any of us survived. I was far from grace at that time in my mind, and I know my family would not have approved, but I always felt the hand of God on my life, even when I didn't deserve it.

It is safe to say that though I was not a good example to others then, I learned a lot of valuable lessons along the way, and I am now in a better place. I have learned not to judge others because of the mistakes I made. Those were not even the darkest moments of my life. Those would come later.

I fear that I have already given enough information to get any number of us in trouble just because they could probably track us down now from dorm records and transcripts. For that reason, I am not going to include any names in any of the incidents I talk about from college. I don't want them hunting me down or me to ruin their lives either. No matter what I say about it, I loved it. I wish I could go back to college and have some of those memories again. They are nothing more than a blur in my mind now. I wish I could go back and get some re-dos on how I lived and have worked a little harder.

Yep, it is official. I met some of the funniest characters and had some of the funniest moments of my life happened while I was in college. The characters were people I came into contact with every day and the people I miss seeing from time to time. I definitely could have been a better witness to them about Jesus, like I was raised to be, but I still had a lot of growing up to do.

One of the funniest people, though, who comes to mind is a guy who lived at the end of the hallway on the opposite end of mine. He didn't have a roommate, and I never saw him come out of his room much except at night. When he did, though, I sometimes didn't know whether to talk to him or run as fast as I could away from him. I wish I could tell you his name, but I am scared of him coming after me. I remember being scared of him then. I don't know if he ever even graduated college or whatever happened to him. I never saw him after my freshman year. That was enough. He was a white guy from the mountains of Eastern Kentucky. He made moonshine in his room and would sometimes light it on fire in the hallways as he downed it from a Mason jar. He never really came out of his room to hang out with us, and most of the time, he just walked past our doors and said hello before he slammed the door to his room. This is the way it was most of the time, again, I say most of the time.

There were those few times, though, that things were not quiet from him and when he did not stay in his room to himself. When the sun went down, he would sometimes throw open his door and the end of the hallway, and we all knew he was coming. This is that point when I always questioned if I should run the other way or call the men in the white coats to come pick this guy up. He threw open his door while we studied or played video games and began stomping down the hallway from one end to the other. This wasn't the problem. The issue of what to do came up when he started screaming, "The South is gonna rise again!"

He yelled this over and over again as he marched up and down the hallway with a sword while wearing a gray Confederate uniform that looked like it had just stepped out of the woods and been taken off one of the soldiers of Robert E. Lee or Stonewall Jackson's Brigades. I couldn't help but laugh at him as he made a complete idiot of himself. We all paid him little attention when he did this, usually as we always kept our guard up. We only had to step in when he would get into arguments with the guy at the other end of the hall from him. Of course, this was the guy who lived right across from me.

The guy who lived across the hall from me became one of my very close friends. He is an African-American man who was always quiet and very rarely bothered anyone. He was a gentle-spirited man who was most of the time timid and barely even spoke. The only time he would really even make noise at all was at night when he was drinking (every night) and sometimes when he was drinking during the day. He was an early riser and woke up sometime before the sun did, sometimes went to class drunk, but always scheduled his classes early so that he could drink the rest of the afternoon.

I remember many mornings being awoken by the sound of a blaring stereo playing "Rocky Top" at its highest volume and echoing all the way down the hallway. You see, he was a huge Tennessee fan who was always boasting about the Vols for as much as we would listen. This was always a fun argument between us because I am a die-hard University of Kentucky fan. He would wake me up for class or, when I was leaving, ask me if I had had anything for breakfast. When I told him no, he would always say that I should have breakfast with him and his three friends.

"Who are your three friends?" I asked him.

"Jack, Jim, and Jose," is all that he would reply. I would shake my head and decline the request for the breakfast meeting with him and his friends.

It was a regular conversation that rarely went anywhere at all but always made me laugh. His problem was that he liked to drink...a lot. His favorite was Jim Beam. He talked about how smooth it was going down and was often seen with his favorite shot glass and a bottle that he must have replaced daily as he offered some to everyone on the floor in the dorm where we were not allowed to have alcohol.

As I said before, these two generally kept to themselves unless they were extremely intoxicated. The guy across the hall from me would never venture to the Confederate end of the hallway, and he rarely ventured to our end. It was when he did that the trouble would boil over like a pot filled with water on high heat. The Confederate would come marching down the hallway shouting his usual comment with his sword pointed toward the ceiling. However, if the two of them saw each other, it was only a matter of time before one of them or both of them said something really stupid.

As would usually happen if these two crossed paths when they were that drunk, they would take turns back and forth and resort to calling each other some sort of racial slur to each other, get mad at each other, and then talk about how the Civil War was either won or lost as it should or shouldn't have been. It truly was a sight to see and something that I must have witnessed over a dozen times.

The funny thing about it was the fact that most of the time, when these two saw each other sober, they would cut up and make jokes to each other, and I have even seen them going to each lunch together like they were best friends. It was only when the Confederate started drinking the clear liquid fire known as moonshine and the guy across the hall was drinking his bourbon or whiskey that they really had words. I can only remember one time when their words resorted to physical violence between the two of them, and that was the time that we had to take the sword from the Confederate's hand for the night to make sure he didn't kill anyone. There were never any threats made about doing so. It was just for everyone's safety.

After they would sober up, though, it was back to normal, and one of them or both of them would say they were sorry, and everyone was back to being friends again. One of them would knock on the other one's door, and they would apologize like men face to face, hug it out, shake hands, and go back to being friends. It was an unusual dynamic. It really was a weird way to start out my college life, but it sure did keep things interesting.

I didn't see the Confederate anymore after we left the first dorm from my freshman year, though I still had my friend, the Vols fan, who once again moved in across the hall from me in the next dorm. I think it might have been better when he did have someone to take out his anger on at night rather than the second year when he woke us up more with that stupid fight song from the Tennessee Volunteers. I hate that song.

My college life is filled with memories and people like that, although most are not as bizarre a pair as those two friends. From dorm life to spring break, we always had fun. I will never forget those guys my first two years of college. We stuck together through thick and thin, in good times and in bad. When hearts were broken, we helped them to heal. We had the most fun any of us could ever ask for. Some of us are still close today, but for the most part, all I can do is hope that some of them read this, think of those times, and smile, and let me wish them the best that life has to offer. Other than some of the guys that I would meet from my fraternity or the Officers I would work with in my twenty-year police career, nothing would compare to my boys from the sixth floor. I learned early in life about brotherhood and how it will support you in times of need.

You will need that support at some point in life. At least, I did. When I didn't feel like I had it, that is when the road got really rough.

Throughout my life, there have been those moments that have defined me. There have been those moments that have helped to shape me. There have been trying times, and there have been crazy times. But through all the crazy, emotionally challenging, laugh-out-loud, good times, bad times, and hope-we-get-out-alive moments, nothing has shaped my life more than the people who have been in it.

If anyone reading this knows you were any part of that, this is me telling you thank you for helping to make me the man I am today. Even if it has not been mentioned because there is not enough time to write everything from my life, just know that you are not forgotten. Whether good or bad makes no difference, healing the heart or breaking it, you have helped to form the restlessness in my spirit, and you have shown me how to survive. I wish anyone who has been a part of the experiences I have shared to have the best that can be achieved and want to thank you for helping to create the symphony of my life. May God give you peace and understanding in everything you do.

You Don't Have to Change Your Accent

One of the things I dealt with in policing a lot was people trying to call you out on what you told them. If you are not honest about who you are, people can see right through that. I learned when I was in college about who I was and what kind of honesty I wanted to portray. I didn't realize until I got into the real world and dealt with real problems just how much being myself would serve me and others well.

While I was in college, I participated in Student Government. During the same time, I was on the Eastern Kentucky University Mock Trial Team when mock trial teams were just getting going in Kentucky. We traveled around the country and competed against multiple other teams throughout the nation. We were a young team at the time, and we traveled to Cleveland, Ohio, for one trip.

We performed the case, and I played one of the attorneys on the team. We completed the whole case and waited for the Judges to come back and grade each team on how they did. The Judges went through their spill about the proper way to try the case and ways to improve. I really don't remember any of that. What I do remember is the last Judge when she got to me to grade my performance on the team.

She was a woman from Germany who immigrated to the United States of America to live. I am wholly in support of this. What I am not in support of is what she said next. This woman basically humiliated me in front of the entire audience and courtroom and made fun of my Kentucky accent, then had the audacity to tell me that when I come to Cleveland, I should change my accent because mine doesn't belong. Admittedly, I have a Southern drawl when I speak. I speak quickly, and sometimes I have hitch words like "umm" or "uh."

This does not show unintelligence or ignorance or stupidity. It was implied in this way to me that day. She said to me, "When you are coming up here, you should change your accent in order for people to understand you and to fit in better."

I was livid! This woman from a country not even of my own with a German accent was telling me to change my Southern boy Kentucky accent when I came up North...in the United States! I have no problem with the people of the city of Cleveland. I just can't magically change my accent without going to acting school or sounding really stupid when I try to change my voice.

From that day on, I decided if I ever went to court (and I ended up going a lot) or if I ever did public speaking (I still do that a lot, too), I would try my best to slow down my speech for pace, but I would not change my accent or who I am just because someone said I should.

In policing, I have learned people are going to do what they are going to do. You have to meet people where they are, not where you want them to be. In policing, we deal with facts and absolutions, but also what ifs. We have seconds to make decisions that affect someone's whole life. Typically, when the police are called, it might be the worst moment of that person's life.

I have decided I want to be a leader who can be kind and lead by example but meet people where they are in life. I am not here to judge people. If Jesus didn't judge someone, what gives us the right to do so? Don't insult people for who they are. Perhaps that is all they know how to be. Reach out to them in love and be someone who empathizes with what they might be going through. I decided that day I was not going to try to hide who I am from people. This is what God has made me.

I apologize for my imperfections when I need to, I take the hits that come to me, and I truly do my best to stand up for what is right. If that conversation were to happen today after I am now retired and worked twenty years of policing, it would likely go considerably different. To the woman who insulted me that day, whoever and wherever you are, I truly hope no one ever did it to you.

I read this quote from Bernard Baruch several years ago, and it stuck with me. "Be who you are and say what you feel, because those who matter don't mind...and those who mind don't matter." That means be the person you are. For me, I was a Southern boy with an accent who took a trip to Cleveland that changed his life.

Some people told me I could never amount to anything and couldn't be a Police Officer standing at only five feet eight. Here we are twenty years later as I finish this part of the book. I'm just a guy who didn't listen to people when they told me I should change who I am to fit where I was. For the record, I didn't change my accent. And I certainly wasn't going to be stopped from being a cop.

The Mayor, the Man, the Chief, and a Pall-Mall Cigarette: How I Got Hired As a Police Officer

I hope to never forget this memory as long as I live, and if I ever meet you, I would love to tell you how it went in real life by demonstration. I am literally smiling as I type this at this very moment. This is how I was hired as a Police Officer. Well, for the most part. There was a lot of work that went into the process and the academy, but this was what I would call "the negotiation" moment that started my career.

As I mentioned elsewhere in the book, I went through a program no longer in existence but was then called the Kentucky Police Corps. It was a program started by President Clinton when he was in office, and there were several states that hosted the program. It included advanced training in comparison to the regular basic academy at the time, and we were trained in other areas just in their inception in the police world. They are now taught like it has always been part of the curriculum.

Anyway, I signed my contract in September of 2001. Everyone knows what happened in September of 2001. The attacks of 9/11. This was just before that. I had signed up for the Police Corps program as a sophomore in college, and they were in the final stages of the process other than background, and we had to find an agency to let me be a part of them. Enter the town of my Alma Mater, where Eastern Kentucky University is located, the city of Richmond, Kentucky. This would later be the city I would retire from, but let's not get ahead of ourselves; I wasn't even hired yet to be a cop.

At the time, I was sitting in the basement of City Hall, where the Police Department was located in the Chief's office. I had the best suit I could afford as a college student (which wasn't much), and I was sitting in the office accompanied by a man from the Police Corps program. In the office was the Chief, the Police Corps recruitment man, and myself. We were waiting for the Mayor of the city of Richmond to arrive so we could get started.

I heard footsteps down the hallway and remember the Mayor walking in and the Chief jumping to his feet respectfully. The man with me also stood up, and I knew I should, as well. So...this was the Mayor of the city. I had never met the Mayor before, but it was very clear very quickly who was now in charge in the room. She was.

The room began to fill with smoke as she smoked through her Pall Mall cigarette. I was not the first Police Corps cadet to work for the city of Richmond, but I was the first one to sign a contract, and they had never been approached before about this. So, the Mayor finished her first cigarette as the details were laid out specifically and in fine detail.

I tried my best not to cough in this room with no windows in the basement with no ventilation. I was supposed to be tough. I was twenty-one years old at the time and was supposed to be in the best shape of anyone in the room. I could not breathe. I thought I would die of second-hand smoke inhalation, and that kept going through my mind as we kept talking and talking and talking.

By the third Pall Mall cigarette, the Mayor began to repeat the details of the entire meeting to ensure she understood what the city was taking on. In a raspy voice and with ash now hanging an inch off the end of the cigarette, she repeated,

"So, you're going to have him declare a four-year contract to the city of Richmond. You are going to pay for his school, his training, and all of his academy expenses, and when he graduates is when we start paying him?"

The man answered, "Yes, ma'am." The Chief said nothing the entire time. They were the only ones working on the negotiation.

She continued and took a long draw on the Pall Mall cigarette, "And you mean to tell me you are going to pay us $10,000 each year he stays with us during that contract, and we don't pay that?" Another long draw on the cigarette she had never exhaled that I saw.

Again, he said, "Yes, ma'am. That is correct."

She peered at me through her glasses and took yet another draw on the Pall Mall cigarette, which was almost to the butt of the cigarette. I was sweating and almost terrified of this woman at this point.

She craned her stiffened neck upward as a smokestack of smoke came out of her mouth and nostrils, and at the exact same time, she somehow still spoke and growled the words in a scratchy voice, "We'll take him!"

That is a true story. I can't make that up. I smile every time I think about that. The Mayor passed away several years ago. Although I never worked for her as an employee, she took a chance on me as a boss before I arrived in the city of Richmond. Whether it was my winning personality or the money and a free Police Officer to be the reason, whatever her reason for hiring me, either way, I am grateful. She was the start of my career and how my life forever changed. It all started in that chief's office, which I would work for, with that enormous cloud of smoke. Here I am. Twenty-three years later, at the time, I am writing this, still smiling and remembering that day in the haze.

The Mayor, the Man, the Chief, the Pall Mall cigarette, and me.

DOUBLE DOWN ON MY DECISION

I had applied many months before for this program they called the Kentucky Police Corps. It was a long and arduous process to get accepted. I had waited and waited to hear back from them. Anticipation was chomping at me. I met the Chief of Police and the Mayor of the city of Richmond and had my interview, and you read how that went.

I signed my contract for my scholarship and joined the Richmond Police Department in September 2001. It was right before that day. If you were alive and old enough to remember, you probably remember what you did that day, too. I got up and went to campus like I usually did, sticking to the usual routine I had. I remember I walked through the Powell Building on the campus of Eastern Kentucky University, and there were large screens set up in the lobby area. It is a huge common area room with lots of couches and chairs for students and guests to sit and congregate. It was a favorite place for most of my fraternity members at the time.

I looked at the screens in horror as I saw people hovering around them. There were no people sitting on the couches talking about trivial, menial, and frivolous things. Everyone was focused on what was taking place on those screens, well...what the screens were showing. There were people on their cell phones (not the smartphones of today) talking to their families. There were people on the landline phone at the desk talking to loved ones. There were people crying. There were people angry. The screens showed America was under attack. Classes were canceled that day, I think. I know I didn't go, even if they weren't.

The screens showed the airline planes turned into missiles and crashing into the World Trade Center Buildings in New York City. Another plane crashed into the Pentagon in Washington, D.C. So many lives lost in the planes. The World Trade Center buildings fell. You can't forget those images if you see them. It is one of those core memories I have in my life. Although I wasn't there physically, I felt like I wanted to be. So many lives lost, and so much destruction. Another plane meant to have a different target was taken back over by the hero passengers who were on board. They crashed the plane in a field in Pennsylvania rather than let the terrorists (cowards) win. Passengers flying to their individual destinations became heroes, and it lit a firestorm of patriotism in this country.

I remember seeing on the footage all the first responders running toward the buildings to save people before they fell. I remember people jumping from the building windows. I remember seeing the images in the days that followed of the ash covering the people and the streets. I remember seeing the buildings falling and seeing all the carnage and rubble as they searched for victims.

I wasn't there. I don't want anyone to think or believe I am saying I was there. I was not. I am not one of the heroes from 9/11/01. I was only an American college student watching on television like the rest of the world. I got to speak to my loved ones that day when others did not get to. My heart goes out to the families still.

I wrote this chapter in September of 2023, twenty-two years after the events of September 11, 2001. Even now, I still remember and feel the rage I felt from witnessing the events. I remember the sorrow I felt for all those involved. I remember the pride I felt when I saw the American flag flying above the rubble. Some people tried to talk me out of becoming a Police Officer a few times, both before and after I signed my contract. I even regretted not joining the military due to 9/11. Looking back now, I know God had a purpose for me in policing, and I was told Police Officers fight for their country every day. If I went back and lived that experience again, I still would have done it. I still would have taken the job for $11.63 an hour, I think. It didn't matter what I was getting paid. I was going to be a cop.

Those of us who were alive during that time and those of us who are alive now and see things played on the anniversary of the day see this slogan every year, and it gets posted all over social media. I keep saying I remember, but it goes deeper than that.

We will never forget.

Know When to Get Up From the Table

In November of 2003, a few of my Police Corps compadres and I were sitting at a café in Morelia, Mexico, in the state of Michoacán. We were eating lunch that day and talking in English as we took a break from speaking Spanish all the time, which we were required to do in the school we were attending for that few weeks, on trips, and when staying with our host families. That is why it was called a Spanish Immersion program.

As we sat there and ate, we were talking about the enormous Morelia Cathedral across the street that was the seat of the Archdiocese of Morelia of the Catholic Church in Mexico. It was an architectural masterpiece, especially on the inside. It is made of pink stone, which gives it an interesting color in the sunlight and at dusk. The courtyard was filled with artists and vendors selling their paintings and sculptures and treats. There is a lot of historical context about it, and I could go on and on, but essentially, the building of the Cathedral began in the sixteenth century and combines the ideals of Spanish architecture and Renaissance along with the Mesoamerican style. It was quite the historical site (remember, I am a history geek. I love it!). It is phenomenal to see!

On the same side of the street as ours and a little further down and above on a second story were offices of important political people. I'm not sure who it was from my memory, but I remember there were guards outside the on the balconies from time to time. Anyway, as we sat there and were in our own world, a crowd had started to gather just about a block from us. Close enough for us to see but far enough for us to be minding our own business.

The crowd kept getting larger and larger as more people, mostly young adults or teenagers, started filling the street. Eventually, I would suspect the street had at least a hundred people blocking traffic or causing a disturbance. Chanting broke out. Some of them had signs and banners and began shouting or yelling in Spanish. I couldn't quite understand all of it, but I understood the message behind it. This was a political protest, and it was becoming less and less peaceful.

Thank God we were not wearing our uniforms for Police Corps that day as we sometimes had to in Mexico. Most of the time, like today, we were in civilian clothes to blend in. We could not blend in. We were Caucasians who could barely speak any Spanish and looked like tourists. We had to haggle on prices all the time in the street markets to not be taken to the cleaners because they thought we were rich. I was a poor college graduate, but in Mexico, I was rich. Perspective.

We were almost finished with the food anyway, so we got the checks.

"La cuenta, por favor."

The waiter with the apron brought out the bills, and we began preparing to pay. Now, I had to figure out in my head exactly how much money to give in Mexican money versus American money. Here goes the math, which I am terrible at anyway. As this was happening, the crowd had grown louder, stronger, and with more intention of delivering their message, whatever that was.

As we finally got to pay the waiter, I saw the Mexican Federal Police and Morelia Police arrive on the scene. It was not in patrol cars, though. They arrived in a black pickup truck with push bars on the front and roll bars in the bed of the truck. Two Officers were hanging onto the roll bar as the truck came to a screeching halt. They dismounted the machine immediately, and all the Officers were out of the truck. Another truck arrived with what I thought was a large dog kennel in the back, but it did not have a dog in it. That was for prisoners who were about to get arrested. Still, another truck arrived on the block, this one with a roll bar and a push bar, too. This truck was a little more menacing. It had a mounted rifle on a swivel attached to that bar, and the Mexican Officer was on the weapon and prepared. There were other Officers running up on foot from the blocks nearby as they were about to engage the crowd. Some people began to scatter and scream about the police. Others did not leave.

It is my understanding from what I have been told they were protesting the Mexican President that day, and I do not know the outcome of how many people went to jail and what happened with the crowds. I do know this. That was not the place or the time for a few guys who couldn't really understand Spanish to be sitting near or around what was apparently about to be a riot.

We got up from the table, even thanking the waiter, and went in the other direction as fast as we could nonchalantly walk. We disappeared around a few buildings and into some alleyways and were out of there.

There is a lesson in all of this I had to learn. In life, you need to know when it is time to leave the table. Not every situation is going to be a protest or a riot, but it could easily turn into a bad situation quickly. Retreat, regather, reorganize, and return at another time.

Know when to get up from the table.

Don't Insult Your Host

I have learned a lot of lessons in life, and I grew up learning manners in my home. Over the years, I have had to learn the hard way on some of the lessons dealt to me. Most of which I have picked up along the way.

While we were in Morelia, Mexico, for the Spanish Immersion and trip and training in the academy, we had the opportunity to go to their police academy, where they train their recruits. I said elsewhere in the book I started at $11.63 an hour. I also had to buy my own gear. My mom even had to help me with that. My agency didn't assist with that back then; they do that for Officers now. Back then, it was gun belts and all the stuff on the belts to hold the gear *for* the belt. Then, I had to have the gear. That included two sets of handcuffs, baton, flashlight, oh...and the pistol. Nothing much, just dropping something around the amount of about $1,500.00 before I became the police. This was not the case with all police agencies, and ours has come a long way from those days, but that is part of my story. To put that into perspective, the Mexican police made less than we did. Their facility was not as nice as ours at the Department of Criminal Justice Training, but it was all they had, and they did great things with it. We were in our Police Corps uniforms, and they met us in their academy uniforms, and it truly was a neat experience. Until it wasn't.

With all that said, on this particular day, we went to their academy and toured it. We spent some time with the recruits and instructors while we still spoke terrible Spanish and they didn't speak English. We went into a gym where they did their training and defensive tactics. Somehow or another, as we were listening to their instructor talk about self-defense and training, one of us was invited to try and do some sparring with the instructor. What a great way to get some practice in for ground-fighting and be able to engage with our fellow Cadets from across country lines.

As we all widened the circle of people to give them more room to engage one another, I watched as they began to move around in the circle and try to gauge how the other person would react in a fight. Once contact was made, there was a little bit of touch-and-shove as they locked arms and bodies. Then came something I did not expect.

Next thing I knew, our recruit had flipped the instructor and taken him to the mat and was on top of him, moving into an armbar hold and trying to get submission. I was amazed and horrified at the same time. I didn't move. Nobody said anything.

The Mexican instructor looked embarrassed as he lay on the ground in front of his own recruits. These were the people he had to continue to train after we left that day. Our Police Corps recruit helped him to his feet and apologized as the Mexican instructor put a smile on his face and laughed it off. Even though he was embarrassed, he took it with grace.

It was a fairly awkward exchange for a few moments of brief conversation before we moved on to the next part of the tour, but the lesson learned on that day: *don't insult your host*.

ANOTHER SIDE OF HUMAN LIFE

I sometimes find it strange what little things we see that will put life into perspective for us. It truly amazes me the simplicity that God sometimes uses to get our attention and teach us a lesson. Sometimes, these lessons are as easily learned as just seeing something that passes in front of our eyes. Other times, we might as well have someone come up and slap us in the face so we wake up from our dream world and figure out what is going on around us. Either way, the message is usually clear once we realize it.

I have been blessed to have had an opportunity that many people have not had in the fact that I have traveled a lot in my life. I cannot say that I have accomplished everything that I would like to while I am alive or that I have been everywhere that I have ever wanted to go, but I have had the opportunity to travel to many of the states here in the United States, and I have been to several places outside the country, as well. I have been able to go to Canada, several places in the Caribbean, and Mexico on several different occasions. All of the travel outside the States has been done since becoming a Police Officer. Although I, just like everyone else, am not as thankful always as I should be, I know that I am blessed.

Before I was in the academy, I had always wanted to go to other countries and see them and see what the world around me was like. I had always dreamed of going to new places and exploring the countryside and viewing the sites. I had always thought it was going to be something that I would have to do when I was older and had saved tons of money to travel. Then, I would go and be this regular tourist with my camera, staying in the hotels and sampling the local cuisine. Don't get me wrong, I have done my fair share of being a tourist, and there is nothing wrong with it, but my experiences outside the United States and my wake-up call from the rest of the world came about in a way that I had not expected.

I have always been the adventurous type who would do all kinds of exciting things in my life. I think there is more to life than just getting up every day and going to work or just staying at home watching television. Life is meant to be exciting and exhilarating and full of new things. This has always been my philosophy, but it has sometimes been pushed to the back corner of my mind and my life because there is most often *something* that always *has* to be done.

When I went into the police academy, they told us that we were going to be learning Spanish for the entire duration of our time there. This was fine with me, and I really didn't think it was a big deal because I had always wanted to speak the language anyway and took French I and French II in high school. In college, I took Sign Language, and that was just an elective class that fulfilled a requirement for my transcript. I had not really had much exposure to other languages or cultures other than those basic things learned in a compact amount of time. Spanish was a welcome change for me, and I had been looking forward to it.

I found out very quickly, though, that the older we get as humans, the more difficult it is for us to retain and learn new types of information. I also found out what it is like to get a migraine headache from learning a new language. *They* say that we only use a very small percentage of our brains, and I thought that I had done well to retain the information I had learned in college, but I was soon to establish an idea that our instructors in the academy were going to push us to the limits on mental, physical, and emotional levels that I had never seen or thought about. I don't know who *they* is, but I wonder if *they* have ever been pushed to their limits at all.

During my training at the academy, we usually had classes all day, physical exercises and workouts, firearms training, legal classes, or some other skills training, and then Spanish would be at the end of the day. Have you ever gone *all day* like that and then tried to learn a new language? This is where those headaches I spoke of earlier come into play. We battled through the learning and the classes for nearly six months and eventually made it as far as we could go within the training schedule because our time at the Department of Criminal Justice Training was almost completed. It was almost time for the trip. We were going to Mexico for what they called an Immersion Program that would completely immerse us into the Mexican culture.

During the Immersion Program, we were going to live with Mexican families, work with the Mexican Police, go on excursions, and go to classes for a period of two weeks. This all sounded well and good at the time I started the academy, but there was one little problem right before we left. I, without a doubt, absolutely did not want to go to Mexico. As I said earlier, I love to travel and experience new things, but I was looking forward to being a Police Officer. We had been in the academy for eighteen or nineteen weeks at that time and had been around the same people twenty-four hours a day and seven days a week. I think we got a few hours on Sundays to go and do laundry. Other than that, we lived together, went to class together, trained together, ate together, and did everything together as a group. This was great, and it brought us all very close to each other personally, but I was tired of being there in the academy, and I was ready to graduate and become what they were training me to be.

Now, there was just one little problem with *my* little problem. It wasn't something up for discussion; I had no choice in the matter, and they told me I was getting on that plane, like it or not, and going to Mexico. My thoughts were: *Well then. When you put it that way, I suppose I will go with you.* Since I didn't have a dog in the fight, I might as well make the best of the situation and get ready to travel. They had made us get our passports for the trip and had pretty much taken care of everything else other than the clothes we were going to wear when not in uniform. And so, on the night before we were going to fly out, we had everything packed and ready to go so that we could be ready to leave *very* early in the morning.

We left before sunrise, at least two hours before. We all sluggishly crawled into the vans that normally transported us when we traveled, and we headed off to the airport. I remember sleeping on the way to the airport. No sense wasting good sleep time when I had the opportunity to do so. I learned that early in the academy, too. So, after being lulled to sleep by the sound of the engine and the fact that everyone else was quiet in the van, I awoke again only as we pulled into the unloading area and the van came to a stop. We all climbed out and began to unload our baggage and meander our way into the terminal. We had gotten there early.

After we all checked our luggage, we headed toward the gate and prepared to depart. It had been a while since I had been on a plane, and I had forgotten how much I love to fly. It had always been a dream of mine to be a fighter pilot in the military, but I had made the decision to come to college and study law enforcement and become a Police Officer instead. But still, it nevertheless brought back the idea, even if only for a moment, when they would soon fire up the jet engines, and the plane would accelerate down the runway.

After going through the extensive security checks that now took place at airports after the September 11, 2001, World Trade Center attacks, we all waited for the others to finish putting their shoes back on, the items back in the pockets, or the belts back through the pant loops. I had never dealt with such invasive security at the airport before, but I was glad that it took place because I was not excited about having a terrorist take over a plane with a bunch of police cadets on it. I simply said a short, silent prayer and prayed for the best. That is all we can ever do anyway. Everything else is out of our hands.

When we all entered the plane and began to take our seats, I watched as those in our group who had never flown before nervously sat down and quickly buckled their seat belts in an attempt to calm their pre-flight jitters. I sat down with my I-guess-I'm-ready attitude and stared out the window of the plane at all the commotion as the crews prepared the plane for the flight. I leaned back in my seat and decided finally that it was better to be there than in the classroom and that this was a trip that was already good because I was leaving the country and I wasn't paying for it.

I saw the crew of the airplane shut the cabin door and prepare the cabin and its guests for flight. I watched as a middle-aged woman in an airline flight attendant uniform began her spill on how to buckle the seat belt, put on the oxygen mask, and use the cushion of the seat as a floatation device. I suppose I was as bored as everyone else as I stared aimlessly at her short presentation and mumbled to myself something about not wanting to have to use any of that stuff and hoping there wasn't going to be any kind of emergency that would require it. I remember wondering to myself what good my so-called seat/floatation device would do if I was trapped inside the plane when it was going underwater. And that was only *if* I survived the crash. I chuckled to myself.

When she was finished, she slowly meandered down the aisle, looking over everyone's lap to make sure they had been listening and had buckled their seatbelts, had their tray tables stowed, and that all seats were in the upright position, although I have never understood what the big deal about having your seat slightly reclined is. Once she was satisfied with the cabin, she took her seat, radioed the captain from a small black telephone hanging on the wall of the flight attendant station, and the cabin lights went dark to signify the beginning of the flight.

The jet engines outside our windows soon roared to life as if they had been caged up and finally let loose. I listened to them like a wild beast; they got louder and louder in one aggressive crescendo. I felt the pressure in the cabin change, and my ears popped as the pilot let off the brake of the plane and we were taxied into position for the initial takeoff. We slowly rolled to the edge of the runway amidst all the different multi-colored runway lights to take off from and came to a steady stop. Eventually, after putting the brake on again before the ascent from the ground, the engines growled even louder and showed immediate destruction toward anyone in their paths.

The pilot let off the brake as the engines screamed to everyone around them to notice them. The jet accelerated quickly down the runway and shot into the sky after several hundred yards, and before I knew it, I was looking as the rapidly shrinking buildings and roads vanished below a ceiling of clouds that were now below us. There was no turning back. We were now en route to a place that would change my life and the way I viewed others forever. After a wait in the airport and a fairly short first flight, we changed planes in Atlanta and then boarded the plane that was bound for Mexico.

After several hours of flight and what seemed to be an eternity of being cooped up in that plane, we finally made our descent into Mexico City in the late afternoon. From thousands of feet in the air, I could see only a glimpse of the city from my window seat. The city seemed to stretch on forever as it grew more and more the closer we got. It was blanketed by a dark smog and haze that made it difficult to see the ground clearly and no doubt made the city seem to be about ten degrees hotter during the summertime months.

As we flew lower and lower, the landscape that had appeared to slowly roll by below us now showed as a fast-moving terrain with a large dark shadow of an airplane moving over everything in its path. The plane shadowed shabby buildings and rows and rows of traffic as we dropped further below the blanket of smog from the enormous city. We were almost there. I could feel the anticipation growing inside of me as the wheels touched the ground and skidded on the pavement while the plane itself shook at the touch to the hard ground.

And it was now official. I could now say that I had been to another country, even though I wasn't even off the plane yet. The feeling went from disgust to boredom and from anticipation to excitement as we slowly taxied to our final stopping point for the trip, and all passengers eagerly awaited the opportunity to leave the cabin and acquire mobility again. I watched above my head as the *Fasten Seatbelts* sign that had been illuminated clicked off and was accompanied by a loud *ding*.

It was like someone had just given an emergency evacuation order as I watched many of the other passengers jump up and grab the overhead compartments of the plane to gather their carry-on baggage. I had to chuckle a bit as I watched them all try to scramble to get their bags before someone behind them could cut in line to get off the plane. When they didn't make it, I saw many of them sigh and give a look of irritation as if that one moment had ruined their entire day. It was quite amusing. Seriously, people, we are all getting off the same airplane. A little courtesy would not kill you to let the older woman in front of you or the woman with a small baby go first. And people wonder why some people in the world want to go live their lives in recluse and solitude.

I wasn't really worried about when to exit the plane; we had everything planned out for us anyway, and it went off without a hitch. It usually did while I was in the academy. They had a reason for everything. They told us what to do and expected us to do it without any question or objection. This occasion was certainly no different and probably far more important than many of the things they had told us prior to this. Before we had gotten on the plane for Mexico, we had been given specific orders by our instructors.

"Mexico City is one of the most dangerous cities in the world. Get off the plane. Get your baggage, and get on the bus. Don't make any new friends with people right then; don't mess around. Just get your stuff and get on the bus."

When I heard them say it like that, I knew that they meant business. They got no other comments from me. I did exactly that. I got off the plane. I got my baggage. I loaded my baggage into the storage compartment below the seating area on the bus. I got on the bus. What I didn't know was that this was the point in the trip (the very beginning of it) when my view on life would forever change and when I would change my way of thinking about human beings. I suppose you could say that I was unprepared for what was to follow in the next few minutes that led to the next few weeks. What I know can be said is that I became a different person by the end of the trip who has a lot more respect for humanity as a whole.

As we all got onto the bus one by one, I remember the sun shining down and casting a shadow behind the various buildings we would pass. The shadows did no more than darken the area and possibly cool an alleyway or a corner in the late afternoon. It did not hide or cloak the filth and dirtiness that I saw on the street corners littered with trash and cigarette butts strewn across the ground. Various signs, posters, and propaganda covered walls, doors, and windows and gave their slogans in Spanish to promote whatever product they were trying to sell. Various beers were advertised and promoted as the name brand was painted on walls in colors that were fading away. It was clear that there was little restriction on advertisement.

A stray dog watched our bus as we passed as it was trying to cross the street. I saw the brown fur that was matted and dirty and watched it limp slightly as it walked. I saw the ribcage protruding from underneath the skin and watched the animal hang its head low as if defeated by everything in life. I looked back to try to see it again, and it just gazed upwards toward us, probably hoping someone would care enough to stop and feed it. I wondered for a moment how long it would live like that and even if it would be better off not living at all. Morbid, I know, but there was a change that had befallen me since landing in that country just a few minutes earlier. It was as if God had draped a cloak of sadness over my heart that I had never felt or seen before.

As I lowered my head and felt remorse for the life I had lived and the way I had treated people in the past, a man in tattered clothing looked at the bus and followed it with his eyes as it passed. It seemed as if he had been looking at me. I felt ashamed as I looked at what he wore and then looked at what I was wearing.

His eyes were piercing like fire and yet had a mournful story behind them that I understood. It was as if I knew his life story, and I had never even met him. His shoes that had once been white tennis shoes now showed the miles and miles of sorrow that this man had walked. He had tan trousers on that were torn from being on the streets and dirty from lying on the ground. His shirt was a dirty and torn white T-shirt that had words in Spanish written on it. His dark, black hair was matted and appeared to have not been washed in weeks. And, just as if he had appeared for only me to see, he was gone. I could no longer see what his expression was, nor the wrinkles on his face that hid the sadness of the world.

I felt as if God was breaking my spirit to show me something and open my eyes to see something that my eyes had never seen before. I am sure that I had seen what my eyes were now recognizing before in a sense, but now I truly was aware of my surroundings and that the life I have had has been blessed.

We have all seen, or no doubt most of us, seen the advertisements on television talking about "Feed the Children" or "Adopt a Child" that talk about the poverty and the hunger in other countries other than the United States. Some celebrities will go on the program or advertisement to endorse it and talk about the pennies a day that could feed a child or put clothes on the backs of people in a village. I was no different. I had seen those ads on television before and done what most every one of us has done at some point or another. I turned the channel and did my best not to think about it as if it was real and there really were people out there in need of help.

Did I feel guilty about it? Sure, I did. I felt guilty because, unless you just don't care, it is difficult not to feel sad about seeing something like that and then turning the channel while you sit in your comfortable living room watching your favorite show on the tube and eating your take-out dinner in your air-conditioned or well-heated home. That commercial just happened to catch you at the wrong time, and it was just too painful to view or think about—or there was just nothing that you could do anyway. So why think about it and make yourself sad or depressed over something that you had no control over?

I have been no different than anyone else. I have seen them, and I have tried not to think about it. I have looked at the commercials that talk about what it would cost to feed someone for just pennies a day. I have tried not to think about probably like many of you have, but sometimes things like that just up and smack you.

That was impossible now, though, because it was all right in front of me, and not just in a faraway land somewhere on the plains of Africa like in the commercials. I was in a country that is right next to my own that has big cities just like mine. The people drive cars just like I do, work hard to survive just like I do, have families just like I do. They go to work every day for low wages and work their lives away while, just like in my country, a small percentage of the population controls most of the money.

Someone might as well have just come up to me and punched me. That is the reality I was waking up to now as I stared out the window of the bus. I saw families outside their homes working in their yards. I knew only barely getting by from one meal to another. I saw children playing with pigs in a pig sty that connected to the front of the house that people lived in. I saw mothers outside cleaning laundry by hand, trying to save every bit of water possible to reuse on another load. Fathers and sons worked the fields as the sun was beginning to lower below the horizon, and the darkness began to creep its way across the lands. I had now observed a side of life that had been before me all this time. I just chose not to see it at all.

It is difficult for me to describe how I felt at that time or the emotional roller coaster that my heart went on during that bus ride. I know, to some, it may not have been a big deal or something that, like me, someone would have given a second thought most of the time. The difference for me this time was that there was no escaping it. There was no changing the channel just because I didn't want to see it. It was right there in front of me. I found myself praying a quiet prayer and asking God for forgiveness those times that I ever thought so carelessly of other people's lives. I wondered why it was that so many people had so much to be thankful for and could care so little for others who had next to nothing.

I found myself in that moment feeling like a spoiled kid who always gets anything and everything that I wanted and feeling awful that I had ever taken so many things for granted. I suppose I shouldn't have been so hard on myself, but the fact of the matter was the same for me as it is for many Americans. We live in the richest country in the world as a whole, and yet most people have never seen anything past their own understanding and immediate surroundings. We live in a place that has boundless opportunities if you work hard at it and the greatest free market in the world, and yet most of us never wake up from our own illusions or step out of our little bubble to see the world as it really is. It is time for us as a whole to finally wake up from the dream that nothing goes on unless it is in our own life and reach out and do something for someone else.

This is not, of course, true for all people. There are so many people who have seen poverty, helped those in need, or even lived in poverty themselves. Who am I to judge anyone on the life they live? I am not perfect, either. I did find myself thinking, though, that every single human being on this planet should go outside their comfort zone and see what it is like to live in someone else's shoes. I think we should all have to experience someone in need who reaches a hand out to us for help. When that hand does get extended to you, what are you going to do? What is the next step to take?

I continued to ask myself questions like those throughout my entire stay in Mexico. That bus ride was the beginning of an experience and a trip that I will remember for the rest of my life. Of all the things we experienced while on the trip, all the time that has gone on since then, and all the things I have seen in my life, I still remember the look on the people's faces and the way the trip made me feel.

It has been many, many years now since my visit to Mexico. Since that time, I have seen a lot of things and have grown up a whole lot. I have seen things that have haunted me to this day in my memories. But no matter what I have seen, I can still see those faces of the people begging on La Cathedral steps in the middle of a busy city. I still wish that I had helped some of those people who saw me as a "gringo con mucho dineros" with my white skin, nice clothing, and ignorance of the situation. I can actually think of something recently that helped bring life back into perspective, just in case I had forgotten since the time I was on those streets of Morelia, Mexico.

I took part in a Bible study group not too long ago that gave us different challenges individually every week that we would have to return and talk about.

104   PROTECTED

One of my challenges for a certain week of the Bible study group was to not turn anyone down who asked me for something. At first, I thought that challenge was absolutely crazy until I was able to talk about it with my group. I was able to help people who asked me, and it made me feel like a better person. I helped and assisted people with everything, from giving a few dollars away to pushing cars out of the road that had car trouble to helping with groceries. I feel like God was giving me a second chance to do a good thing for anyone I encountered.

I was always told as a child a verse that now serves me well in my adult life. Hebrews 13:2 says, "Do not neglect to show hospitality to strangers, for thereby some have entertained angels unawares." Although not always the safest thing to do for some people these days, I have truly learned to feel better about myself when I do help someone. The way I see it now, it is not *my* place to judge someone. I just need to do the best that I can to help someone in need, if at all possible. Sometimes, it takes nothing more than that of a kind word to change someone's life. Think about that.

Open a door for a stranger. Pay for a young couple's meal. Pay for the person behind you in the drive-through at your favorite fast-food chain. Help someone other than yourself, and you will discover a joy that you never knew existed until you did.

As I now return to the flashback of memories I have of Mexico, perhaps you might begin to see the change this could have on a young man's life, who has hopefully become a better man because of the entire experience. I only hope that there might be some sort of event like those in my life that might help you to decide that you want to be a good person, too.

When we finally finished the seemingly never-ending bus ride to our destination in Mexico, those feelings of excitement began to return to me as we pulled into the parking area. The sun had long since disappeared behind the now unfamiliar horizon and had given in to the darkness that surrounded us. There were numerous lights that lit up the street in a dull, pale orange glow. I remember looking out the window of the bus and seeing lots of people standing around. I saw families with little children, husbands and wives, teenagers, and the elderly. These could only have been the families that were there to pick us up and take us to their homes to live for several weeks and during the duration of our training.

The instructors had explained everything to us prior to the long ride from the airport, so we sort of knew what to expect. What I wasn't ready for were the grueling classes every day, for hours at a time, to teach me how to speak Spanish so that I didn't get myself into trouble. I found out very quickly that the adult mind has far more difficulty retaining information than that of a young child in the developmental stages. I had severe headaches every single day from the plethora of information that was being thrown at me so that I could learn it. My only hope was at the end of the trip, and while I was there in Mexico, I might be able to regurgitate any bits of information so that I was able to be confident on the streets of both the U.S. and my current location for its duration. But all that aside, it was going to be a wonderful trip.

In the parking lot, all the families gathered underneath the street lamp, each group of people waiting to welcome their respective houseguests. We were going to be staying with them in their homes. We were taken in like family, treated like family, and yet, to me, there was one problem that arose from this: we had to speak Spanish like the family. I quickly found myself in a communication nightmare and did my best not to sound like an idiot in the things that I spoke in my own dialect of the language.

My host family was absolutely wonderful, and I loved staying with them. The family included a divorced mother of three children, one of whom was an adult (who spoke English), a teenager, and a nine-year-old boy who loved soccer. We ate with them every day and experienced everything that the family did for two weeks. I had another one of the academy cadets from my class who also stayed in the home. We even got invited by the family to come back whenever we could if we ever went back to Mexico.

The trip to Mexico absolutely was a blessing to me and completely changed my life. Up until the trip, I had a very distorted view of the world and had not really experienced anything out of my comfort zone. The trip opened my eyes to new ideals and a culture that I had never dreamed of seeing or experiencing. From learning the language and seeing the enormous Catholic churches and cathedrals to experiencing Noche de Muertos, it has been an experience I will never forget.

I remember seeing the enormous city of Morelia from up on top of a mountain, both during the day and at night. The Catholic churches climbed up from various areas of the city and appeared to be reaching toward heaven and trying to touch God. The aqueduct that wrapped halfway around the city told stories of hundreds of years past as they loomed in silence, where they once provided water to the masses of people living there. There were statues and fountains in parks that were so inviting that they seemed to be from the pages of a storybook themselves, each one painting a perfect picture on a real-life canvas. The food was excellent, the taxis drove crazy, and the setting was that of a romantic movie in most places.

It was not all romance and glory from times past, though. We frequented the central area of the city, where many of the shops, main streets, and the over 600-year-old cathedral towers with its bell towers and Spanish architecture. We often passed the always-open gates of *La Catedral* to the outstretched hands of the poor and the needy. Waiting outside the church for any signs of help and hospitality were the hoards of homeless men, women, and children that would gather in front of the church near the time of Mass. It was the saddest thing that I had ever seen. I guess I had observed things and people less fortunate before, but it never really sank in for me until I was there.

I remember specifically an elderly woman sitting on the steps as I walked by. I reached into my pocket and withdrew 50 pesos worth of money to give to her as I placed it in her small, woven basket. She had silvering black hair, a face of saddened wrinkles, and dark skin. Her hands were frail and small and looked barely able to lift the basket that she held. Her clothes were old and worn out, with a history of the hard times she had suffered. She spoke in soft tones as she said "Gracias" to me as I put the money in the basket.

As I walked away, I couldn't help but look back at the number of people growing on the steps in the shadow of that church. I wondered how many of them couldn't afford to eat, how many of them had no home or family. I wondered. I felt my heart sink into the pit of my stomach as I remembered some of the times that I had complained about some type of food that was put before me or complained that my home wasn't nice enough. From the appearance of things at that moment, these people had nothing. Who was I to complain about my life? What better place than under the watchful eye of Jesus and the saints on the glyphs of *La Catedral* to repent for my shortcomings? I did.

On many of the days that we went to class in Morelia, we would later in the day leave to go on various excursions to help train us in the culture. This was my chance to be that tourist with the camera. Many times, it would be a trip to a museum or a government building that was rich with history and architecture and told stories from times gone by. The *hacienda*-style of homes and buildings allowed us to view the building from various floors and balconies that surrounded a large courtyard below. The echoes of voices beamed off walls as we asked our questions and tried to learn more about the depth of knowledge that enveloped Mexico.

It was quite enjoyable for a history buff such as myself to experience something other than the local fast-food restaurant of the American culture I knew. The city in which we were standing was two to three times older than that of the United States. That is not to say that I do not enjoy the history of my country. It was just a different kind of history. From the strong Spanish Catholic influence to the indigenous people of the land, Michoacán, Mexico is an amazing state.

Another one of the day trips we took led us to a little school for elementary children. Our mission that day was to do as much clean-up of the school as possible and make it a safe place for the children to study and play. I remember the high, chain link fence that had barbed wire across the top that separated that little school from the rest of the ghetto that it was placed in.

We arrived there on the bus we usually traveled on, ready and eager to help. When we got there, we saw a saw school yard overrun with weeds, rocks, and the occasional scorpion and snake hideout. There were old tires in the yard that had been discarded there because no one wanted them. The gutters and the roof were being torn away from the building by tree branches that were growing out of control. The walls of the school had become dirty and covered with graffiti that now covered up certain areas of the murals depicting school children holding hands. It was definitely a sad sight for the eyes. But now, there was work to do.

We had a great deal to accomplish and only a short amount of time to get the job done. We had arrived on the bus with about ten of the Mexican police cadets who were there to help us, along with our instructors who accompanied us on the trip. We divided off into groups, and the work got started. The next

108   PROTECTED

thing I did was start climbing as we cleared out the tree branches and the gutters of the school. I remember one of my classmates nearly falling off the roof with a chainsaw in his hands as he cut away the limbs.

While this was going on, some of the other cadets were mowing and cleaning up the yard. Now, when I say mowing the yard, I don't really mean it that way. There was no mower to be found. The grass was being cut with a sickle. That's right, a grim reaper, giant hooked blade, sickle. That was how we had to cut the grass, hoping not to get attacked by scorpions. It was one of those things we just had to laugh at.

We took the old tires and painted them white after we buried different portions of each tire in the ground. Now, the kids had something for them to play on. We got rid of a mountain of trash that rivaled that of a landfill. We painted walls to cover graffiti and painted the trunks of trees with paint that doubles as an insecticide to protect them. And after three and a half hours of blood and sweat, we stood back and looked at all the work we had accomplished, even with a language barrier between us.

Although that sense of accomplishment was great, I will never forget the looks and smiles on the faces of all the little children who had continued to study even while we were making all kinds of noise and racket to do a good deed. The warm eyes and the dark hair of the children, along with those cute little smiles, are enough to bring a tear to even the strongest person. For once in my life, I could see what true gratitude was supposed to look like. I was able to learn from little children who could barely read and write what it meant to be a thankful person, and from that point on, throughout the trip, no matter what happened, I kept thinking about those little children and the impact a few gringos had made in their life. Since that hot day in Mexico, my life has never been the same.

Noche de Muertos en Michoacán...
I Gained Respect for Religious Freedom

Day of the Dead. Honestly, I thought it was the Latino version of Halloween at first. I was so ignorant at that time. It typically occurs November 1–2 of each year. That day of the entire excursion to Mexico was probably the best out of all the trips we took. There had been several, but this one had the most culture, the most information, the most historical sites. I couldn't wait as we boarded the bus to see what we were going to get into. There was a vast amount of difference in the experiences we had seen thus far. This trip was sure to be rich in culture and would clash beautifully between the indigenous people of Mexico and the Spanish and other European influences that arrived only several hundred years previously.

We visited three towns: Santa Clara del Cobre, Pátzcuaro, and finally Tzintzuntzan. Each was rich with its own unique history. In the State of Michoacán in Mexico, it is considered one of the most beautiful places and festivals in the world to see this. My words cannot even come close to describing this, but I will certainly try. Death and sadness are brought back to life for a time. Long-lost loved ones are remembered, and cemeteries of gray and bleak darkness are illuminated with beautiful colors, flowers, and light from candles, but I will get to that. To put it simply, it is a religious holiday.

I had never seen anything like it. I had always been brought up in America with a watered-down version of what holidays are supposed to be like culturally. Other than the fourth of July, most of our holidays (maybe not all) are shared with other countries in the world. This was a new experience for me. I was new to the country, new to travel, new to what other cultures did. We have the right to religious freedom in our country, though it seems to be more and more persecuted. This was the first time I had experienced a holiday from another culture's perspective. Skulls normally symbolize death and evil, yet they were celebrated on this day. Again, death given life. Listen, you are just going to have to do some research after you read all this.

I can't remember the specific order of towns we went to first, but either Santa Clara del Cobre or Pátzcuaro was first. When we went to Santa Clara del Cobre, it was quite the stretch of miles (or kilometers) from Morelia, where we had been staying. Also called Villa Escalante or Salvador Escalante, the names are interchangeable and understood to be Santa Clara del Cobre. What was so fascinating about this town was its people and the history prior to the Spanish and European influence. It is part of the Pátzcuaro region and mainly populated by the Purepecha indigenous people. The town and its people were dominant in creating crafts and goods made from copper prior to the nineteenth century. They were some of the most advanced copper smiths of the era until the Spanish arrived, who introduced new techniques that made them even better at their craft. The artistry from the copper in the fires to its finished and painted products could take anywhere between days and months to complete, and well over 75 percent of the small population worked in the industry when we were there. I had never seen such craftsmanship and artistry from start to finish in handmade fashion. It was jaw-dropping. We even got to hammer out some copper in the fire with hammers, which you have to do really fast and try not to hit your buddy with a hammer. We screwed it up.

In Pátzcuaro, some kilometers away, it was a street festival. There was dancing in the street, a parade with vivid colors, and street vendors everywhere. They had candy skulls, churros, brittle. They were cooking meats, roasted corn, and other vegetables, and the smells took us to a period in history when time stood still. There was no hurry or rush this day.

The warm smiles greeted the American tourists, and they tried to sell us anything they could. We were not allowed to buy any food products from the street vendors unless they had been packaged. Nothing cooked on the streets or from the water could be purchased. Montezuma's Revenge, you can look that one up, but the bacteria or whatever it was in the water in some countries is very real and can make you very sick. It broke my heart. I wanted to buy from the street vendors.

I remember the colors and the street dancing, the costumes and the mariachis. I remember the smiles and the fact no one was working other than to work as a vendor for the festival. Our Police Corps cadets stayed together and were walked through the streets and shown the various sites, such as significant churches and religious sites. We visited Basilica de Nuestra Señora de la Salud and other beautiful old churches. Of course, this was one of my favorite parts, and I could not soak up enough of the history of it all in that amount of time. Before we knew it, it was time to load up the bus again and off to the next location.

We were on the bus for a while, and it was getting dark outside. From the bus window, I looked out, and I remember seeing something way off in the distance. I could not tell what it was at first. Our instructor or guide or someone got up and told us we were arriving in the town of Tzintzuntzan. I couldn't even say the name right. I had to spellcheck it for this book.

Then, I realized what I was seeing off in the distance across a lake. It was candlelight. Candles lit up an entire hillside. I later found out that it was the cemetery. This was one of the most beautiful things I had ever seen thus far in my life. I was seeing this from probably a mile or two away.

Tzintzuntzan comes from the Purepecha language, meaning "place of the hummingbirds." When we got off the bus, we were shown a series of small temples and what appeared to be a pyramid dating back centuries. The temples had been reconstructed, and it is the former capital of the Purepecha empire when it had thousands of people at its height. They were part of a people called the Tarascan civilization. We had been transported to the past in this small town. Even the Spanish here was difficult for us to understand, and we could barely speak Spanish as we were new to the language. I loved the adventure.

Tzintzuntzan is famous for its celebration of Dia de los Muertos and the festivities. On this night, we were introduced to the old culture clashing with new culture and even modern society. In one area, you had the pyramids and temples trapped in time with a mysterious haze hovering over them.

Then, in another area, the tranquil cemetery was decorated with yellow flowers, colorful scarves and garments, and archways of color adorned the walkways as candlelight illuminated an entire hillside of gravesites. Family members sat at the graves of their loved ones with their loved one's favorite foods, having picnics and displaying photos of people who passed away. There was singing and praying and the soft strings of guitars being plucked in hushed notes while families huddled in blankets to keep warm.

I said nothing here, yet we were allowed to walk through. We paid our respects with a nod, a slight bow, and a smile. I had an old woman reach out at one gravesite to take my hand. Her face was wrapped with a shawl around her gray hair, and her skin sagged over her face. Her eyes had seen a long life. Her hand was cold. Her eyes were saddened, and she sat alone, but she seemed appreciative of us walking through. She did not know me, nor I her. The man in the picture at the gravesite appeared to have been her husband. I recognized her in a photo from another time, a black and white photo. It looked like a wedding photo. She had decorated her husband's grave and was having a picnic with him. I walked on.

As I exited the cemetery on the other side, I could not believe I had not seen this before. How had we not noticed or heard these ridiculous differences between all the worlds we were viewing? Just across the street was an enormous street party. People were drinking. There were more street vendors. I saw a man spit fire! How had I been so focused on these other things that I missed this? It was truly like Mardi Gras just across the street. Knowing this was a bad place for the cadets to be and there would likely be trouble to ensue, we did not stay long there. But when I tell you it was a party, I mean it was a party!

Prior to us leaving, we were all brought back to the pyramid and temple areas. We sat down in the area of this ancient archaeological site, and I wondered what was going to happen next. *What's going on?*

Juego de pelota con fuego. That was what was about to go on. Purepecha Ball, similar to the Mayan tradition. Its deep and historical symbolism shrouded still in mystery. As we sat there in the near-dark, awaiting whatever would happen next, I then heard the sound of hollow drums, animal skins stretched over the drums, and possibly a tambourine. The sound of gourds hollowed out with its seeds as a rattler. Whatever was about to happen was starting now.

Men and women marched into the middle of the arena, as we should call it, since we were between the pyramids and temples. Dressed in white, adorned in feathers and robes, and carrying various items of some significance, a parade of people marched to the beat of the drums into the middle. Lit up by torch lights all around us and carrying some sort of ornate fire, they went to the center and stopped. A ceremony began. Very fast-spoken Spanish was spoken (which I didn't understand but a few words). Sun. Fire. Mother. Father. God.

Then, there were the words that caught my attention..."fire," "hot," "be careful." All of this in Spanish. I couldn't speak much at the time, but I could speak enough to know something crazy was about to go down. And down it did. A group of men marched out next to the center to the beat of the drums, each one carrying what appeared to be some sort of shorter version of a hockey stick. Okay, I like hockey. Let's see where this goes.

Praying ensued, and then the shirtless men in regalia began to circle very fast around the ball of fire that had been placed on the ground. The other people had left the arena ceremoniously, and when the circling stopped, the men clicked their sticks to stop. Some sort of warrior's howl ensued, and they all broke away from each other. Game on!

The next thing we knew, these men were hitting this ball of lava and fire with the sticks, each group of men trying to get it to the opposite end of the field in front of us to a hole about three to four feet wide. Apparently, that was the goal. We were playing field hockey, with no pads, in the dark, in a pyramid, with a ball of flaming hot lava and fire. This was awesome!

The crowd erupted in cheers, and the drums kept playing. Chunks of rock would fly into the crowd, and the announcer would yell "Look out" or something in Spanish on a microphone. The crowd would gasp and cheer, and if one team got the fiery ball into the hole at the end of the field, the crowd, including us, were on their feet! I remember pieces of rock flying past our heads into the stands. It was intense. It was dangerous. It was the most adventurous sporting event I have ever been an alleged spectator for.

So, why even include this chapter in this book? It was part of my Police Corps experience, but really nothing notably having to do with any calls for service, specifically in my career. I guess the reason I wanted to include this was because I had lived such a sheltered life I had never seen anything like this before. I had never understood about other cultures or religions. This holiday is based on religion.

It ultimately caused me to do more research and have greater respect and understanding for other cultures I don't understand or even those I might not agree with. Just because I wouldn't agree with something doesn't mean someone is any less human or deserving of love and understanding. My views are not always going to be someone else's views. Their views will not be mine. This does not mean either of us should not learn from each other. Maybe if our world spent more time learning about others and respecting each other, we could witness to each other and find some common ground and peace. We are too busy trying to force others to our own point of view. That is not respect. That is not love. That is persecution.

I HATE WATER POLO:
THE KENTUCKY POLICE CORPS EDITION

Let me start this chapter by saying to anyone who loves water polo this is not personal, and I have nothing but respect for the athletes who play the sport. I am fascinated with watching people play it now that I had my experience. Second, to whoever my Police Corps friend was who said it was a good idea to play this, best to just keep it to yourself.

There are very few fears I have in my life. I am not a fan of snakes, but I am not terrified of them. I am a public speaker, so the fear many would have of public speaking doesn't even phase me. I am, however, somewhat afraid of drowning. I love the water, grew up around water, and considered myself a water dog...until the day in the academy we played water polo. It was a generic version of it, but all the same to me.

We received specialized training in the academy from what most other recruits did. This included police mountain bike training, learning Spanish, ground fighting before it was really a popular thing like it is today, and water rescue tactics. Or, as the instructors so appropriately called it, "drown-proofing."

This was how we spent several Saturdays in Police Corps. In a pool. Several times in full uniform. We learned how to go fetch bricks deep in the pool. One person doesn't come up for air unless the other one is down with the brick, that kind of thing. We learned how to work together to accomplish a task and breathing techniques. We turned our pants into flotation devices in case we were ever stranded in the open water, and we learned water rescue tactics to help others.

"Reach, Throw, Go" was the order of the rescue tactics.

If someone is in trouble, reach for them first. If they can't be reached, throw something to them to help them. If that doesn't work as a last resort, go get them. I must say, in all my career, I have never had to utilize this, but I know some Police Officers or first responders out there are heroes because they did. It is better to not risk your life unless you have to. You are no good to anyone if you are dead.

Anyway, on this particular fine Saturday, when we could have been doing anything else less life-threatening, we were training as we had for some time now. We were being instructed by a separate instructor Police Corps brought in who was ex-military, Special Forces, or something. I can't remember, to be honest, but I do remember how tough he was. We trained all morning and ended a little bit early for the day, or so we thought.

I have never forgotten what he said that day. He said, "Hey guys, we are done with the rescue training for the day, but I am not allowed to let you leave because we have to have a certain number of training hours and time. Does anyone want to play water polo since we have to stay a while longer?"

One of my Police Corps compadres spoke up vibrantly and was like, "Yes, let's do it!" Many of the other cadets agreed as I said nothing. That was the first and the *last* time I played water polo.

The instructor blew the whistle and said, "Listen up, here's the rules..." The next thing I knew, we were treading water in the deep end of at least twelve feet of water, and there was a ball being thrown in the air back and forth. We had split into teams, and clearly, I should have been the last one picked like we were on the playground as kids. The ball headed my way, and I was trying to score a goal at the end of the pool. Herein lies the challenge. When you have the ball, everyone on the opposite team is trying to *take* the ball by whatever force necessary to do so. Stealing the ball, drowning, whatever.

My head was under the water as I held onto the volleyball as I held onto it like a floatation device in the ocean and like my life depended on it. It might have. After the exhaustion set in and I lost the ball, I swam to the side of the pool to grip it for just a moment and catch my breath. I was greeted by the instructor, who started screaming at me to get out of the pool and immediately give him twenty-five push-ups. I welcomed the push-ups and was willing to pay the price. However, the toll went up in price every time we touched the side of the pool.

This fiasco called water polo, although it really wasn't water polo, went on for about an hour. I thought I was going to die that day. That day, my fear of drowning was realized, and all over, a volleyball going into a makeshift goal at each end of an indoor pool on a Saturday. There was no saving the volleyball like Tom Hanks did in "Castaway" and naming it Wilson. I would, to this day, take a knife to that ball and pop it so I could have some satisfaction that no one would ever play with that ball again.

Yep, I hated that game, and it taught me a humbling lesson about me not being as much of a water dog as I had perceived. Lesson learned.

<u>FINAL SCORE</u>

Water polo/volleyball Win
Josh   Loss

I'm sorry to my teammates for letting you down. I nearly drowned with as much grace as a rock sinking to the bottom of the pool. To all my peeps out there who play water polo for real. I have real respect for you. Good luck in all your endeavors.

—∞—

Night Terrors

Are you afraid of the dark? I want you to really examine yourself and ask yourself if you are afraid. It is not so much the dark that most people seem to be afraid of. It is what lurks in the darkness. It is what hides in the shadows of the night and takes our breath away. It is the fear of the unknown. It is that feeling that you get when you *think* there might be something out there watching, waiting. As humans, we tend to fear what is immediate, what we cannot control, and what we have readily available in our memories. The night is often a natural everyday occurrence that brings about some of our worst fears.

Even words that are often associated with the dark often bring emotion to our hearts. Darkness. Shadows. Night. Fear. These are words that tend to go hand in hand when it comes to describing the nighttime hours or the things that we don't really want to think about. And what is darkness? It is the absence of light. It is the time when most people tend to go into their homes and lock their doors safely and securely and put away any thought of what might be outside those walls. It is the time when most people don't want to walk anywhere alone, especially in an area that they do not know or are very familiar with.

Why do people like scary movies? Why do we like roller coasters and big theme park rides? Why do people enjoy dressing up in costumes on Halloween, telling ghost stories, or going to haunted houses? We like to get scared...a little bit. None of us really likes to get scared to the point where we are not in control of ourselves, but we all like to have a little fun and challenge our minds. We like to take our minds to the verge of our comfort zone and see how far we can push ourselves. What happens when we find out where the border line of that zone is and cross over it? How easy is it to go back to that place of happiness for you or that *safe place*?

Have you ever ventured past your comfort zone at night or gone somewhere that makes your skin have goosebumps? Have you ever looked out into the darkness of a backyard and quickly closed the curtains or shut the door because you didn't know what was outside, or better yet, you knew there was nothing outside, but you didn't want to think about it or take any chances?

If you are completely honest with yourself, you will know what I am talking about. It doesn't matter how tough you are or how much you think you are not afraid. I would almost bet that at some point in your life, you have been afraid of the dark. I will be the first to say that I have, and you might be surprised to find that the last time I was, I wasn't a child at all.

Although not as stellar of a student as I might have wished to become when I was in college, I did learn some things that stuck with me, and I have readily applied them to my career or the things in my life that I have encountered. As I learned when I was in my psychology classes in college, fear is a natural emotion that our bodies go through. When we feel threatened psychologically in situations, our bodies will react accordingly in a physical manner.

There is a part of our brains called "hypothalamus." This part of our brain controls basic needs such as thirst or hunger. The hypothalamus also sends certain signals that activate the Sympathetic Nervous System. When those signals are sent, the Sympathetic Nervous System will release certain hormones into the body that will prepare the body to deal with any emergency or dangerous situations that it may encounter.

I have heard in many classes and throughout my training as a Police Officer that this response from the body is now known as the "fight or flight" response and will prepare the body to either fight through the situation— mentally or physically—or it may prepare the body to actually flee from the situation that it is in. It is one of the most simple explanations for something that I have ever heard. When the body is threatened in any way, it will either decide to fight, or it will decide to run away. Pretty simple, huh? This is controlled by a part of the brain called the amygdala.

The human body does an amazing thing at the point when it may feel threatened. Physically, the body may begin to have certain reactions, such as the heart rate increasing, the lungs dilating or widening for more airflow, the digestive system may temporarily shut down, and goose bumps may rise on the skin. Other reactions that the body may have include sweaty palms, dilation of the pupils, a decrease in saliva or dry mouth, and secretion of sweat or adrenal glands. The hormone called epinephrine or adrenaline is released into the body, which will cause it to trigger all these responses. Epinephrine is the body's main chemical that is released during its reaction to fear.

Me? I like the night. I don't mind the darkness or the fact that there are shadows. Don't get me wrong, I am by no means a man to enjoy it all the time. I do enjoy the daylight hours also, but I don't mind working at night. I never have minded it. At night, you find out who you really are and how to adapt to a different environment. It is at night when you face your fears and the things in your life that you have always dreaded. I have learned, though, that the night has its uses and that it can serve a purpose. Take some time one day and pay attention to what happens when the sun goes down over the hills. If you will stop and look, you will see that the world goes through a metamorphosis each and every day. Of course, it depends upon the season and where you live as to what the hours of daylight or darkness may be, but in essence, it is the same occurrence every twelve to sixteen hours or so in most places.

Let me take you on a journey and prepare you for the night as it slowly brushes across a brilliantly colorful sunset sky. Close your eyes and let your imagination run wildly as the concept of the night envelopes you and draws you in. Take yourself beyond the place that you know and explore a side of the world that most never do and allow yourself to be freed from the turmoil and ideals that sometimes haunt us in the hours of light as we hurry from place to place. As the light begins to fade, the shadows slowly and gently careen their way across the ground upon which you place your feet. Your emotions and your senses heighten as the darkness seems to wrap around you in a cool sensation that your mind and your body cannot control. The tumultuous sounds of the day all but vanish little by little, and for a brief time, it seems that the world around you becomes still. As the darkness begins to take over, your mind is awakened, and the place that you once saw becomes entirely different. Has the world changed color around you?

The absence of the busy sounds of the day now dissipated and dispersed, your hearing seems to become more acute to the tiny noises around you as they echo in your ears like a rising storm of thunder. Your sight changes as it becomes more honed in on minute detail due to the lack of light and colors. Your smell seems to amplify itself as you are now able to smell even the slightest change in odor as it blows through the wind across your face. An apparent transformation of life is now before your eyes that was not there before. New creatures, both large and small, now creep through the woods, grasses, and streets that you might not even see were it not for the obscurity of the now-darkened world around you. These things are brought to you by the mere change of light and the lack thereof.

Oh yes, I like the night. I am not alone in my endeavor of sorts, and I know that there are many others who enjoy it as well. From my fellow co-workers to the night creatures and their sounds, to the thief that stalks the shadows and the dimness that manipulates our minds when the sun fades from the sky, there are many who enjoy the night like I do. Some enjoy it for hours, some for the thrill of the hunt, and some for the chance to camouflage themselves in the blackness that takes over for that amount of time every twenty-four hours. Whatever the reason, it all comes with a certain mindset that must be achieved in order to effectively conquer that time when the world is, for the most part, unlit.

They say it takes a special person to be a Police Officer. I would most definitely agree with the statement, but I always like to add my own little twist to the comment. I think we are all a little crazy in the same respect if you think about it like this. Police Officers and all Emergency First Responders and personnel are running toward a problem or situation that everyone else is running away from! If you think about it like that, there has got to be something wrong with all of us, right?

Now, with that said, make no mistake on what I am stating. I think that it is noble, honorable, and very necessary to have those people who are the ones who are going to be the people who get there first and help others or, in essence, save the day if you want to look at it that way. However, if you look at it from the standpoint that I just introduced, you have to wonder if there isn't something wrong with all of us because we are running toward dangerous situations that no one else wants to be a part of. I often sit back and think about that or look at people's reactions sometimes when I tell them stories about the things that my fellow Officers and I have encountered.

I often hear the questions, "Well, weren't you scared?" or "Do you ever get afraid?"

More times than not, I am able to play it off without a second thought because I have gotten past those situations that I was in and am now able to laugh about it. But there are times in my life and certain situations I have been in and then been asked those questions that I have no choice but to answer with a resounding *yes!*

That is not to say that it happens often or that I have never been afraid. I would be a liar if I told you I have never been in situations that have scared or startled me, but most of the time, we are able to laugh about it afterward and just learn from the situation that we were in at the time. That is a key factor to anything in life, not just police work. It is important to learn from what happened and do it better the next time. Police Officers are not perfect, and we do make mistakes, but it is not always about making mistakes and learning from them. Sometimes, we could have done something differently that would have worked just as well, if not better, than what we did at the time of the incident. And sometimes, some of the best lessons we can learn is because of something that happened when we were afraid. It will always keep us on guard and prepared.

For example, let me tell you about an incident that myself and another Officer had when we had to do a search of an apartment. You should know, first and foremost, before I tell this story, that a building search is one of the most dangerous things that an Officer may have to encounter in his or her career and that we may be called upon to do it sometimes daily throughout the career we have chosen.

Let's take a look at the facts that surround a building search. Imagine yourself as the Officer, and then imagine that building search performed at night. This is where that fear I talked about earlier can come into play. So, here are the facts. It is nighttime, which means it is dark outside, which means it may be and is probably dark *inside*, as well. As an Officer, you would be going into a place that is most likely unfamiliar to you and unknown. There are probably multiple rooms inside wherever it is that you are searching, and that includes closets, bathrooms, or any other type of small area. It is possible that there may be some sort of alarm going off, if it is a burglary call or a fire alarm

JOSHUA HALE 125

call. There is probably a lot of furniture or items that are inside where you are searching that you may or may not be able to see. There may be multiple levels that need to be searched, and the rooms on those levels, too. You may have to use a flashlight. Oh, and one more important thing, there may actually be someone inside the place that you are searching that you don't know about. If there is, they probably know the place better than you do, and they might have a weapon of some sort.

So, with that in mind, put all those factors together plus the possibility of other factors you may have forgotten about or omitted by accident, and you might have a slight idea of what it is like for a Police Officer and what they might be thinking about before they enter into a residence or a building looking for the bad guy. Does that get your heart rate going any faster? Did you experience a chill down your spine when you thought about the fact that there might be someone in that darkness hiding and waiting for just the right moment to catch you by surprise? That is the fear. That is the feeling that we go through every time we go into an unknown place.

On the occasion that I was speaking of earlier, it was a hot summer night, and my zone partner and I had been dispatched to an apartment where someone had seen an open window next to the front door and thought someone might be inside. At the department where I work, the city is divided up into different sectors or *zones*. Although we ride alone in patrol cars, there are usually several Officers who work in one area in the city, and then there are the Supervisors who can go anywhere in the city as needed or as necessary.

On this particular night, it was just my zone partner and myself in that area that responded to that call. I remember when we got there, I broke into a sweat just getting into and out of the vehicle. That is how hot it was that night. Sure enough, just as soon as we both got out of the vehicles about four houses up to walk to the apartment, I noticed that there was an open front window, and inside that window was nothing but darkness. My mind immediately started racing and going through possible situations or scenarios in a mental rehearsal of sorts, and I began preparing myself for the task at hand.

The other Officer and I began by creeping up to the front door and the open window that was situated beneath an overhanging porch. Oh yes, as Officers, we learn to adapt to the environment that we work in just as much as the criminals do. We have learned to use the darkness and the shadows to hide us and keep us from being seen, as well. It is sometimes somewhat of a game to me just to see if, when on a call, we are able to disappear into the night to avoid detection. I always joke with people, saying that when it gets dark, we turn into and move like a group of ninjas.

As we moved almost silently toward the apartment, I took a keen sense of my surroundings and anything that we might encounter. Before we got any closer to the apartment, my zone partner got on the radio and told our dispatchers that we would be on a different channel than everyone else was and that he wanted the channel to be cleared of any radio traffic. If we were inside hunting for anyone in there, the last thing that we needed was for someone to come squawking over the radio and giving away our location as we moved through the darkness in the apartment. The dispatcher then advised all Officers to clear the channel, and we began to inch our way toward the open window again.

When you work with people for so long, you know their moods and their signals and what to do when they react to something. You understand what they want to communicate to you without any words having to be said. This was one of those times. Non-verbally, we both were able to establish that I was going to enter into the window first and secure the immediate area as best as could be done until he was able to enter into the residence also. I drew my firearm from my holster and peered into the window as we ventured up onto the front porch. I looked into the window further as much as I could see without going in and then nodded to my partner as I began to enter the open, darkened, ominous blackness that loomed before us.

I did my best to keep my weapon pointed in various areas of the first floor of the apartment as I lifted my leg over the window sill and, as quietly as possible, pulled the rest of my body into the dark room. Immediately to my left was an open area that appeared in the dark to be a living room of sorts. I could tell that it was a large space and that it did not have much furniture, if any, inside that room.

Now, inside the room, my eyes had begun to adjust to the darkness and to the faint lights that were shining in from another room about fifteen feet away. I could tell then that the area where the light was coming from was

Joshua Hale

a kitchen and dining room area, and I could observe the reflection of the street lights from the street behind the apartment, shedding a dull yellow glow across the walls and the tiled floor. My eyes, constantly scanning for dangers, took in as much of the rooms at a time as possible. Watching. Barely breathing. Waiting. Gun always ready to fire. To my immediate right and somewhat behind me was a flight of carpeted stairs that went to an upstairs level. I could see the first few steps that led up, but then the rest seemed to disappear into the blackness and the unknown again. It is in these moments when you see things like this that you really reflect back on the training you receive as an Officer. It is only natural to have a certain amount of hesitation when faced with nothing but darkness, but you can overcome the darkness if you put your mind to it. It is important to remember, though, that you must always be on your guard. There may be something hiding *in* that darkness.

I stood by and on the ready as my partner crawled through the same window that I had just entered through. Even as he and I both entered the apartment as quietly as we could have, once inside, we knew that it was still too much noise. Once he was inside the room with me, we stopped for a moment and listened. Nothing. Silence.

There is sometimes nothing more deafening to the mind than the sounds of silence. The only sound I could hear was the faint sound of both of us breathing in the hot, stagnant summer air and the sound of my own heart beating inside my chest. I remember then that the summer air, as humid as it was, was no match for what followed. My nostrils began to almost burn with the smell as it entered my nasal cavity. No question about it: the stench was almost undeniable. It smelled rotten and disgusting as it seemed to hang inside the room like an invisible cloud. I looked at my partner as he entered the window and smelled the same thing that I had. It smelled almost as if something had died, not quite as potent, but awful nonetheless. Cat urine.

It was horrible, but at the same time, it put my mind at ease to a certain extent. It is never good to relax your mind in those kinds of situations until *after* you are actually *out* of the situation, but either way, I did, and it almost cost me later on. You see, the way I thought about it at the time was like this. *If there is nothing in this room and this place smells this bad, there probably isn't anyone that lives here and nothing alive in here at all other than myself and the other Officer.*

Now, I am certain that you can already see what kind of trouble this type of thinking can get an Officer into. If an Officer starts thinking like this, he or she may become complacent with the surroundings or think the situation itself is not dangerous. Bad idea. You never know when something could change or when you might have missed something. In essence, there could *always* be something there that you might have missed, overlooked, or just didn't see to begin with.

With that idea aside, we began to perform a search of the apartment. We cleared the first floor, sweeping around each and every corner of the apartment, inside closets, open spaces, and the bathroom. We backed our way toward the stairwell and turned our attention to the upstairs portion of the apartment. Using periodic sweeps of the flashlight and then again extinguishing the light, we crept up the steps to the next level.

Immediately in front of us at the top of the stairs, we stared into a bathroom. The floors were dirty, the sink was filthy, and the room was all-around disgusting. There was no time to take notice of why things were not cleaned. On to the next room. The two remaining rooms upstairs were bedrooms. Various pieces of dirty clothing littered the floor, along with trash and other discarded items. Old posters hung on the walls and throughout the entire upstairs, and that unmistakable smell of cat pee followed us everywhere we went like a shadow. That wasn't all. Not only was the smell undeniable, but the sights were disgusting. Cat poop was strategically placed throughout the upstairs as if it were supposed to be there.

My partner and I gave a disgusted look to one another when we took notice of it and were careful not to step on the land mines as we tip-toed our way through the rooms. Once all of the rooms had been cleared for anyone inside them, we quickly headed back downstairs to complete the final level of the dark labyrinth through which we made our way. Slowly, quietly, we softly stepped on the carpeted surface of the steps. Looking down, I saw the same type of droppings that had so eloquently been established in the upper portion of this dump. Again, it sickened my stomach as the familiar stench slithered its way towards us and began to squeeze as it wrapped around us. I did my best to remain focused and on target.

We cautiously peered around the bottom of the steps and into the living room area again. After establishing that there was once again nothing to be worried about, we tactically moved toward another set of steps that led to a lower-level basement. I stepped off the last step from upstairs and was now in the center of the living room, preparing to move downstairs. Now, it was at this point that I questioned whether or not we should have gone downstairs before we went up, but I suppose that it really wouldn't have mattered because what had already been done could not be undone. We were exposed. We were out in the open.

I don't think, in all my experiences or situations I have been involved with, I can remember being so startled by what happened next. I have been in situations involving people with guns, knives, suicides, murders, traffic accidents, rapes, car chases, foot chases, and anything that you could probably imagine. Not much has made my heart leap or jump into my throat, so much as what happened when we began to descend the obscured staircase that was before us. I think it is because neither of us really expected it and the fact that it all happened so quickly.

From out of the darkness below and in what seemed like a split second, a black cat jumped up the staircase and ran into another room of the house as it let out the most horrific and silence-splintering shriek. It lunged at us so quickly that it was a wonder we didn't shoot it, each other, or anything else in the room. I cannot even begin to describe to you how much it scared the life out of us as it jumped at us. I think *I* lost one of my nine lives that day, not the cat.

Of course, it was only for a moment that it alarmed us, but the concept that it did is still funny to us today. See what I mean? You never know when something else may be lurking in the shelter of the gloomy blackness. There is not even a question about that one.

As amusing as this may sound, though, I think it would be safe to say that there was a lesson learned by us when this happened to us. Sure, we make all kinds of jokes about it now, but put yourself in our shoes and imagine what you would have done if that had been you. If you would have been the one sneaking around in the dark trying to catch the bad guy while being virtually undetected in the process, something that makes you jump like that is not something you want to have to deal with.

It turned out that there was no one in the apartment and that it had pretty much either been abandoned or the tenants had been kicked out, leaving behind a mess that looked like it had been there for some time. One way or another, the front window had been left open, and stray cats had moved into the apartment, which explains our newfound friend that neither lost his life when he scared us like he did and also that awful smell of cat urine throughout the entire apartment. Someone had a lot of work to do before the next tenants could live in there comfortably.

I learned that you can never check something too much in this line of work. We have stepped over bad guys, on bad guys who didn't make a sound, and even walked with K9s who passed right by bad guys. It happens. We have been lucky. We have been blessed. We have been protected. It might seem somewhat overzealous to think that you can learn something from every situation, but that may not be far from the truth. One thing is for certain in police work: there is a definite need for problem-solving skills and the need to be a chameleon of sorts in many different instances. You have to be able to work with the elements and the weather around you...and work in the weather around you because it is a job that does not stop for any type of weather. It is also important to utilize the environment around you for what is known as concealment or cover. Using the world like a giant playground is one way that I like to look at it. One definitive, solemn thing that I was rudely awakened of when I became a Police Officer is that most of the metaphorical kids that I deal with do not play nice on the playground...ever.

As a Police Officer, I have talked to people from what seems to be all walks of life, at many different stages in their lives. The ability to talk to anyone on their turf is a skill that needs to be acquired early on in the police career and will benefit someone throughout their entire life. Knowing when to act or react to certain situations will help in the ability to control emotions both personally and will aid in the recognition of other people's emotions, as well. This does not just apply to that fear that I spoke of previously but to all emotions in general, although the ability to control fear will make someone a master of the game. I strive every day to be better at controlling my emotions than I was the day before.

So, what else has there been? I assure you that there have been many, many more incidents that, looking back, were far scarier than that of a black cat jumping up from a dark stairwell. I only used that as an example of how any situation could change in an instant and how, as Police Officers, we must always be as prepared as humanly possible. I think that there is more to it than that, though.

I grew up in a rural town and went to a little country church that my grandfather was the pastor of. I feel there is a whole lot more that goes on around us than we may see or know about. If you are reading this, I don't know what your religion is or what you believe in. I don't know if you grew up in church like I did or if you have never been at all. I don't know if you believe in Jesus, God, or angels or if you don't. Perhaps if I tell you my past experiences, you will better understand my thinking and the way that I was brought up to understand things in life.

After growing up in a Southern, mannerly, God-fearing household, I believe beyond the shadow of a doubt that there is a God and that he places his angels around us every day. I especially believe this as a Police Officer. I feel also that almost everything has to have an opposite, which means that if I believe there is a God and a Heaven, I also believe that there is a Devil and a Hell. I sometimes question whether we, as Police Officers, fight off demons every day in our own manner. Let me explain.

Another Officer and I were once having a discussion about our jobs and the way that our lives are affected by the things we encounter. At the time we were speaking, I was having a particularly difficult time getting past a suicide scene that I had just worked on the day before. To tell you the truth, I can still remember the details with vivid structure to this very day. I will not go into all the particulars of the case, but I feel that if I am going to get you to understand some of the things that we deal with, I need to somewhat describe to you what it was like.

The most basic fact of the case was that a young man had just shot himself in the head with a 12-gauge shotgun on the day after Thanksgiving. I don't think I need to go into any more depth than that because I feel your imagination and your mind will take care of the rest with ease. To be somewhat descriptive about it, there was not much left to identify the male subject by means of facial features. I remember his mother running around the yard in a nightgown and screaming, "He's upstairs!" as we entered the home. I remember the movie "Full Metal Jacket" being played on the box television in the room and the smell of the shotgun and marijuana mixed in the air. I remember the Marine Corps anthem blasting over the speakers and the Confederate flag and military regalia draped all over the room. I remember it all.

Now that I have explained the situation, let me inform you of why it was so difficult for me. I remember every suicide, dead body, or murder case that I have worked or seen, but this one stuck with me in more specification than the rest. The victim was twenty-five years old. At the time of the incident, I was twenty-five years old. We both went to the same college. We were both in fraternities in college, and, as it turns out, we both knew some of the same people. This was especially hard for me because I watched people that I knew coming into the home to console the mother of the young man as we were finishing up our responsibilities on scene. I don't remember much conversation with those people. From what I recall, it was no more than a polite nod and an acknowledgment of sorrow for the loss.

It was *my* case. *I* had to write the report. *I* had to take the photos and gather any evidence, and *I* was both the first and last one to leave the scene. I had seen a few other scenes like this before this one, but this one still haunts me today. There was a certain music that was blasting on the radio when we entered the room and a certain movie that was on the television screen. I will never forget those details. I remember what the room looked like and how it smelled. I remember hearing his mother crying at the base of the staircase below me. I even remember the look that one of my fellow Officers returned to me as he was holding her back to keep her from coming upstairs and the way that she just melted into his arms. I remember almost everything, and even today, when I drive by the house, I silently say a prayer for the family of the young man. I went outside after the Coroner told me he would meet me out front to talk to me after a few minutes. I remember it was really cold that night, so I got into my car to stay warm. I got into the cruiser and turned off the radio station that was projecting Christmas music from all the speakers surrounding me. So there, in the car on the street in front of this house, alone with no one around me but God, I did the only thing that my body and mind would allow me to do at that moment.

I broke down.

The tears of sadness that ran down my cheeks were not only for the man inside but for everything that I had encountered since taking on this job to help people. I desperately and deeply prayed to God to help me get through the moment quickly so that I might be able to stand strong for those around me. *How can someone get so far into the darkness that they can't find any light around them? How many lives will be hurt from now on because of this one moment in time tonight? Why, God, why does it have to be this way?* I could not help but ask these questions silently as I dried my own tears.

Yet, from somewhere within my spirit, I regained my strength and was able to bring myself back to the reality that I was in. My eyes stopped crying, and I composed myself yet again to continue the quest. I saw the Coroner coming down the front steps of the house, careful not to slip on the large patch of ice on the sidewalk. He began walking toward me to finalize any last details for the case. We spoke briefly about it, and he wished me a happier holiday season and hoped that we did not have to see each other unless it was for a happier reason. I wondered if he could tell that there had been a change in me. I wondered if he could tell that I had broken down and lost control for a brief time. I wonder if he could tell I had been crying. Did he know?

There have been more times than not that I know that either I or my fellow Officers could have been hurt badly or, even worse, if it wasn't for someone looking out for us. Can I explain it to you? No. Do I have all the answers to my own questions sometimes? No. What I do know is that no matter what kind of things I have encountered in my career thus far, I have been able to go home safely at the end of my duties on a shift, and I have been blessed to have family and friends that have supported me in my endeavors and accomplishments.

I do not feel that this is by accident, nor do I feel that it is by mere chance that such things have occurred. I could tell you scripture after scripture from the Bible that could apply to my life as a Police Officer and how there are incidents that reflect everyone. I feel, though, that if I can be a good man every day and exemplify that ideal with the people that I may encounter, I have made a step in the right direction to be the Police Officer that I feel that I should be.

I just felt it important to talk about the things in my life that have made an impact on me and those things from my career that have affected me. I don't think, however, that it would be fair for me to tell you about all the darkness, fear, and scary things in my daily job that I, as an Officer, encounter if I did not also explain my heritage and how it affects those things that I may have to deal with. Even though it sometimes rears its ugly head, the fear does not usually win with me. It rarely has any major effect on my mind, and I daresay that most of the other Police Officers that you may come into contact with have also learned to master the art of bodily emotions. But as I stated before, I want no one to call me a liar about what I have learned or experienced or how it has come to pass. I do make mistakes, and I gradually adapt and overcome the odds. We, as Officers, have demons that we must battle every single day and every time we put on the uniform or get into the police vehicle.

What I feel is difficult for people as a whole to understand is that we, as Police Officers, are not these mysterious robot-like creatures that are *always* in the spotlight and the public's eye, show up when we are called upon, and then disappear once the problem is solved. We experience emotions beyond most people's understanding, and it is sometimes more difficult than not to just let it go. I heard a politician say once that the police are a necessary evil. No one wants us around until they need us. No one wants to get a speeding ticket. People tend to freak out when they see a police car in their neighborhoods because they automatically think there is something bad going on. People, as a whole, do not understand that there is a lot more to the job than just responding to the calls that go out over the radio and, for the most part, do not want us around unless those calls are going out over the airwaves and magically sending us to save the day. But what happens when we are needed?

People call us for *everything* you can think of, from barking dog complaints, domestic disturbances, or fights to "legal" questions that have nothing to do with the law at all. I am always amused at the reasons why I respond to certain places, and I sometimes cannot help but laugh at it all or even get annoyed at times. It's a natural occurrence in this line of work. What I feel the public needs to see is that we are people, too. We have families and personal lives outside of work and general responsibilities that do not include anyone except those who are close to us.

There is one thing that is certain: it is not the same as being an accountant, a bank teller, an insurance salesman, a student, or a teacher. Don't get me wrong at all; these are very wonderful and noble occupations, and I have even had the privilege of being several of those things, but the fact of the matter is that being a Police Officer is *not* a job that you can just "leave at the office."

I was a Police Officer twenty-four hours a day, seven days a week, and 365 days a year. I have sworn an oath to always be moral and upright and to hold myself to a higher standard while protecting those around me. I have had to give up things in my life to be in this career. I have struggled financially or only been able to just barely get by on my wages. I have spent time away from my family and friends. I have lost many of the people that I once called "friends" because of decisions I have had to make with my job. I have had those haunting nightmares and memories that seem to never go away from my mind. And I know that I am not alone when I say that there have been years when I have had to work every single holiday or had to be alone on them because of my job.

While children are opening their Christmas presents on Christmas morning, we are working. When people are gathered in church listening to the preacher or singing hymns, we are working. When families are gathered around a table eating Thanksgiving dinner or having birthday parties with friends, we are working. When it is raining, sleeting, snowing, the sun is shining, it is extremely hot, or bitterly cold, we are working. We are working when the world is awake and when they are asleep. We are working. We are there protecting, sometimes seen and sometimes not.

Please understand that I am not complaining about these things at all. I knew what I was getting into whenever I signed on, but between these things, the initial stress of the job, and the fears we go through, I often wonder why it is that Police Officers take the oaths we do, to begin with. Why do we choose to go out there and be the ones on the front lines for those people we don't know? Why do we choose to face the fears of our own and of others when no one else wants to?

After being an Officer for two decades now, I watched myself change and grow into the man that I have become, and I know that I will continue to grow spiritually and emotionally the older I get. I strive every day in my life and my job to be better or to do something differently to make someone else's life a little happier. I now watch as the new Officers are trained and then take to the streets with a new and refreshing breath, hoping that they will save the world and help everyone in the world around them.

It is an amazing sight to see and even brings that spark of life into those who have become less like the torch that they so once brightly burned. I love to watch the anticipation before going on calls and the reactions that they now have to situations or the way their problem-solving skills evolve. It makes me strive to always be better. It is that new blood that washes out the old bitterness that sometimes infects police agencies and other types of employment. I've found that if a person stays somewhere long enough, they can find something to gripe about.

It's that new blood and young attitude that helps the older Officers continue in their days. Although still young and full of mistakes, as is expected, if the older Officers are honest, they will tell you the same thing because it does bring that go-get-em attitude back. Officers who are seasoned need that. We need that young rookie who keeps calling you "sir" no matter how many times you tell them not to.

Maybe with that refreshing breath to all departments, we can help prevent the nightmares we have at home when we sleep, or the stress from the health problems we face, or even help us to laugh a little bit more in roll call since we have become so cynical toward life. I know this. This calling takes heart and guts with very little glory to go with it. I know that this career is hard on a family and hard on the person behind the badge. Sometimes, with these challenges, we have to face the demons on the outside while battling the demons within.

Jesus, Superheroes, and People Just Trying to Do the Right Thing

Indulge me for just a bit as I stray from the normal path, which I have a tendency to do often if you know me or ever meet me in person. I will bring it back around to a point, I promise. For a moment, I just want to reflect on my childhood, and you can do the same. Superman is absolutely my favorite comic book character and superhero. He has always been my favorite, probably since I was a kid watching Christopher Reeve playing Superman in all his movies over the years when I was younger is the reason. Then, after his accident, I had even more respect for the Man of Steel before his death in real life. It broke my heart, but I remember how he fought until the end, and they still call Christopher Reeve *Superman.*

I remember, as a kid, putting on blankets and sheets as a cape, trying to jump off of things in the house and my treehouse while trying to "fly." As you can imagine, it never really worked out for me. This did not stop my attempts or my favorite comic book hero being Superman.

It is interesting to me how our culture has set up Superman to be very similar to Jesus Christ in recent years. Movies and shows portray him in many ways, but, of all ways, he is portrayed as someone for truth, integrity, morality, and love for mankind. This is an interesting dichotomy because it was not what I believe was originally intended by the Jewish teen creators of Superman in the 1930s. Or maybe it was.

Jerry Siegel and Joel Shuster originally created Superman, and the first issue was released in 1938 by Action Comics. He became very quickly one of the best-known characters in the world after Siegel and Shuster sold their rights to Superman to Action Comics for less than $200.00. It really is sad for the creators, but look where their creation is today!

Eventually, with World War II on the horizon, Superman was portrayed by the Jewish men protecting the weak and those who could not defend themselves. This was the hero the world needed at that time in the comic book world. He has changed a bit over the years with different directors of movies. Christopher Reeve, when I was growing up, Dean Cain, Brandon Routh, Henry Cavill, and more have donned the cape. Gave people hope. In movies like *Man of Steel*, Superman even says the "S" is not an "S." He says, "In my world, it stands for hope."

I can't explain how it happened over the decades since I am not as knowledgeable as other fans, but it seems Superman has, at least in American culture, been compared to Jesus. I am okay with that, but let me be clear on something.

Superman is a comic book character. Jesus was a martyred Lamb of God who died for all our sins. However, the comparisons of our cultures are quite fascinating. By the way, stay with me. I promise I will bring this around to a point.

Jesus is from heaven. Superman is from a heavenly place (at least to humans). Jesus came to this earth and was raised secretly by essentially foster or adoptive parents, Joseph and Mary, and given a human name, which was Jesus (in English). Superman came to earth and was raised by foster or adoptive parents Jonathan and Martha Kent and took on the human name Clark Kent rather than his name Kal-El. Jesus and Clark Kent were taught both by their fathers in heavenly places, as well as their earthly fathers, allowing them to learn to be human.

Jesus died on the cross for the world's sins. He rose from the dead three days later and conquered death. Superman died saving the world from a villain named Doomsday in the comic published in 1992. Eventually, he would be brought back to life in the comics, as well as even in the recent movies— "Justice League" (both versions of it)—after he was killed by Doomsday in the movie "Batman vs. Superman: Dawn of Justice." If you look carefully, in the background of the scene, you will see there are telephone poles or beams from buildings that form the shape of crosses, like on the hillside of Golgotha, where Jesus Christ was killed. Coincidence, maybe if I ever meet Zack Snyder, I will thank him for casting Henry Cavill as Superman and ask him that question. I doubt it, though.

Even Brandon Routh, who played Superman in Superman Returns, was pierced in his side, similar to Jesus being pierced in his side at Calvary. The spear was made of Kryptonite, but it was seemingly symbolic all the same. And when Superman rises in these movies, he goes above the earth with the sun in the background. He stretches his arms outward as if on the cross, again symbolic of Jesus. Now, this could just be the directors' style, and I recognize that, but there is no denying the appearance. However, I bet this changes the way you will view a Superman movie from now once you have read this.

Now, I am nearly a hundred percent certain Siegel and Shuster never intended Superman to become an icon similar in pop culture to Jesus Christ, but that is what has happened. Now, these are the comics, and there were twists and turns to make Superman bad, blah, blah, blah...I stopped reading at that point. Sometimes, in life, people just need a little hope.

Well, bringing this whole Superman thing home and refocusing on the point. Let me again clarify: Superman is not real. I love the character, but it's not real. Jesus Christ is my savior, and I was raised to believe in Him my whole life. I have been through a lot of dark and scary moments in my personal life and with my police career, and I have not always been as pure as God would want me to be or as I should be, but one thing is certain. I have not been alone through all of that, and neither are you.

Someone reading this book may not believe in Jesus either, and that is absolutely your right to believe that. However, think about it like this. We literally base our time B.C. and A.D. on the life of a man whom we have historical documents showing He walked the earth. He is acknowledged by historical documents in numerous religions such as Christianity, Islam, and Judaism. And although these religions may not agree with one another regarding the role He played, there is no denying His existence.

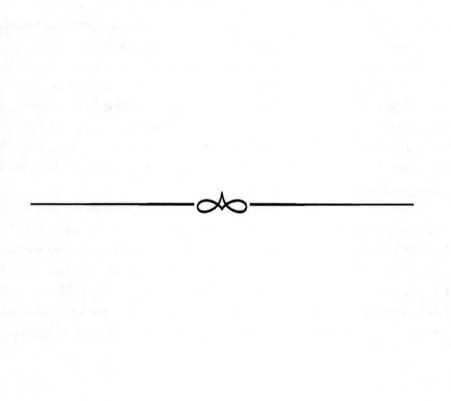

Just People Trying to Do the Right Thing

When Jesus began His ministry, as documented in the New Testament, He first had to pick His team. And—I am not gonna lie—it is like the "last guys you would pick on the playground" kind of team if you think about it. I mean, come on, we had guys like Peter (Simon), who was a fisherman by trade and operated a boat most of his life on the water. Peter gave all that up to follow Jesus, but he was someone who ended up betraying Jesus, he cussed a lot, and he even cut off a Roman soldier's ear. But Jesus kept him as one of His closest disciples.

Matthew was a tax collector by trade until Jesus came into the picture. Let's face it: nobody likes paying taxes, and Matthew was one who worked for the Romans to tax his own people. He also gave all that up to follow Jesus. Every other disciple has a story like that. They gave it all up to follow a man who they believed was doing the right thing.

Police Officers are not superheroes. We are not perfect. We are human. We are just a team of people put together (Avengers, assemble!), and overall, 99.99 percent of all Police Officers are just trying to serve and protect and do what they feel is a calling. For me, much like discipleship, this calling comes from deep within. I cannot explain it. It is a feeling I could not hold back from continuing to serve while I was working. It is truly something God put in my life to utilize for His kingdom and to help others. I have messed up along the way, but I have overall tried to be a good man.

I have worked with a lot of Officers over the years. As a matter of fact, in twenty years of policing, I saw over 275 men and women leave policing, retire, or worse...pass away. This is from my agency of around sixty-five sworn Police Officers. Some left for retirement, like me, because it was time. Some left for money and other jobs. Some left because they were forced to leave. Some left because they were weeded out...yes, I said it. Some left because they wanted to do something else. Either way, they served.

In those two decades of policing, I have worked with some of the finest men and women in law enforcement from the Commonwealth of Kentucky and, dare I say it, anywhere in the country. I am biased, of course, because I have seen the changes come through as an agency has evolved into something great. Some might disagree, but that is what the First Amendment is for, and the freedom of speech. Besides, I am the one writing this book.

I remember being in the Police Corps Program (I spoke about that at another point in the book), and when I was in the academy, an instructor from Basic Training asked me, "What agency are you going to?" I proudly held my head up at twenty-three years old and said, "Richmond Police Department," as I smiled. I remember the instructor rolling his eyes and saying, "Oh my God. Why?"

This was crushing to me since I was so excited and was only about four weeks into the twenty-three weeks of fun-filled adventure we had in store for us. That was sarcasm, by the way. I remember asking myself if I had made a wrong decision. But I also remember telling myself, "If this is true what he said, I am going to change that." And I did my very best over the next two decades to make a change for the good. Again, not perfection, and I didn't always even live like Jesus wanted me to. I still don't sometimes. I have tried, though. Many times, people quit trying to do good. That is when we fail.

Make no mistake, this came with a price. A huge price. It has nearly cost me my life a few times. It has cost me some relationships. I have not always been the best husband or father when I should have been. I have not always been the best brother or son or grandson or nephew. I have not always been the best son-in-law, brother-in-law, uncle, or even a good friend. The list goes on and on. But hey, this book is about my life as a Police Officer, and this is the truth about it. I have a lot of "I'm sorry" to say to people, and I hope that if they are reading this, they would know I tried. I know there are other Officers who may read this, and they need to prepare themselves for some of the things I talk about. Don't repeat my mistakes.

I missed meals, holidays, practices, games, and concerts and got called out at all hours of the night. I have not worked nearly as hard as I should, and the men and women I had working for me toward the end of my career worked circles around me on investigations. I was an aging man whom God had shown the door to, but we will get to all that. I never knew my limits, and I would not listen to those who cared about me telling me to *slow down* and *rest*. I thought I was unstoppable. I should have listened to those people, mostly my wife, who was telling me to slow down and take it easy. Instead, I did the total opposite of that and ran on little sleep, working long hours trying to get ahead for my wife and girls and chasing what I thought was the right thing to do. I think that is all most Officers do. We just try to do the right thing.

As an Enneagram 2 with a 1 wing (you can look all that up later), I felt like it was my job to help people. I selfishly get joy from helping others and making others feel good. I take on tasks and won't quit until I accomplish the task. Here lies the problem: I take on too many things, and I end up dropping the ball somewhere. I end up overwhelmed. I end up frustrated with myself or others who will not perform to the task. This is not a healthy way to be. I am trying to be better. I am trying to find a way to slow down. I am working on my walk (not run) with God at His pace and not mine.

As I wrap this part up, just remember that first responders, and especially Police Officers whom I know well, are just people. We are human. We get tired. We get hungry. We get grumpy. We have good days and bad days. We make mistakes. I know a lot of cops who had bad days, but keep in mind all we respond to is other people's bad days. That is generally it for us. Every now and again, we have something really great happen *for* the good. Generally, we try to *be* the good.

Remember I told you as a kid I wanted to be Superman? I really did! I learned I was not him at an early age. It took me a little bit longer...ahem... forty-two years and multiple mistakes as a grown adult, to realize how to listen when God tells you to slow down. I was just trying to do the *right thing*. I didn't have to be everybody's *everything*.

I found that out on April 25, 2022. I was humbled by God and He made me lay down, but we will get to that in another chapter.

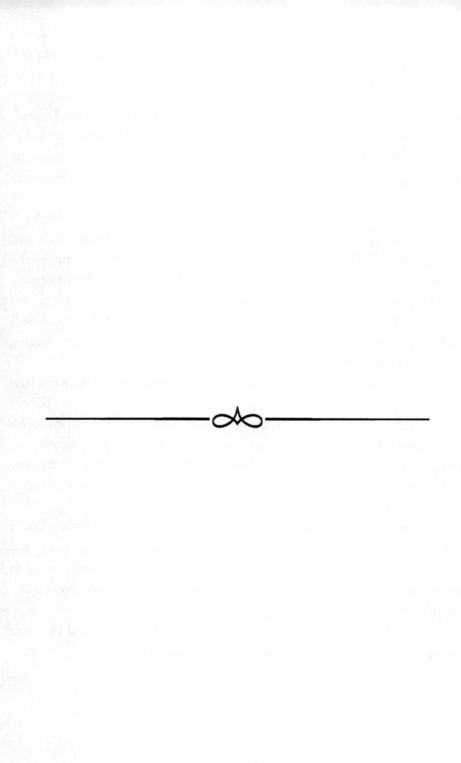

Trains and Railroads

I have always loved trains. I am fascinated by model train sets. For as long as I can remember, I have had model train sets. I still have the HO scale train set from when I was a kid. I switched to the N scale when I became an adult due to space constraints in my homes I have lived in. I even built a temporary model train set for our public library of Polar Express to show off one year while the library read the book, showed the movie, and gave out milk and cookies.

One of the coolest presents I ever got was a few years ago when my mom gave me my late Grandfather's Lionel O Gauge scale train set from post-World War II. Metal tracks, electric steam engine, the boxes, and all! As an excited adult kid (now having been a Police Officer for many years, as well), I did what every kid would do: I opened the boxes to try to play with the toys. I set all track up in a big oval—no reason to go overboard to test it. Then, I put the train on the tracks after making sure the wheels were aligned and everything linked up. Then, I plugged it in!

Have you ever immediately regretted doing something and hoped there was a way you could figure out how to fix it? This was one of those times.

The electric box on the train and tracks started to smoke, and a small spark of fire began to flash. I rushed over to the wall and yanked the cord out of the wall in order to avoid burning my house down. Thankfully, it was in the basement of our house, which is kind of the play area and not the main living area, and there was no damage to our floors or major infrastructure.

Needless to say, I did not play anymore with the train that day. I made sure it was not on fire and completely damaged, and I boxed it safely back up to work on another day. I will get my Grandfather's train up and running, though it has now become a goal of mine.

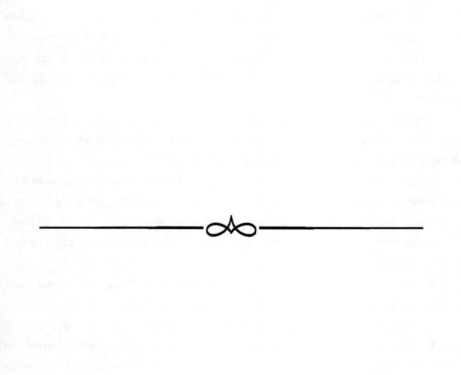

REAL WORLD DANGER

Trains have also played a fairly significant role in my police career at times. Perhaps that is part of the reason why, while I was still an Officer, I could not find myself the energy to pick up the hobby on a regular basis. There are always thoughts in my mind of the things I have seen, and something so simple as train tracks on a train set brings those thoughts back to the forefront. I am able to function, and it does not stop me from my daily activities, but these are intrusive thoughts that take a bit to go away again.

One of the more exciting stories is when I was told I cost one of the railroad companies approximately a million dollars for shutting down the trains for too long while we worked on an investigation. A man had been involved in a shooting, and when our Officers saw his vehicle, he fled across a major bypass from the Walmart and Lowes parking lots where he had been seen. He pulled down a side street with a cul-de-sac and a dead end at the railroad tracks.

It was one of the shortest pursuits I have ever heard on the radio. This fantastic officer did everything correctly, and we expected him to turn around in the cul-de-sac and come straight back out towards us in the vehicle or bail out from the vehicle on foot and take off running. Nope!

Well, actually, he did bail out of the vehicle, but not before he took his little rally cross-racing car up the gravel road to the railroad tracks and turned left by pulling a move from "The Fast and the Furious" or "The Dukes of Hazard." Yep. That's right. He drove his car onto the railroad tracks, and it was small enough to fit down the side of the tracks, and he was able to get a significant distance down the tracks on the gravel before he was forced to bail out of the vehicle. Now, the car was blocking the tracks, and at this point, we could only approach the vehicle on foot and not get other police cars up there. Let me rephrase that...as the on-duty Supervisor, I was *not* sending my police cars up there onto the railroad tracks with my Officers in them.

About 150 yards down from the gravel entrance to the tracks was the abandoned car. It was red. I still remember. We assembled a team to approach the vehicle and slowly made our way toward the vehicle. There were woods on both sides of us, and it was broad daylight, but a suspect in the woods with a gun could have easily ambushed us. God was looking out for us that day. We challenged the vehicle upon getting there as we hid behind the other side of the tracks at a lower elevation. The car was crashed into a tree on the opposite side. After several challenges and no response, we approached the car. It was unoccupied. We cleared it anyway. The gun was observed in plain view on the driver's side floorboard.

The suspect was apprehended a short time later that morning by our K-9 and his handler when he was hiding in the bushes, acting like he was supposed to be on the tracks and didn't have a clue what was going on. People really do think we are stupid, I guess. He had tried to kick a door into someone's apartment and hide but was met with a weapon and a homeowner who didn't want another guest. The suspect then fled back to the tracks where we had apprehended him.

Now, after all this fiasco and everyone was safe, we had to process the vehicle for evidence, and we had to get it off the railroad tracks. This was the problem. I couldn't get a tow truck to the location where the car was located, and the car was blocking the tracks enough to where a train would have hit it. This is where the railroad companies started getting upset with me on the phone because they were losing money and had trains stopped. I was told I had cost the company about a million dollars that day as I got screamed at on the phone. Good times. Well, if it was going to be one million dollars, it might as well be more.

After about two and a half hours of processing the vehicle as a crime scene, dealing with tow companies, getting chewed out over the phone, and having the railroad people on scene to finally assess what had happened, we were able to get the tow truck down to the car just enough to put a wench on the car and pull it away from the tree down the tracks to be loaded up on the truck. This was no easy task.

And for the record, I know we had heard train whistles in the distance at least two times. The distance was not that distant at all.

150   Protected

The Serious Side of the Tracks

Several times in my career, I have been dispatched to calls involving pedestrians being hit by a train. They were all suspected suicides. These images are still horrible to me, and I wouldn't wish this fate upon anyone. On one particular occasion, I was a very young patrol officer and was working third shift. I was on scene with the Coroner, and we were walking the tracks, looking for evidence and assessing the scene.

The Coroner was walking with me, and we had to pick up a foot that had been severed from the body of the man. Now, as I am writing this chapter, it is at least eighteen years later this occurred, and I remember the details from that night. We have one of the best Coroners in the entire nation, in my opinion. This man has seen and dealt with so much I have no idea how he continues to do what he does. Maybe one day, he will write a book, too. We have worked many scenes together over the years now.

On this particular occasion, he recognized the rookie officer before him and knew I had never dealt with anything like that. He knew the gruesomeness of what we were dealing with, but as he always did when working a scene with him, he was teaching, even up until I retired.

"We have to collect the foot," he said.

I didn't want to be the one to pick up the foot, but he told me to, and on a crime scene involving a death, the Coroner is in charge in Kentucky. Besides that, I had so much respect for him already. Even the few times we had met, I would do what needed to be done.

"Treat the foot like it is the entire body itself, with respect. We will send the body off to Frankfort for an autopsy even though we are almost certain what the cause of death was. They will be put in the bag together for the medical examiner to perform the autopsy."

I had gloves on and did as he instructed me as he watched a young Police Officer collect the foot from the railroad tracks. We carried it approximately twenty-five yards to where the victim was located, and the body bag was next to the tracks.

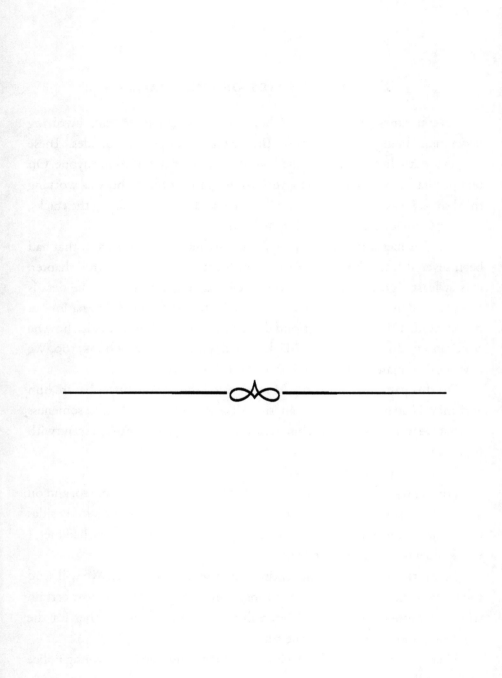

The Aftermath Memories

That is something seared into my memory now like a brand every time I look at train tracks. I push the thought down mostly. After all these years, it really doesn't haunt me like it used to do. There were more victims throughout my career, more foot chases on the railroad tracks, more tracking of suspects.

I guess I never thought as a kid who loved trains they would eventually have such a real impact on my life. I am still fascinated by them. I still love model trains. I still watch the real trains roll by and try to count the cars when I am stuck in traffic at a railroad crossing. I still hear the *clickity-clack*, *clickity-clack* on the wheels and the tracks. I still see the flashing lights and crossing gates at the railroad crossings.

I still hear the train whistles way off in the distance.

The Unmistakable Sound of the Thunder Stick That Can Go Boom

We had a problem nightclub nearly the entire time I was a Police Officer. Over the years, it would be run by different people, but it was owned by one man. They hadn't had a liquor license to sell alcohol since who knows when, so basically, the owner signed a rental lease to whoever would rent the establishment, and it was BYOB. There is no way it was up to code. There was water running down the walls, and there were only three exits, one of them blocked and the other closed off. It was a coffin for anyone who would have been trapped in there if something had happened.

It was BYOB since they didn't have a liquor license. Bring your own beer, beverage, or however you want to say it. And boy, did they. That's not all they brought there. People used that place as a location to sell illegal narcotics under the guise of a "club," thinking the police wouldn't notice. They brought their guns, prostitutes, and juveniles they would sneak or allow into the club. College kids would show up thinking they were going to the hottest place in town, mixing in with drug dealers and gun runners while the music played until two or three in the morning, well past the noise ordinance-allowed time. We issued citation after citation to the owner; several of them have my personal autograph on them over the years. Then that would get tied up in court, or some attorney would pay someone off (yep, I said it), and the carousel would go round and round and round. It was ridiculous and went on for nearly my entire career. That place was a real five-star location, if you can't tell.

Hundreds of people sometimes would show up from in town and out of town, mostly from out of town to attend. The owner of the establishment wouldn't even park near his own building. He would park several blocks away and walk to it. I got into multiple fights over the years, and we had fights nearly every weekend it was open, and it was always only a matter of time before we had a shooting. It was always a ticking time bomb. It was a dangerous place for Officers to go, even in groups. We had multiple shootings there over the years I worked for the agency. One night, we got the call.

One male had been shot inside the club, and they had dragged him out into the street in front of the building onto the sidewalk. There were multiple people on the street when we got there in other fights, and it seemed nobody was in a hurry to leave. People stood by drinking, playing their music, and smoking dope while a man was dying on the sidewalk. It was anarchy on the small, one-way street.

There were only about nine Officers who responded to the scene, five from ours, I think, and a few from other agencies. We were right on the edge of campus, and there were university police close by, but they didn't have the "clearance" to come and assist us...not just yet. The Officers soon threw that order out the window and did it anyway. Thank you, guys. All in all, there ended up being about ten Officers, including all agencies. Ten Officers and over 200 people in the streets refusing to comply with any Officer commands.

I assisted two other Officers in rendering aid to the man who had been shot multiple times. He kept passing out and nearly dying on us. We kept waking him by saying stuff like, "Don't go to that light, man! Stay with us! We will help you!" The ambulance couldn't get there fast enough. We asked what his name was, and he wouldn't tell us. Did he not hear us from the pain of being shot? We kept asking. He finally gave us a name, so we started calling him that.

"_____, stay with us! You have got to stay awake!" We kept saying stuff like that for several minutes with no response when we said his name. Finally, one person behind us said, "That's not his name. He lied to you."

They had formed a circle around us like a football huddle over us and kept getting closer and closer, even trying to pull him by the leg away from us at one point. We were in a bad spot regarding officer safety. I had told one of the people in the crowd I knew (professionally from his life choices) to get these people off of us. Hindsight 20/20: it was probably a terrible idea and had been a gamble because he started yelling and screaming and shoving people back off of us, but they listened to someone from the streets. They knew who he was. I will leave it at that. I didn't trust him, but he helped us in that moment and kind of stood guard over us to make sure people didn't try it again.

Our Officer, who was a medic, had gotten agitated and asked the victim of the shooting why he lied to us. We were trying to save his life. He told us he had just got out of prison the previous week, and he didn't want to go back to jail. We would deal with that later. Back to work on saving him, for now. Who cares about jail?

Meanwhile, it was getting bad with the crowd. We had asked for more units, but there were none to give. Dispatch put the jail and hospital on standby because eventually, one way or another, we would get there with someone. Our K-9 handler was there on scene, and the dog was out of the truck. I hardly ever saw the dogs get out of the truck by the handler. They are a tool, not a weapon. You don't wield weapons until you have to, but it was time to start showing force.

Officers were fighting with people, and one woman even went straight up to the K-9 after being warned, and he went after her to bite. He was barking, and she was given warnings. People were not listening. It was scary for us. I heard someone in the crowd at some point in the next few seconds yell, "He's got a gun!"

I looked at the other Officers with the victim; they had it under control, and I knew I was not a medic. I got the nod to go. I got up from the group, and I saw my Corporal and heard the Corporal yell, "Hale, get your shotgun out!" I looked around, and Officers were coming closer together as if circling the wagons in the old west. We were getting surrounded, and no one cared about anything we said or commanded.

Let me pause for a moment in this story and tell you this was early on in my career, and I was on third shift. It seems in the deterioration of our culture, this type of incident has gotten worse and worse. Seemingly, there are no consequences for the anarchy people cause. That is why we have businesses and cities being burned and peaceful protests where the instigators are bussed in just to start a riot. Adults who were never disciplined as children are now taking out their temper tantrums on society, all while encouraged by politicians with an agenda and the media. It has worn away the core of what the freedom of speech and right to assemble peacefully truly means.

I looked around me as I rushed from the circle of people. I ran to my cruiser and grabbed my shotgun out of my trunk. At the time, we did not have rifles at our agency. This was the long gun we were issued. Man, I love that weapon. A Remington 870 12 Gauge shotgun, or as I love to call it, "The Thunder Stick."

Everyone knows police have pistols and rarely pay attention if you think about it. It is a part of their uniforms. But when a long gun or specialized weapon gets deployed, people notice.

I deployed the shotgun and kept it in the high ready, pointing straight at the sky, never once pointing it at anyone in the crowd. Some people saw it as I got it out of the car, and I heard people yelling things like, "Holy crap, he got a shotgun!" They didn't say the word crap. Then, I performed my favorite action with that weapon. It is an unmistakable sound even those who know nothing about weapons understand. It was old-school, it was like the old west, and it sent a message the moment it was heard.

I racked the weapon as loudly as I could and chambered a round. Did I have bean bag rounds for less lethal? Did I have rifled slugs? The crowd didn't know, and they didn't care to stick around and find out. Immediately, we heard lots of expletives being uttered, and people started to scatter in all directions. Car doors began slamming, and engines were started, loud stereos playing from inside some of them. The college students ran back to campus, or at least ran until they were out of sight and off the block.

I looked back over to the Officers, and the ambulance had arrived. EMS was rendering aid. The victim was going to live and was going to be transported to the hospital, probably going back to jail for violating his parole but going to live all the same. I walked around carrying the shotgun high in the air for everyone to see for some stupid reason, probably thinking it was cool (which I did).

The crowd was all but dispersed, and I heard my Corporal yell at me, bringing me back down to earth. "Hale, put your shotgun back up. Store it the right way." And just like that, I was back in reality, and the high-intensity moment that was like the Wild West was over. Several people went to jail that night.

I learned a few things from that one incident that lasted maybe 15 minutes of my life. First, sometimes it doesn't matter how nice you are to people, you may still never get their cooperation. Second, no matter how much I love Westerns, I was not in one. This was real life with real people and real consequences. I dropped officer safety when I shouldn't have, and I should have put the shotgun away sooner. I admit that. Third and finally, there is an unmistakable recognition and realization in the sound of a man racking a Remington 870 12 gauge. Or, as I call it, "The Thunder Stick," that can go *boom*.

Is That a Monkey?

First off, I am not an Animal Control Officer (or whatever it is called everywhere else). I was a Police Officer on patrol, expecting to do "patrol things." This was *not* in my job description when I got hired, nor is it in the job description now. We are not snake charmers, deer chasers, possum catchers, bear trackers, mice hunters, rabid fox killers (even though we actually had to do that once, so I guess we are), or pest control specialists (I *hate* bedbugs so much!!). Police Officers are not cattle wranglers (done that), nor are we supposed to chase horses around a neighborhood in the middle of the night (Done that, also. Then I tied him to the tree in the front yard of my Supervisor after I caught him.) We are not supposed to herd goats in the street (been there, done that), nor chase chickens to get them back into their cages (also done that).

Okay, okay. Based on the above stories, which are wild in themselves, I guess it is safe to say we get called for everything, and maybe we do have to do a little "Animal Whisperer" stuff while we are on duty. But never, and I mean *never* in my life, did I ever expect to deal with one dispatched call the way it went down.

One day on first shift, I was on patrol, and we got a call for a welfare check on a suicidal female. The particulars are that she was supposed to be at work and never showed up. She had been suicidal recently, and she also had a doctor's appointment she missed. Her family had contacted her repeatedly, her phone went straight to voicemail, and she was not responding to any texts. There had been no contact with anyone on social media, even through various attempts, and all communication had stopped with her. See where I am going with this?

I arrived at the house to do the welfare check and found a vehicle in the driveway. I knocked on the door. No answer. There was a storm door and a regular front door. The storm door was locked. I knocked louder. No sound. No answer. I knocked louder, with the knock I had been taught while working third shift. It is the kind of knock to wake people up from their sleep in the middle of the night. That...rude knock, if you will. Still, no sound, no answer.

I called for another unit on the radio, and my Sergeant and another Officer who would later become a Supervisor with me through the ranks of my career showed up. All doors locked, six-foot privacy fence that was locked, no way to make contact with the woman. I knew what was coming next in the process. We had to make entry into the house somehow.

On the front porch, there was a window next to the door about two and a half feet up from the porch with a small ledge. Unfortunately, I had to break the latch on the window in order to make entry. No screen on the window. I lifted the window and pushed back the mesh curtains.

Remember I said there had been no sound or response when I knocked repeatedly on the door? The next part must have taken away at least part of my next four heartbeats. When I opened the window and was starting to climb my way through (smallest guy, and it was my call anyway), by the time I had my right leg through and touched the wooden floor, I was committed, and there was no turning back. I remember the odor of dank, musty, and what I thought was an unmistakable memory from dispatched calls in the past. It smelled like death. The odor wasn't what made my heart skip, though.

Now, keep in mind this is a terrible way to have to do things tactically, and I did not want to be doing this. As I stepped onto the floor, I was met with a pair of glowing eyes and an animal with a head larger than mine. Have you ever seen the movie or heard about the two Tsavo lions called the Ghost and the Darkness? They killed a lot of people in Africa. This was not them, but the animal was in my face like a silent ghost from the darkness.

It was not a Tsavo lion, thankfully. It was much better. It was a huge Bullmastiff dog who had not made a sound at all when I had knocked on the door, and we never knew he was in there. We were face to face, and now I was in his house, and he was staring at me with yellow eyes, drooling. There was no excitement, no licking my face, no tail wagging, no snarling or teeth bared, just his yellow eyes trying to decide what to do next while he was about six inches from my face.

I pulled my banana yellow-colored taser (I hated that color taser because it stood out so much on the uniform, but they had told me that was the point) and pointed it directly at the dog in slow, methodical movements. I spoke softly and said something like "good puppy" or something dumb like that would help if he decided he was going to handle this intruder to his territory. But it wasn't just *his* territory. I prayed silently not to get bitten while I was climbing through the window at a disadvantage. I backed myself over to the door while keeping my eyes on the dog, and I unlocked the doors. They started talking, and I said, "Shut up," in a whisper while trying not to freak out and still keeping eyes all around me to make sure there wasn't some other threat. I probably shouldn't have said that to my boss, admittedly. I apologized later.

I walked my way through the living room carefully and led the dog gently into the garage while trying to do a quick sweep with my eyes for safety. Admittedly, it was not a thorough search like it should have been. I backed myself out of the garage and closed the door, breathing a sigh of relief. The dog had never made a sound.

We continued our search through the house for the woman, following the stench through the house. The house appeared to be in decent order. It was not too messy, lived in, and someone had apparently recently been there. It was a home that should be expected. The smell, not so much.

We made our way down the hallway slowly deliberately, until we got to the last door. No dead body yet; that was a good thing. The problem was, the smell was coming from beyond that last door. We could hear a television on inside the room. We had cleared the whole house up to this point—no turning back now. Anticipation and familiarity with apparent circumstances began to set in my mind as I prepared myself for the other side of the door. I was not prepared in the least and nearly urinated on myself at what happened next. (Yes, I said it.)

The order of Officers in the hallway was the other Officer, me, and then our Sergeant. We had each checked doors while the other provided cover as we swung doors open. At this point, anything living would have absolutely known we were there because we had announced ourselves about ten times. It was not a secret now, and we were not being quiet. If there would have been a bad guy behind the door, he had us. It wasn't a bad guy, but from my memory, what was behind that door had bad intentions for us!

The Officer opened the door slowly, and I held the cover position with my pistol at that point in case something happened. *Something* did! When he opened the door, a small furry, black and tan and white colored creature about two-and-a-half to three feet in height jumped in front of the doorframe and stood up on its hind legs while using its tail for balance. He (we could tell it was a he) lifted his arms and showed his claws on his little black-colored hands in attack mode. He opened his mouth and bared his sharp teeth with his wide, crazy-looking eyes and then, after all this time, with no sound. We got sound.

He started screaming and hissing at us in a high-pitched tone and jumping up and down like he was going to kill us all. I almost shot him. Maybe I should have included that in the number of times I have almost had to kill someone. But I didn't have to. When he started screaming, my vision saw a blur start bouncing around the room off the walls like something out of X-Men in the comics. More screaming and hissing and howling. There was more than one of these things! They immediately went crazy and were banging and jumping everywhere.

The Officer holding the door put an end to the madness in a split second when he slammed the door as he said,

"Welp! She's not in there!"

We all stood there in silence in the hallway as the chaos ensued inside that room, too stunned to even react in that moment. Not including me since I was young in my career at the time, but between the other two Officers on scene, we are talking decades and decades of police experience. Even they were too stunned to say anything. I know one thing, though. At that point, I don't think any of us knew for sure if the allegedly suicidal woman was in that room or not, but I wasn't going in there to find out! My Sergeant was standing right there with me. I would have taken my insubordination write-up!

After the initial shock wore off in a few moments, we still had to find this woman. I had gone outside through the back door after we told dispatch we could not locate her. When I got outside, I discovered the complexity of the entire situation in this house. This woman had turned her house into basically a zoo enclosure. A portion of the back of the house was attached to enclosed wire cages, and the window to the room where we just were had been lifted up and was wide open so monkeys could go in and out as they pleased. There were things for them to climb on and play on, food and water sources, and boxes to hide in. It was truly like a zoo exhibit. It was impressive.

Even more impressive were the signs on the cages outside for anyone who could see them, clarifying the legality of the monkeys and how they had been grandfathered in under a previous city ordinance and not the current one, allowing her to have exotic pets. I was floored. Of all the animals, monkeys?

Word had somehow traveled fast on the radio and cell phones that this was the type of call we were on. A Supervisor at the time on the Command Staff decided he would stop by and "check on us." I was getting ready to leave since the homeowner was not there. We had done our job there, and there was nothing left to do and no reason to be there anymore. We were securing the house and getting ready to leave again when we got a phone call from dispatch confirming she was okay and safe. Good news. Meanwhile, as I was leaving and walking past the cage, that Supervisor walked into the backyard with me and saw the monkeys. The female monkey was still jumping around all over the place. The male monkey was still following us everywhere we went and exerting dominance in a series of gestures to show us we were on his turf. Semi-aggressively. I won't detail the gestures.

He was crawling on the chain link fence everywhere we went and following us as we moved. I had seen enough. Cool experience, different call, but I was over it. Not the Supervisor. He walked up to the cage, right next to the sign that said, "THESE MONKEYS ARE LEGAL," and he started to extend his arm. I had this feeling of dread for what was about to happen next, but in a split-second moment, it would have been too late to react.

He stuck his finger out toward the monkey, who started to bare his white, sharp teeth, neared the cage, got directly next to the monkey's mouth, and said, "Is that a monkey?"

At that moment, the eyes of the monkey grew wide and then fierce. His eyes became aggressive, and the primate hissed and snapped his mouth shut, clamping his jaws tight. The angle upon which I was standing in relation to what was happening did not allow me to see the exact situation for what it was, but I saw the monkey snap his mouth shut. I turned quickly and had a momentary freak-out as I checked on my boss.

The monkey had missed, although not for lack of trying to make contact with his skin. Then, I heard the colorful language as my boss started yelling about the monkey trying to bite him. He said, "Did you see that thing try to bite me? Is that a monkey?!"

"Yes, sir. That is a monkey," I said as I walked out of the backyard, shaking my head and rolling my eyes.

The names of the monkeys will be spared to protect the innocence of them. I won't say they were sweet because I didn't know the animals, and they certainly were not sweet to me. But I heard another story about the monkeys after that. One of them died a year or so later from a fire and smoke inhalation. The other monkey was so broken-heartened. I felt sorry for the lady who owned them. We talked to her on the day we had gone to her house. She had been going through some things emotionally. Thankfully for her, she had some companions who, although not the ordinary or what was expected, probably gave her more love and affection than most humans are capable of. It is pretty sad, really, that we are like that.

I've seen a lot of things in my career, dealt with some crazy stuff. But never since that time have I ever had an encounter like we did that day, which became such a core memory in my life. That was the day in policing we met those two monkeys.

The Great Masquerade

"And the award for best actor goes to..." is the start of a phrase that many of us have heard if you have ever watched any great movie award shows. After the announcer says that, he or she would then insert whatever name may be appropriate for the award at that particular time. It really goes the same way every year on every awards show that you watch on TV. They will usually arrive at the show in some fancy car and then schmooze the media, other actors, and onlookers as they strut down the red carpet. After that, all the actors, directors, producers, and movie people go inside for the show and then have an after-party of some sort.

I had never really thought about it until recently, in one of my training classes for policing, when my instructor told the class to forget about how good the Hollywood scene may appear. The people there were no match for the skillful acting of the police. He said that the police were the greatest actors in the world. I sat there and pondered that thought for almost an entire day and thought it was very necessary to include it in this work.

We have all seen people on Halloween dress up for a party or dress their children up for Trick-or-Treating. More than likely, most of us have done it ourselves at some point or another. If it wasn't that, we would have been in a play or acted out a part of a scene at some point in our lives. At whatever point in life it has been done, it is all about hiding behind a mask of sorts as a disguise. And that's the point, isn't it? I mean, no one will know the real person behind it if we don't want them to.

Police work is just like that. Most people who view the police see us as these people who show up on scene in a uniform, perform a certain task, and then leave. What *most* people do not realize is that things do happen after we leave. There are often and almost always case follow-ups, interviews, or interrogations of different people involved, court testifying, and always massive amounts of paperwork to go with that. That is the nature of the beast, and it should just be expected if a Police Officer is going to do his or her job.

There is more than those things, though. It goes to a much deeper psychological level than most people will ever know. This chapter is called *The Great Masquerade* for a reason. The biggest masquerade of all is the one that the police put on every day when they put on the uniform to go to work. This job changes you as a person. Ask any Police Officer, and they will tell you that it does. The only problem with those changes is that it is, most of the time, not something you can control. I am not going to tell you that everything is easy for us all the time, and I am not going to tell you that everything is totally difficult for us all the time, but I will tell you that a line is drawn that you never know you cross until you have done so and are looking back at what you wish you didn't know.

Think about it this way. Do you think you would be able to go into an interview room to talk to someone who has murdered his "friend" in cold blood, someone who has burned down a building for fun, and someone "accidentally" got hurt, a voyeur who became a rapist, or a child molester who thinks it is okay to sexually molest little children? Could you show restraint and empathy to one of these people to gain their trust and let them tell you something that may be their deepest secret and the darkest place that your mind has ever traveled? What would you do? Or maybe the better question is, "What would you want to do?"

The list could go on and on about the different so-called "types" of criminals, what they do, and what makes them tick. The problem that we face as law enforcement Officers is that we *must* find a way to talk to each and every type of criminal and do so without the suspect seeing any kind of weakness. We have to be able to look at graphic and violent crimes as if they were nothing and then prepare cases on them. Most importantly, we have to be able to return to our homes and families and leave it all at work. Could you do it? I will be the first one to tell you that it has been more difficult than I ever imagined, and sometimes, things haunt me that I wish I would never see again. You can't just leave it at work.

It could all be considered one big game between Officers and criminals. Just like Officers are gathering information on the bad guys, the bad guys are gathering information on us. We have to be better, stronger, faster, smarter, and more prepared for anything than they do just to be safe and go home at the end of our shift. That doesn't include being ready for court cases, civil lawsuits, and the good-ol'-boy system that plagues the criminal justice system like a virus and allows the thugs, gang members, and predators to go free.

Most people don't want us around unless they need us, even though they never openly say that. Many lawyers are only out to try and prove the Officer did something wrong as opposed to their clients, who get presented as saints once in the courtroom. How disheartening is it for a Police Officer to be confronted on all sides by opposition? That is why it is imperative for any young Police Officer to never take things personally, although it may be difficult at times. This is something I had to learn very quickly out of the academy. It is not personal. It is business. It is a dirty business that Officers have to accept will not always go the way they want it to go. It won't even be that way most of the time. We have to remember to keep a firm belief in what is right, do the best we can, and let it all go when it is over. There is always another day to fight the bad guys, and chances are, if you don't get them this time, the criminal will almost always screw up again.

If you, as an Officer, get so lost in the job and the world we face, I promise you, you will lose yourself. As you read this book and in certain chapters, I even talk about that. It is imperative that we learn as Officers to put on the hero's mask and yet be real at the same time. Don't make enemies out there, but don't be a doormat, either. Keep your family and your faith sacred and just do what's morally right. If not, there is always a vicious media out there that is waiting for the fall of a hero.

Be able to take that cape-of-the-hero mentality off and just be a normal person. But always be ready and prepared to go right back into it. If you are sick or physically ill, admit it and get well. Stop trying to be the invincible person you are not. I only say this because it seems to be a common theme with men in general, and especially the Type A personality Police Officers. You need to take care of yourself first. Then you can save the world. I had to learn this difficult lesson the hard way. Try not to do it like me.

**Straight from the photo album.
Here's me one day shy of a year old.**

Smiling for the camera.

170   Protected

Picture collage. Top picture is me as a Boy Scout. The other picture is me sitting in the dune buggy that I don't remember ever getting started, Boo-Boo in the passenger seat. (I'm not really sure whose arm that is from the top of the dune buggy trying to pet the dog. Oh well.) This was about the age of the bullying incident.

Just an older kid now and his dog Boo-Boo. She was such an amazing dog. I was headed back to college again and hated to leave her. She died not long after this. She had lived a good, long life.

My Old Kentucky Home….well, not mine that is in the picture. Here is the sign at the entrance to our neighborhood when I was growing up. This would be somewhat of a boundary for me as a kid to go no further than this on our bikes. Our dog Boo-Boo would wait near this sign when she saw the school bus coming, and then race the bus down the hill while cutting through yards to greet us as we got off the bus. Truly, it was a wild little kid's playground.

A young, 23-year-old police cadet. Kentucky Police Corps Class 5. Department of Criminal Justice Training

Here is a photo of a Michoacán Police truck as it cruised the streets one night during our trip in Morelia. This was not during the time of the political protest, but several of the trucks looked like this, as well as those from Policía Estatal. Some of the trucks had more prominent roll bars and cages on the back with Officers riding back in the bed of the truck.

Mural painted by our Summer Camp kids and Officers in 2014. The handprints serve as the signatures of the artists. It is still there to this day and looks just as vivid. It is one is my favorite in town.

Speaking at the Anti-Bullying Rally and ceremony to make October Anti-Bullying month in Kentucky. Purple in the ribbon for Domestic violence awareness, and yellow for suicide prevention awareness. It was a packed auditorium with hundreds of students and other people attending as the Governor ceremoniously signed Senate Bill 20 into Law.

Prayer before Turkey Bowl V. Police and Fire Department members praying together before the game. 2015

Turkey Bowl V Game play action. This is definitely before I broke my pinky finger. I'm the guy in the right corner near the hash mark on defense. 440 is my badge number on my back at the time this photo was taken.

Filming "Healed By Horses" Documentary. You can find it at www.vimeo.com . Search for "Healed By Horses" by Chris LaForet. Pictured here are Chris and Sherry LaForet as we are filming the documentary. What is not pictured is Eclipse standing in the shade behind me.

Eclipse.

Hometown Heroes Charity Softball Tournament - Police Department vs. Fire Department

The friendly trash talk never ends with us and we wouldn't have it any other way. My love for sports never stopped when I grew up and it is a place where we can have fun and turn off the seriousness of what we see and deal with on a daily basis as we all work the streets together as first responders. Sometimes, though, these games get a little intense. Photo courtesy of Kim Owens.

Operation: SAVE BAMBI Here is proof there really was a baby deer we rescued in the execution of a search warrant. My Detectives were awesome and I loved working with them, and of course I took my opportunity to hold the deer!

Throughout my career, I had the opportunity to work with some of the best men and women from law enforcement. At the end of my career as Support Services Commander, I was blessed to have a great number of people who worked together as a cohesive unit. On this particular day, we were training at the firing range with a vehicle by shooting through it at various angles with various types of bullets and weapons. We also shot through windows. We then worked these trajectory shots like they were a real crime scene.

The entire team included our Detectives, most of our Firearms Instructors, Bike Patrol, Crime Scene Technicians, Collision Reconstruction Unit, and even our Drone (UAS) Unit. This picture is only a glimpse and a portion of the great team of people from that day and every day.

We usually take a selfie with the kids when I travel and speak at the schools. They love to participate. Since 2013, I have spoken to thousands of kids about bullying and teen suicide. We must find a way to give hope to people when they have none.

Frankfort, Kentucky at the Capitol. This photo was taken after having marched in the Governor's Inaugural Parade in December of 2015. Two other Officers and I from our agency marched in honor of Officer Daniel Ellis. There were Officers from other agencies representing their fallen Officers and Troopers, as well.

April 25, 2024 – Exactly two years to the day from the date I had the stroke from the brain bleed, I was blessed to be able to attend the Police Department's annual awards banquet with my wife and daughters and I received my shadowbox with my uniform for the rank of Major. I retired from policing on August 1. 2023.

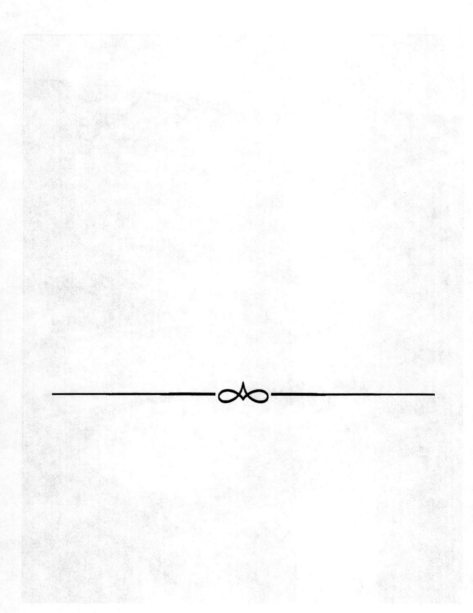

Chasing Demons

There is a line in a song by a favorite country singer of mine that goes like this: *"When I'm not chasing demons, there's demons chasing me."*

I have seen some dark...and I mean *dark* stuff in my career, some I have talked about in this book, but most of it I haven't. It has taken a toll on my health and well-being. I know I am not alone in this journey and endeavor. This short chapter is my reflection on a period in my life and career when I truly struggled. There were winding turns and dark paths taken when I felt like I was walking alone. Law enforcement chases the bad guys and fights the evil in the day and night. It doesn't stop there. But hey...like the song says, "When I'm not chasing demons, there's demons chasing me."

The year was 2004. I had a permanent residence! I had bought a home and everything! I never thought I would do it at such a young age, but with the wisdom of my mother, she encouraged it. My roommate moved into the house with me, and there was a backyard we quickly fenced in to contain my Husky puppy, Kaylee. It felt good to have a home to call my own. I bought it from two married Police Officers on the force with me for a good price, and the sale went fantastically...for my first home buy, anyway.

We moved into the home, and Jared got his room, and I got mine. We organized and put things away after moving (the one thing I hate doing more than probably anything in the world), and the home was established. It still had wallpaper border, hunter-green carpet, and one bathroom, but I didn't care! It was my home. I ended up living there for ten years and started my family with that home. I drive by it sometimes just to think of the core memories with my wife and two daughters.

A while after moving into the house and after college, as I was a new Police Officer, Jared took a job in another state, and so now it was time for me to support the mortgage on my own. Some of my other friends also moved away to start their lives, but my other best friend, T.J., always knew he was welcome, and the first thing he would do when he got there to visit was raid my pantry and steal my favorite snack, *The Little Debbie Fudge Brownie*. Not those stupid *Cosmic Brownies*, mind you, the good ones with the English walnuts on them. They don't make them anymore, sadly, upon me writing this book.

Side note: If anyone knows the people at Little Debbie, please have them bring back my favorite snack. Thank you.

At first, I was fine about Jared moving on to start his life. The college roommate thing had to end sometime. However, as a new Police Officer, I started at around $11.63 an hour working and went into debt buying my own gear because I wanted to do it that bad! I thought I could support the mortgage on my own and had too much pride to ask for help. Anyone else like me in that aspect? Eventually, though, I got behind on my bills, and the worry of not getting the bills paid began to weigh heavily on me. I was serving all portions of the population, rich and poor alike, yet I couldn't pay my own bills. Thank God the city went to home fleet shortly, about a year after I was on the road. I never told anyone because I was ashamed that I could not make it on my own and didn't want to disappoint my parents.

So, this was one of the first things to come with growing up for real and the job: financial responsibility. My family lived nowhere near me at the time, and I had to survive. Alone. Officers all over the world serve for pennies on the dollar compared to the private sector, and they get treated like garbage if they make a mistake. They serve for the act of serving, not for money. Law enforcement is not a career you just *try out*. Law enforcement and being a first responder is a calling, whether you believe in a higher power or not.

Insert *stress* Here

Now, I have always had a few amazing friends in my life, some of them closer to me than my own family. Some people who might read this have been in my life, came for a time, stayed for a bit, and moved on, just like I did in your life. That's how life is. Some people moved on in my life, or the closeness in my heart because you didn't come to stay—you came to go—but not before I had to learn some really hard lessons with it.

Sometimes, I have been the person who has gone out on the town to places just because I didn't want to be lonely and I wanted to hang out with people—the needs of an extrovert. Most of the time, I was the designated driver in my college years, although there were several nights of regret and a lot of forgiveness from God and other people I had to ask for.

When I was around seventeen years old, I was introduced to alcohol in the form of a bottle of Jim Beam. I tasted it, and it was horrible. I went home and told my mom and swore to her I would never drink or smoke cigarettes. I'm sorry, Mom. I broke that promise, but it led me to where I am today. I drank some in college, and I was often the life of the party, or I thought I was—probably not the case. God spared me and kept me out of trouble on several occasions when I deserved nothing less than to go to jail for alcohol intoxication or disorderly conduct...the very thing I arrested lots of people for later on in my career. Do you know how difficult it is to admit this?

Alcohol never really got to take hold of my life until I became a Police Officer. The stress was piling up on me mentally, though I would never tell anyone at twenty-five years old or a little older that I couldn't handle it. I had this. My walk with Jesus strayed, and I became a lost sheep of the ninety-nine. I remember Jared telling me I needed to get back into church. But my faith was fine. I was good. And I was having fun.

I was on third shift for several years, and my days off were Tuesday and Wednesday. I worked night shift, then would go to another job to try and work sometimes, and rarely did I sleep more than five hours. Again, I had this. I had parties at my house, and I would come home several days a week in the early morning after work, start drinking, and then fall asleep (if that is what you want to call it). Then, I would wake up in the evening from doing that, make sure I was sober, and go to work.

Let me be clear: I was never, and I mean never, drunk or intoxicated on duty.

I share this deep, dark secret because I know there are others, law enforcement and not, who are struggling right now. There is help for you. There is a life beyond the bottle or whatever drug you have consumed, and God's love is *real* forgiveness, no matter what anyone says. Eventually, after I got ripped by a certain Sergeant and cussed at because he cared, I had my wake-up call. It was a core moment in my career. I am proud to say now I have moved on from that life, but there are others who still need help. I plan on still helping others and lifting them up.

Learning how to control your emotions and how to deal with people is only the beginning. The next big thing is knowing when and how to say certain things and when to shut things down. This has always been one of the more difficult concepts of communication for me to ever achieve. And I *still* struggle. You see, police work is unlike any other profession. Police work is an emotionally exhausting job every day due to the high stress level and day-to-day jobs we perform and the wear it does on the body. Our bodies tell the story of our stress. Sometimes...oftentimes, we bring our jobs and emotions home with us, whether we want to or not.

This is a part of my life I am not proud of. This is a part of my life where I didn't want to look at myself in the mirror or discuss my problem. But if you are truly going to be a Police Officer, this is something you may or may not have dealt with. If you are truly getting a window into my life, this was part of it.

Although my family lives within a few hours drive from Richmond, it was not easy to just pack it up and leave to go home when I worked second and third shift. When I graduated from college, my sister followed me to college and went to the same university I did. We became a lot closer, and it was great because now my family would come visit frequently, or if we needed anything, we were together in the same town. This was great during college, but when she graduated and I became a Police Officer, it was shortly after that she moved away. She now lives about three hours away.

It's really no one's fault. It just is what it is. My trips became less and less to home because I worked all the time, almost every holiday for several years in a row. I am not proud to say this, but at times, I felt like I was facing the demons on my own. I know Jesus never left my side, but in the silence is where we grow. In the dark is where the seed begins to change.

Alcohol has ruined the lives of so many people and caused so many complications to relationships that would not normally have happened. And I was on the downward spiral to its path of destruction. It is not a life choice some would make, but it seemed harmless at the time. I have felt very judged by Christians and other people, and even I didn't know where to turn at that point in my life. I was losing hope. I was also carrying a gun every single day in service to others to save people and give hope to the hopeless. I wanted help from someone but didn't know how to ask for it or where to go where I wouldn't be judged. When someone doesn't know where to turn to or cannot turn to the church, they won't go. Period.

But in the stillness and the loneliness, God never stopped loving me and kept working on me, sober or drunk. I always had my conscience telling me right from wrong. Sometimes, I would listen; sometimes, I wouldn't. I *knew* I had a problem. I became more reclusive and removed myself from interacting with other people more and more. This was one of the lowest points for me. I began to pray deeply and desperately for God to rescue me and not turn away from me and help me fix the mess I had made of my life. I didn't believe God wanted me anymore. Sometimes, I didn't know if I believed in God at all from everything I had seen. The bottoms of liquor, wine, and beer bottles were all I found at the time. It left me nothing, and there was no real joy found in it. I began to question myself and had to make the conscious decision to become a better man and not give in to temptation. The idea itself sounds like motivation. The temptation comes when a man is alone with his thoughts, and the silence is an opportunity for the enemy to creep in.

Please understand I am not here to preach to anyone. Christians today have become so high and mighty and preachy we won't reach people where they are like Jesus did. In my career, I saw a whole lot of people who needed love and could use the love of Jesus. And yet, the church never reached out to them. I am not better than anyone, and I fight my own battles every single day, but the church could always do more if we were not so religious. Religion comes from man, not God. Maybe if we stopped worrying about what someone looks like when they come to church or when we see them on the street, we could realize they need help. Remember, Jesus took the time to wash people's feet when He should have been the one who received that treatment. That says a lot about the church today and the priorities of society.

I had decided something had to be done in my own life in order to save myself, my career and just be happy in general. I had been quietly taking a path leading to destruction, and no one even knew it. Or, maybe they did know but felt it was not their place to intervene or tell me and help. Who knows? All I know out of it all is I wanted to change and needed to change no matter what. My only hope is that I never let anyone down in the process, but if we are being real, I know I did, but I am not afraid to admit it.

I am telling you this part of my story to tell you there are a vast number of unseen pressures in police work and for all first responders. I address some of them in this book. The pressure takes a physical, mental, emotional, and spiritual toll on you, and sometimes it wins. When this happens, humans look for ways to release the pressure valve. We have to cope somehow. I didn't do it the right way. I found no answers on the road I was traveling. Perhaps mention of this in my own life might be the chance for someone to look at their own life and find hope in their darkness. Those demons with you in the darkness, you don't have to be afraid when you know Jesus walks through that dark with you. He never left my side.

Everything happens in the spiritual world before it happens in the physical world we walk in. We all have a past. We all have mistakes and things we wish we had not said to someone. Satan knows exactly where and how to hit you and when. We all suffer silently in our own ways. The key is to understand God's forgiveness for us, and therefore, we should learn to forgive ourselves.

I really, *really* did not want to put this chapter in this book. I really wanted to hide this part of my life and hide behind the facade of goodness we all put on for other people. We know how to act and when to act the right way. Not doing so is a choice.

Unexpected Answers When
I Didn't Ask the Question

I have a former instructor from the academy who became a person I think very highly of in regard to leadership through all the training I took as I was moving up in the ranks through my career. I had many of the courses he taught. He has known me since the time I was beginning my career. He knows my faith. He has seen the growth, and we have disagreed many times over the years about leadership and the *right answer*. And yet, I respect him so much and still learn from every conversation we have. In one of the trainings, we discussed how many people we all are in life. He said we have the public version of ourselves everyone sees, the private version only those closest to us see, and the intimate version only God sees. He asked if it was okay to be all three different versions.

Stay with me. I'm going somewhere with this.

We all discussed it in class, and all agreed it was okay to have those different versions of ourselves because not everyone should get to look at exactly every part of your life. The public should not see what the Police Officer's home life is like. The public should not get to see or hear the conversations with God.

Then came the reality check. He said if we were truly to be good leaders and men and women of integrity (a word many leaders say they have), then we should be one person. There should not be three versions of us. We should be that person all the time. People should see the person you are from the moment they meet you.

MIC DROP

Here was our instructor and now my friend who had shut an entire class of leadership within police agencies up with one single statement. He further went on to describe how we are either that person or we are not. There is no in-between.

I never dreamed I would one day tell anyone in the world about one of the things I am most ashamed of in my life. I had to learn to face the fact I cannot change what is in the past, though the past may still haunt us in many ways. The problems I faced in my past are just that...*in* my past. I cannot change them. I can only learn from the mistakes I made and hopefully earn forgiveness from others I have wronged. Forgiveness is not guaranteed from someone just because you say, "I'm sorry."

I had to learn to forgive myself. I still struggle with forgiving myself. I forgive others for me, not for them. I forgive them so I can move on, and it is still hard to press forward. Shame is a way Satan holds onto your life. Jesus takes that away. I am not ashamed of this anymore. I am stronger now than I was then.

I have lost family relationships, friends, and nearly my own soul because I did not keep my eyes on heaven. We all have a choice to make. Mine was simple. I did not want to be the man I was becoming, and all I needed to do was admit my own mistakes. The chain of addiction (and that comes in many forms, not just alcohol) was wrapping around my life and was taking a stronghold in my life. There is always help out there, and I was afraid to ask for it.

I am so sick of society telling people what to believe or how they are wrong if they believe differently from someone else. I still believe in the freedom of speech and religion. But for a society that acts like we have all the answers, we sure are hypocritical of others and don't lend a hand when someone is drowning. Then we blame everyone else for our own problems we got ourselves into. Take some accountability and help someone in need. The choices are up to the individual as they make them, but maybe if we all showed a little more compassion and grace and stopped hating so much, people would have a chance to be human and make mistakes. Would the first people who have never made a mistake please stand up? I'll wait.

Closing Note: The demons can't win if you don't let them. You can have a relationship with someone who will walk with you every step of the way. I wish I could tell you it gets better. But the spiritual attacks won't stop coming at you as long as you walk this earth. You are always either coming out of a storm, in a storm, or going into a storm. Just remember, there is hope in the darkness. His name is Jesus. You can be free.

Healing from Unexpected Places

Have you ever lost your way? I don't mean to lose your way on a trip or on the highway. I do that all the time. Ask my wife. She is the navigator. I mean, have you ever lost your way emotionally? Have you ever had depression or anger and didn't know how to deal with it or didn't even know where it came from? Have you ever had grief and you didn't even know you were still grieving? What about hatred for someone, and you know you shouldn't hate people? Come on, if we are all being honest, even about the hate part, we know we have dealt with one or all of these things. You may even be dealing with them still.

There is hope.

Throughout my career and even when I was in college, I had the opportunity to do some work at a horse stable in my area. This place has never paid me but basically got free labor out of me. I eventually got to ride the horses whenever I wanted to, and I learned a few lessons along the way.

It was all worth it to me. When the barn was empty, and it was time to call them up in the mornings or evenings for their meal, we would holler or whistle. Then, the sounds would slowly arrive. Like a slow, rolling thunder. The sounds of hooves to sometimes over forty horses! If you have heard it, it is unmistakable.

The owners go by the Natural Horsemanship philosophy. They also live much like the Native American cultures do regarding the barn and the things in the barn. This is where we sometimes disagreed, but I would always respect their wishes. For example, if there is a snake in the barn, I am not allowed to kill it. I think this rule is one that could be broken. However, they do not and believe the snake has a purpose. The same goes for spiders, etc.

Over the years, I went to this barn and worked with the horses, never being very good with them at first and definitely not having the trust of the owners to do anything other than clean and shovel manure or throw hay. When I was younger, I had more edge and an attitude to boot. I found a horse I really liked but wasn't ready for this horse. This horse's name is Eclipse.

She is a dark, wild spirit of a horse, now one of the alphas at the barn last I heard. She would run and kick and bite. Right up my alley. I thought I could handle her, and she would sometimes allow me to get close enough and be tame enough to ride, and then she would take off through the pasture to do whatever she wanted. Little did I know through these wild rides, God was teaching me a lesson.

He was healing me in a sense I never knew was coming. There were emotions I was dealing with because of my new career, the struggles with substance abuse, depression, and the things I was not used to seeing because of my sheltered life. God was giving me an outlet.

Sometimes, we would walk through the woods by the creek. Sometimes, we would gallop through the fields with the wind blowing through her mane. Sometimes, I just dismounted and let her graze the grass while I sat on the porch of this old abandoned cabin on the property or looked at the headstones of this old cemetery with headstones back to the 1700s. It was Eclipse and me.

As the years went by and I would visit Eclipse less and less, it seemed she would still remember me every time I would show up. It wasn't as if I didn't want to go, but it was timing. I would go weekly for a long time, and then sometimes, it would be a year or more. She wasn't my horse, but every time I would go back, it felt like it, and then I felt guilty for abandoning her. One day, she made me pay for that. She remembered me. I had brought an apple that day. The owner told me to ride Eclipse bareback through the pasture. She had calmed down a lot since I had last seen her. This seemed legitimate at the time.

It turned out to be a terrible idea. I remember being thrown from the horse and Eclipse coming back and standing over top of me as if to check to see if I was okay, drooling on me, walking away about ten feet to go eat some grass. Hey, at least she checked on me. Nothing was severely hurt except my pride.

When I was assigned to the schools, we were able to partner with multiple organizations and create a juvenile equine psychotherapy program. I have seen known gang members who would have been on their way to prison become like little children when working with the horses and develop a respect they never had or never knew. There is something about getting an attitude with an animal that is 2000 pounds that will change your perspective on life. Equine therapy works!

Shortly after all that happened, the owners of the barn were contacted about a documentary for the program we had started. The documentary is called *Healed by Horses*. You can still find it on www.vimeo.com. I was asked to be in the documentary among the other people in the program due to my law enforcement background and having worked with the juveniles, some at the barn. Ultimately, it became one of the things that jumpstarted my public speaking career (if you want to call it that), and the rest is history. We hosted a public showing in a high school auditorium and even handed out posters for the movie. To me, it solidified everyone's belief in the idea of healing from the horses, some of God's greatest creatures.

Every year, our Police Summer Camp goes back to the barn, and we let our kids have a day to experience what it is like to work with and ride the horses. They only get a limited amount of time, but maybe it will teach them to have respect for an animal they never got to be around. They can always go back, but you have to lay the foundation.

For me, it was about going to a place where I could get away from all the crazy calls and just be out in the open in God's open country with the horses and the sky. I wasn't a cowboy in Texas, but that never stopped me from trying here in Kentucky. I can ride a horse a little better now than I used to be able to, and I am a lot older now than I was. I found that undiagnosed equine psychotherapy helped me to find some healing in unexpected places.

My favorite place was with a horse named Eclipse.

The Good Ole Days of Policing

Do you ever wish you could go back in time? I mean, even for just a simple thing, to relive something? I do. I wish it all the time. Not just to try and change some of the things I did wrong but to relive some of the hilarious things that happened along the way throughout my career. The drunks. The craziness. The adrenaline dump. The fun stuff.

In the early stages of my career, we were a poor police agency because the city spent the money on other things other than public safety (we won't go there). We didn't have home fleet, and I had to buy all my own gear except the actual threads I wore as a uniform. But even in those days, I had a lot of fun as a cop. We dealt with mostly the same drunks, and it was always an adventure when dealing with them.

I remember the first cruiser I got to drive. It was a Ford Crown Victoria with dip spit running down the side, and the seat sunk in and ashes inside it from others who used it before me. The cars rotated out through the shifts 24/7 and were always breaking down. It was comical and a disaster.

When we finally got our home fleet, and I was allowed to drive my cruiser to my house, I got one of the older cars in the fleet, a Chevrolet Impala. I didn't care in the least and was so excited. I cleaned it up and drove that front-wheel drive car like I was in the rally cross. There were some "defensive driving skills" practiced in an empty, snowy parking lot on a slow Christmas night one year when I was young in my career. At least, that's what I tell myself now. Don't worry; no damage was done to any property, and I really did learn how to drive better from it.

We had changed the stripe package on the cruisers, and I remember when we got our first few cruisers in. The Crown Victorias were beautiful, and although I wasn't a huge fan of the design, what I did like about it was the fact it was different from other agencies and made us stand out. Several of the Supervisors who had been there a long time got the new cruisers. I didn't expect or even care if I got one. I liked my Impala. It was like night and day or driving a small plane versus a big boat on the road, with the power pushing from different areas of the car. Anyway, one of my Sergeants got one of the first new cruisers issued out for home fleet, and he responded to a call with me one night. I can't remember if it was second or third shift. I just remember laughing in the dark a little while later. Like, really laughing.

We got a call from a pizza place in town about a man who had stolen a pizza and ran out the door. I could just hear the tone and dispatch rolling their eyes as they gave the description of a local drunk we dealt with all the time. Nearly every day.

He was a homeless man who would fight, run, spit, or do just about anything else, and he usually did. I had caught him breaking into buildings with his butt in the air, breaking into soda machines on the street with a boombox strapped to his body by a belt and headphones on before the days of Bluetooth (that is how I snuck up on him). This time, however, he stole a pizza. And decades later, I can't stop smiling about it.

It wasn't my call to go to that, I recall, but if it was, I didn't get there until second on scene due to where I was geographically in the city. All I know is when I rolled up, I saw one of our female Officers chasing a man (guess who) down the street while he was wearing old tennis shoes, raggedy shorts, and a torn T-shirt.

The man was carrying a pizza in his hands, and as I got on scene, he flipped the lid to the pizza box up and started shoveling pizza in his mouth by the handful. Now, this was a full-on, running through the middle of the street foot pursuit. The Officer was gaining on him because, let's face it, he wasn't exactly a gazelle on the plains. He was a drunk running at an angle down the middle of the street. That is not to take away credit from the Officer. She did a great job in the pursuit.

I heard her screaming at him, saying, "_____! Stop! Police!" (For the record, I know his name. The names have been redacted.) He looked back at her with the lid of the pizza box flapping in the wind as he shoveled the pizza into his mouth. With a mouthful of pizza, he screamed back at her over his shoulder and yelled,

"It's mine!"

And then, it happened.

Excuse me for just a moment. Let me pause to laugh and take all this in. It makes me remember the fun times of policing.

Okay, I'm back.

Like a slow-motion camera, it all plays out in my mind as I watch this all unfold still to this day. As he was looking back at her and shoving the pizza in his mouth from hunger, he couldn't focus on what he was doing, and he tripped over his own feet. Then, in the middle of the street, I saw the pizza box start to leave his hands, and he went down, skidding about ten feet.

Now, if this had been one of my kids when they were little, there might have been some tears, and that would have been the end of it. Not with him! Before I knew it, he was trying to get up and get back to his feet and that pizza box. Seriously, I would have bought him the pizza.

He didn't get the chance to get up, though. By that time, I was not a spectator anymore and was out of my car and assisting the other Officer. It was a dog pile on the rabbit, and he was detained and put into handcuffs, the pizza about ten to fifteen feet in front of where we were. He was handcuffed behind his back per policy (this comes into play in a few minutes), and immediately, he began his usual berating of us in a slur of drunk, colorful language.

As he was being walked back toward a cruiser, my Sergeant pulled up to the scene in his brand new Ford Crown Victoria with a new stripe and light package. Newly washed, too. He told us to put the man in his cruiser.

In typical fashion for this man, there was always more to come. He asked if he could keep the pizza because he was hungry and homeless and because we were going to charge him with theft anyway and could not give it back. He actually had a valid point for once in his life. What happened after this, though, was completely unexpected from him...except that it really wasn't given who he was.

For some reason, he was allowed to keep the pizza, and it was put in the back seat of the cruiser with him. What harm could that do? He was in handcuffs, and he was going to jail, which was only about a three-minute drive or so since it was so late and there was no traffic. Well, we didn't leave in that amount of time. The Sergeant had to figure out what happened and talk to the Officers, restaurant staff, and witnesses. So, needless to say, for about five minutes, the drunk man was left to his own devices in the back of the brand-new cruiser...with a pizza.

I have heard the expression, "Idle hands are the devil's playground/ workshop." The proverb suggests that someone who is bored or unoccupied will get into trouble or mischief. And that is exactly what happened. We didn't have cages over the windows of these new cruisers, so thankfully, he didn't kick the windows out or anything. When we would check on him within the five-minute timeframe, he was just looking at us through the back seat window, appearing to just be his usual drunken self. Nothing suspicious.

Unbeknownst to us, he had slipped his handcuffs from the back of his body to the front and now had access to that pizza. Rather than eating the pizza we had allowed him to have for hunger, he chose the mischief route instead. He took that pizza, every slice, and smeared it all over the back of the cruiser seat, cage window, door handles, and every other part he could get to on the side of the cruiser we couldn't see at the time.

Two things: First, this is a major safety issue for law enforcement. This could have been much worse than it was if he had wanted to hurt us. Second, when Sarge came back to the car to drive him to jail, he opened the door to check on the man and talk to him, and that is when he saw all the collateral damage from the pizza sacrifice.

Sarge blew a gasket! I thought he was going to yank him out of that cruiser right then and there. Instead, colorful language ensued, and he got into his car and took him to the jail before something worse happened to the man. A wise move. In the darkness and shadows, I could not stop laughing afterward. I am *still* laughing decades later.

Those were the good ole days of policing. They were more simple. The drunks understood and still halfway respected the police. Even the drug dealers had some honor and wouldn't allow other drug dealers to set up shop in their town. Sure, it was dangerous, and there were dangerous moments, but most of the time, it was still fun.

Times have changed in policing.

America's insatiable appetite for drugs, violence, child pornography, and its other vices have made it one of the top (if not *the* top consumer, depending on the category) consumers of each of those. The national media has turned against policing or used it as a political platform, and celebrities who live lavish lifestyles use their influence to state whatever narrative they see fit without having actual facts. They partner with politicians and organizations and shout "defund the police" while our streets are being overrun with crime.

Our streets are flooded with drugs from other countries and cartels, and our people, young and old, die from overdoses and murdering each other. Do we hear about that on the news? Do we hear about that from celebrities? Hollywood continues to have people die from overdoses, but still, there is silence. They would rather rally around those who would prey on children and spin a narrative of acceptance than face facts that our world is in trouble and needs Jesus.

Yes, those were the good ole days of policing. Those were the days when men and women signed up for a career and served until they retired. When a Police Officer is killed in the line of duty saving a life, is that run on the national media, or are we too busy fighting about the next election and how to swing votes for politicians? Politicians line their pockets with big companies, and the working class suffers more and more.

The luster and shine of the badge are gone in the eyes of the world, or at least to those keyboard warriors who would never say this to an Officer's face while we live in a digital age of people who think they know better. The bodies are piling up, and families are being wrecked by the actions of what we do, and we have yet to see all the ramifications. Families turn on their Officers while they serve, never asking what we feel. Then we, as a society, wonder why the whole policing field is falling apart and we can't recruit or retain like we used to.

Maybe society has made its bed and now has to lie in it. We write laws about guns and criminals and how we will take away rights written into the Constitution as it was breathed out by our Forefathers. Please let me know how that goes and let me know how it works out since criminals are so good at following laws.

Meanwhile, those who would call themselves Christians or religious are the very ones who are silent when they should be vocal and vocal when they should be silent. This world has become lukewarm and afraid to offend anyone with a different opinion or background. We defend what we shouldn't, argue about frivolous things, and don't defend or fight for what we should. It makes me sick.

If you can't tell by now from this book, I am an opinionated, imperfect person called by God with a purpose. Sometimes, I don't get it right. And often, I don't do it the way God wants me to do it. I was a Police Officer who enforced the law, and sometimes, I messed up, too. But don't we all? In policing, in politics, in the church...

Romans 3:21–23 says,

> "But now the righteousness of God has been manifested apart from the law, although the Law and the Prophets bear witness to it, the righteousness of God through faith in Jesus Christ for all who believe, for there is no distinction; for all have sinned and fall short of the glory of God."

What I mean by all this is, what if we all gave each other some grace? What if we forgave one another and didn't criticize what we don't understand? I laugh about the man stealing the pizza because it is a funny police story from my life. I don't laugh at the fact he was homeless, a drunk, had nothing good in his life to turn to, nor the fact I could have been a witness to him more than I was. I look back and realize I could have done more to help him. Maybe he would have taken the help. Maybe he would not have. I didn't even try. That one is on me, and I live with it every day.

What if just one of us tried a little more to be a better person? What if we tried to do better and everyone tried to make a difference for others? Imagine what a world we could have for our children. Imagine the kingdom we could build for Jesus.

Imagine what it would be like.

"Have You Ever Killed Anyone?"

This is the question I got asked most often by little children over the years of being a Police Officer. My answer, thankfully, is no, but I have come really, *really* close to doing so on about three occasions that immediately come to mind.

The first time I almost had to kill someone was when I was a young Police Officer, and I responded to a trailer park for a domestic in the middle of winter when there was about two feet of snow on the ground. There was a man who was fighting his family out in the driveway with a 2x4 board, and I could not make this up. All he was wearing was his tighty-whitey underwear in the freezing cold winter!

I drove lights and siren through the night and turned off the siren as I turned into the driveway to try and avoid detection, leaving the lights on so my fellow Officers could find me. One would think he would have heard the siren and would have run or stopped fighting or something by this time. Apparently, this drunk guy didn't get the memo he was supposed to do that. When my feet crunched through the snow and gravel up the driveway and around to the back of the trailer where all the commotion was, I saw the man in his underwear swinging the 2x4 around and cussing at about three or four people.

He was headed toward a particular female, later found out to be his girlfriend. He raised the board over her head, and I yelled, "Stop! Police! Drop it!"

This drew his attention away from her, and he quickly turned around as I yelled, "Police!" again in my loudest voice I could. This still didn't really register with him, but at this point, I had drawn my firearm. Now let me give a little pause here and tell you that at this point in policing, all we had was pepper spray and batons as less lethal weapons. There was no such thing as a taser at that time.

So, as he turned toward me and began to charge me from about twenty yards away, I raised my firearm and, after having already been professional in my announcement of "Police!" and "Drop it!" for some odd reason, the next thing that came out of my mouth as I stared him down and stood my ground was, "Tell me how you want it!" My pistol was pointed center mass to him, and he might have truly been able to hit me with the board before going down, even if he had been shot. Studies have shown someone with a knife can travel twenty-one feet in a few seconds and still stab an Officer. This guy had a 2x4 about four feet long! I had a clean shot at that close distance with a building behind him, not a trailer. If I had to take the shot, I would have.

Not realizing the stupidity of what I had said until later. That didn't matter right now because it clicked in his mind what was about to happen. He was about to get shot by the police. He immediately began to cuss me, but I continued to order him to throw the board to the side away from him and get on the ground. He continued to yell at me and talk about how cold it was, how there was snow on the ground, and how he was in his tighty-whitey underwear. I proned him onto the ground anyway, went over to him, and thankfully he did not resist anymore. I would have hated to fight a man in the snow in only his underwear. The other Officers showed up from across town just as he was getting handcuffed.

He was handcuffed and put into the back of the cruiser, still cussing and spitting at me because I couldn't drive him somewhere else to get him some clothes to take him to jail. You win some, you lose some. But hey, at least I didn't have to shoot him.

On another occasion, a man had a domestic fight with his girlfriend at their home, and it got very physical, so much so that she fled the residence almost completely naked except for a blanket and underwear out of fear for her life. She ran to the neighbor's house, and they called 9-1-1 for her. It was at this point he kicked in the door and basically took his girlfriend and two other people as hostages with a handgun. He knew we were coming to the residence, and when we arrived, we parked down the street to approach on foot. He was drunk, and for some reason, he came outside into the front yard. I was hiding across the street behind some concealment with a 12-gauge shotgun. Not cover that was safe, concealment to hide where I was located. At that point in my career, we had not been issued rifles. It was probably thirty yards away, and the shotgun had slugs loaded up.

206   PROTECTED

The girlfriend and the neighbors had run out the back door when he came outside the front door. I remember his nickname because I knew him and that is what he answered to. I remember hearing them screaming from behind the house, but that doesn't mean there was no one else inside that I knew of at that moment. That shot, if I would have had to take it, had better have been spot on.

I yelled from across the street as I popped up just enough to get a clear shot and show him I was armed with a long gun. The yard he was in was very well lit up, as was he. I was hiding in the shadows, and he could not tell exactly where I was based on his looking around. The pistol was in his right jeans pocket, and he started to reach for it.

"Don't do it! Don't reach for it! Get your hands up!"

He was held at gunpoint just like that until a few seconds later (which seemed like an eternity) when other Officers heard me yelling and arrived next to me. We approached him and gave him specific orders, keeping his hand away from the weapon as we moved forward. A contact/cover team established, we made our approach, and he was taken into custody without incident. Again, God kept everyone in that situation safe. As far as I know, that man has cleaned up his life today, and there were no other incidents with the police, although that one was almost his last either way.

I have been in a lot of tense standoffs throughout my career. Some of the men and women I worked with, or even those who may read this book, could have had far more intense situations than this. Another incident I had was one in which a man we dealt with on what seemed like a weekly basis had a domestic fight with his girlfriend (are you sensing a pattern?) and ended up burglarizing her apartment. Again, I was on third shift at the time, fairly early in my career.

He had kicked the door into the small apartment and had barricaded himself inside a bedroom in the hallway. He had his body pushed up against the door with his back, and his legs braced against a dresser and a bed. At first, when we entered the residence, all we saw was darkness and heard silence. I felt like my heart was going to jump out of its chest. It was stressful.

We searched the apartment, and as I passed by that bedroom, I heard someone speaking inside the bedroom and then someone yelling for help—a female voice. A male voice cussed her and yelled back at her and tried to silence her. More screaming. More intense this time. He was actively stabbing her, trying to kill her. She was defending herself by putting her hands up. We later found this out from the severe lacerations to her hands.

We challenged from the hallway. His attention was diverted to us for the moment. Now, what transpired all happened within about a minute and a half total. We tried to force our way into the bedroom while he was seated below us, below the doorknob, still actively trying to stab at her. He could not do both very well, though, as he was trying to keep us out, too.

My Supervisor at the time was a huge guy in that small hallway, and there were three of our Officers in the hallway, a Deputy with us, and a trooper on his way. We just didn't know it. Imagine, if you can, the top one-third corner of a wooden door splintering inward while the door stayed intact at the bottom from the suspect's body braced against it. Now, we had progress. First light into the room.

The suspect stopped trying to stab his girlfriend, had stood up, and was now trying to stab us. I was first in line. I had a clear shot of him, and my pistol was in the room as we were breaching the door. He was coming at me from about three feet away. Finger on the trigger, I almost pulled it. What happened would have haunted me for the rest of my life if it had occurred. The Deputy on scene, with all of us likely having tunnel vision, stepped in front of the barrel of my 9mm handgun, reached into the room, and began spraying pepper spray.

This only made the situation worse in the long run, as we were all hacking and coughing from the exposure to the OC spray. I thank God that, for some reason, I recognized this would have been friendly fire, and I almost shot my friend. I reholstered my firearm, and we dove into the room as the Deputy knocked the knife out of the suspect's hand. One of our Officers got the female victim out of the room, and the fight was on with the suspect. He kicked, spit, punched, tried to bite, tried to get the knife. I felt like that fight lasted forever, and he was not that big of a guy.

Remember that trooper I told you about? At some point during this time, he popped up in the room, and all I remember is hearing the words "Taser, taser, taser!" I heard the spark of electricity throughout the room and the screams of the suspect as we gained compliance during this painful time for him. Tasers had just become an item being issued to law enforcement; our department just hadn't had any issued to us yet, but it was soon after this we did. The fighting dropped astronomically when this invention became a tool for our law enforcement agency to use. Not many people really want to ride the lightning.

Once the suspect was in custody, he had to be carried to the car because he was still kicking and screaming. He kicked a cruiser window out that night and everything. But he still went to jail, and no Officers were hurt. The victim survived her injuries and, after multiple surgeries and physical therapy, was okay.

She was okay, so much so that when the suspect decided to take this case all the way to a jury trial about a year and a half later, she testified, as did expert witnesses like doctors, trauma nurses, and physical therapists. The Officers, including me, testified in the case, and we thought it was going to be over. It was time for closing arguments, and the Commonwealth was about to rest its case.

Then, something wild (and that is the only way I can describe it) happened. The suspect, now the Defendant in the case I was the arresting officer for, wanted to testify. I was floored. The other witnesses were shocked. The jury was shocked. The Judge was shocked. The Commonwealth Attorneys got excited unexpectedly, and his Defense Attorney was not ready for what was about to happen next. To be fair to her, her client did not tell her this, and she did her very best to advise against this.

The Judge had counsel, and the Defendant approached the bench and explained there would be no appeal if this happened. He asked him once, then twice, "Are you sure you want to do this?" He said, "Yes, I want to tell my side of the story." The Judge threw his hands up and said, "Okay, Defense Counselor. Call your witness."

The next twenty minutes or so were a courtroom drama that should have been aired on television in a series or played in a movie. The Defendant went on to talk about how trained Police Officers wouldn't take the knife from him and how he was trying to save the victim from the police. I couldn't believe my ears as the Defendant spun his story to make him sound like the victim.

The jury wasn't buying it. At all.

He pleasantly smiled at the jury as he finished his direct examination. Now, it was time for cross-examination from the Commonwealth. It was a very simple cross-examination. The attorney only asked one or two questions for clarification.

"Mr. _____, you said in your testimony that you tried to hand those Police Officers the knife, and they just wouldn't take it. Is that correct?"

"Yes," he said.

"About how long would you say you held it out there for them to take, and they just wouldn't take it, did you say?"

"I believe I said about thirty to forty-five seconds I held it out there."

Then, the Commonwealth went and got the bloody knife still in the bag tagged as a piece of evidence after getting permission to approach the jury and stood in front of them holding it up. She asked the other Commonwealth Attorney to use the stopwatch to time out just how long thirty to forty-five seconds really was while holding it in front of the jury, and no one in the courtroom saying anything.

Nothing.

I heard the clock ticking on the wall. It was so quiet. At the end of the time mentioned, the cross-examination got rougher for the Defendant as she stated to the jury it was impossible to believe that trained Police Officers would just "refuse" to take a weapon safely during a stabbing. Genius cross-examination.

The jury ended up giving the Defendant thirty years in prison because he was a persistent felony offender.

I have friends whom I have worked with who had had to return fire to take someone's life. To anyone reading this who believes Cops are all gun-happy and want to go shoot people, think again. This is something that weighs heavy on our hearts, and in law enforcement, we have split seconds to make decisions no one else would ever be in a circumstance to make. The stories you read above are all before today's time of body worn cameras, and they are in memory like it was a movie I just watched.

And let me be clear: I support body worn cameras, and they have helped law enforcement tremendously to accurately tell the story. If the police screw it up, we are held accountable. As a matter of fact, those good Officers (which is 99 percent of the Officers in the career) don't want the bad ones giving us a bad name.

I would say this, though. Today's media is not the media it used to be. Anyone and everyone can get on social media and think they know everything about a case and make a decision on it when they were not even there. I would encourage you to put yourself in the shoes of all parties involved, not just those you may align with your current viewpoints. How can we, as a society, ever learn to grasp new changes and challenges if we cannot see it from another's perspective?

And if anyone would like to know from those stories above, the suspects in all those cases above were Caucasian males, just like I am. It had nothing to do with race. It had to do with the preservation of the life of a victim and stopping a threat. I am a Caucasian male, too.

Silent Machines and Life-Changing Surprises

Remember I told you about my love for that show, "Pacific Blue"? Well, as it turns out, Bike Patrol in Kentucky is nothing like it is in California and *nothing* like it is on TV. We did get to do some really, really awesome stuff, though. It was probably my favorite thing I ever did at the agency other than working with kids in schools. Supervision is okay, and I loved it, but it is a lot of stress. Bike Patrol is about working the streets.

Street-level narcotics busts, undercover vehicles, stakeouts, special assignments, and getting our own office away from everyone else so we could be left alone to do our job. There was a lot of trust in us, and we had to work really hard. We were a high-production specialized unit. If we didn't produce results on the street, the unit would get disbanded. Period.

I loved working with those guys on Bike Patrol. We chased people both on bicycles and on foot. We would sneak up on criminals in the dark. I loved working with those guys. I am still close to them today, even after retirement. I could always call them if I needed anything. We got into so much stuff. The criminals hated us on the Bike Patrol. When we would roll into a particularly high-crime area of town, no one heard us coming.

We were nearly silent on the bikes. Silent machines. By the time we were close enough for you to hear us, we had you. If they did see us, they would start to scamper and scatter in every direction, yelling, "Bike boys! Bike boys!" Then, we would chase whoever threw the closest bag of dope onto the ground. We pulled traffic stops in high crime areas and got drugs out of cars and took drunks to jail (not on the handlebars, we called a car). We worked our own search warrants and produced high numbers and closed a lot of cases. We had a close group of three guys, and we looked out for each other and drove each other nuts! I think the only bad part about it most of the time was the terrible schedule we had to keep, but we survived it.

One of the requirements of Bike Patrol was that we needed to be at nearly every single community event. We always did a lot of community service events. That was fun. I usually enjoyed interacting with the public. One event I did not enjoy working every single year was the Fourth of July Extravaganza. Herein lies the problem: nearly everyone worked that event, and definitely every Bike Patrol Officer worked it.

By the time I retired, there were many Officers in the agency who had been police mountain bicycle training certified. So, lots and lots of Officers were able to be on bikes. In July of 2008, though, there were four or five of us certified throughout the entire agency. So, guess who got to ride a bicycle while every other Officer rode around in a golf cart? That's right, the actual Bike Patrol guys. I get it. The reason for the bikes in policing in the first place is because they are fast and mobile through crowds. They can sneak up on you and go places other police vehicles cannot go, even a golf cart.

I was assigned a specific area of the park that year with another bike officer. It was an area of the park where most of the people would later congregate for the fireworks as they watched under the stars with their blankets, chairs, and tents. It was near the food vendors, and there were lines and lines of people either trying to get food or trying to use the port-a-potties. It had the most people in it, but at least it didn't have most of the juveniles who liked to fight on the basketball courts because that's what they did. They came to a park when there were thousands of people there on our day of Independence and got into fights. It was ridiculous. Still happens every year.

Prior to the fireworks, there were live bands who would play on a large stage set up, and then when the fireworks went off at exactly 10 p.m. every year, a loud melody of Lee Greenwood, Bruce Springsteen, Toby Keith, and others would play while fireworks and colors exploded and lit up the skies to the *oohs* and *ahhs* of the crowd.

At this particular moment, though, it was hot outside, and there was a lull in the action. I was tired because I had worked the night before on bikes. I was sweating in every place on my body, and I was over it already. Forget the fireworks; I want to go home. What happened next stopped me in my bicycle tracks, quite literally, actually.

As I was snaking my way through the crowds on the bicycle, forcing a smile and saying hello to everyone, especially kids who loved the bicycle, I came through a large group of people, and there was finally a clearing. When

I cleared the crowd, I was going to take a moment to just stop and get off the bicycle. If you have ridden a bicycle for any length of significant time, you understand it can literally be a pain in your butt.

Then, I saw her. Orange spaghetti strap tank top, khaki shorts, flip flops, long dark hair, tan-skinned, and she looked up at me with beautiful, dark eyes. There was a little blond-haired girl who had probably just learned to walk recently, running around her legs like a carousel. When she looked at me, not only did the bicycle stop, but my world did. I feel like I almost fell off the bicycle; I might have if I hadn't caught myself. Call it cheesy if you want; I don't care. It was a moment out of a Nicolas Sparks novel, except I was not some strapping actor from Hollywood. I was a Kentucky boy with chicken legs on a bicycle.

I stuttered and tried to speak. I was nervous all of a sudden. I had a dry mouth. Was I dehydrated from the heat? Probably. I was able to get one word out of my mouth, and that is all, and I bet even it sounded stupid.

"Hi."

I got a response from her. She spoke back. "Hi." I could tell we were getting somewhere. I went to speak again and start whatever goofy thing I could come up with to try and impress her, and then I heard it. Stupid, stupid radio.

A tone drop. The ear-piercing screeching it always gave when we were being dispatched to an "emergency." This time, the emergency was kids fighting at the basketball court next to the playground. I could have screamed. Let those kids fight it out. I have more important things to take care of. They will figure out who the winner of the fight is.

No, instead, I mounted my trusty Gary Fisher Sugar model full-suspension bicycle and turned my wheel in the direction to pedal fast and leave. All I could get out of my mouth was, "I have to go to a fight call. I will try to come back."

That woman with beautiful dark hair and eyes smiled at me, and all she said was, "Okay." Then, I was off to find whatever kids were fighting and ruined my moment. I felt like if there hadn't been a fight at that point, I was going to start one with them. Perfect moment ruined.

When I got across the park after going around the fence to the main playground, I got to the basketball court and found a bunch of juveniles who had already been separated by some Officers who had been assigned to that area and had been driving a golf cart. As it turns out, in this instance, the golf cart *was* faster than the bicycle. First time for everything, I guess. The fight was already broken up, and the crowds of onlookers had already begun to disperse. I was so aggravated. I had wasted energy getting over here only to find out it had been handled, and to top it all off, I had left what appeared to be the start of a good conversation with a woman who literally had stopped me in my tracks. Never in my life had that ever happened before. After the situation was cleared, I had to get back to my zone. What did I do next? I went to try and find the woman again and pick up where we left off!

When I got back, I went back to the exact location she had been with the little girl. She was gone. I searched and searched in that area, riding all through the crowd. I looked for a long time and couldn't find her. It made me kind of sad for some odd reason. But it was getting dark now. I had a job to do. It really would have been nice to have gotten her name, at least.

At the end of the fireworks show, there were people everywhere! People were walking to their cars, there were families with children in strollers crossing the street, there were cars parked in the grassy areas of the park trying to pull out into the road. There were thousands of people trying to exit from the park's two exits. It was gridlocked traffic.

Lots of people were honking and cussing, carrying on about how traffic was moving slow. First of all, let me stop you there. No one *told* you or *made* you come to the park to watch the fireworks. Don't blame that on the police, who are just trying to get everyone home safely.

I went to a specific intersection to start directing traffic within the park and hoping to prevent some chaos and anarchy...more importantly, trying to get myself home at a time earlier than 0100 hours. Inch by inch, people would move onto the roads, most of the time letting others enter the road first as a sign of courtesy. We are in Kentucky, after all. I had stood in the intersection for a while, moving vehicles as I could, blowing the whistle to get the attention of those who were not paying attention. Sometimes yelling if that didn't work.

Of course, you always have to have *that* person who says something like, "Excuse me, I know you are really busy, but can you tell me how to get to such and such place or if these intersections are shut down? I'm not from around here." If you are a cop reading this, you understand what I am talking about. Never fails. I try to remain polite, hunger and dehydration taken into consideration, then give the best professional answer I possibly can in a polite manner.

As traffic was moving forward at slower than a snail's pace, this little black Suzuki passenger car pulled into the intersection. I didn't pay attention at first, but then someone caught my eye because the window was down. Orange tank top, dark hair. It was her! I had taken off my helmet, and I *know* I had helmet hair going on. I am certain it looked terrible, and I never even thought about that. In the passenger seat, there was another lady sitting with her, and in the back seat there was this little blond-haired girl in a car seat smiling at me. But it was not the same little girl.

I was shocked. I was floored. How could this have happened? How, out of all the intersections or cars in this park, could she be stuck in gridlocked traffic at mine?! (Here's a hint...it was God.) There is no way I could have planned this, orchestrated it, or even tried to pull it off without divine intervention. It would have been impossible. I looked at her, and she smiled at me. This time, I wasn't missing my chance and said, "Hello again."

"Hi," she smiled shyly and sweetly. From the passenger seat, I heard the other woman say, "Is that the cop you were telling me about?" I looked away and got embarrassed but flattered. The beautiful woman in the orange spaghetti strap tank top shot her mother a look, and I heard a loud, not-so-whisper saying, "Yes! And he can hear you." I smiled. Thank goodness the little girl in the backseat saved us adults from that awkward moment and ourselves.

She sat up as big as she could in her car seat and smiled with those cute dimples and said, "Hi, my name is _____, and I am four years old."

"It's so nice to meet you. My name is Officer Josh. I am just a little bit older than that."

She grinned that unforgettable grin of hers. It's the grin I know before she breaks out into a laugh or when she hears a joke, even as an adult now. It's the smile when she is happy and when someone has made her day. That unforgettable grin. She wasn't the only one smiling. I noticed. We talked small talk for a bit, and I still kept trying to keep my focus on working, though at this point, it was nearly impossible. I was so distracted. I would yell at a few more people and blow the whistle when I needed to since there were still people everywhere. The only people I wanted to talk to were right in front of me in my own mind.

After what had seemed like such a short amount of time, traffic started moving again, and she had to move her car with traffic. I should have held them up. I told them to have a good night and be safe, and it was so nice to meet them. I didn't get her number that night, and she didn't get mine. I was working. I kicked myself for not getting it.

We had all carried on a conversation, and I found out the woman's name, and she was the little girl's mom. And the other lady in the passenger seat was the grandmother. The woman I met in the orange tank top would eventually become my wife; the little girl became my stepdaughter, whom I raised as my own and call my own. The other woman would eventually become my mother-in-law, but not just yet. More time needed to pass. At least, that is what I feel was God's plan. Or, it could be that I completely dropped the ball again when He handed it to me. Not to worry, God would give me yet another chance or two to get it right. He has always been so gracious when we don't deserve it.

We had a Safety Officer at the time who kept telling me there was this girl he wanted me to stop by and see at this medical office he attended. Little did I know, he was talking about my future wife. He also could have told me, and I was too idiotic to catch on. Then, in October, we had an event called the Halloween Hoedown. It is one of the biggest events of the year. Wouldn't you know it? We were assigned to work Bike Patrol for the event. Big shock.

I remember riding that evening on one of the side streets we have off Main Street and hearing someone say my name. When I stopped and turned around, there she was. She was there at the event with her daughter. I was *not* missing my chance this time. I didn't ask for her number, but we talked for a few minutes, and I offered mine. I told her what time I was off work and I would love to talk to her later. I remember asking if that sweet little girl knew her numbers, and she said she did. I helped her to write down my phone number in her handwriting and gave it to her mom. She called that night, and we talked for hours, until around two in the morning, I think.

We started dating shortly after that, and we haven't looked back since. We were married on August 7, 2010. We truly had a fantastic fairy-tale wedding. It was beautiful. Looking back on everything now, there is no way I could have arranged any of the encounters, and even when messed it up, God directed her right back into my path. He wanted her to be my wife. We had our youngest daughter in 2011, and both of our girls are fantastic!

My wife has her own spectacular journey, and maybe one day, she can publish a book about that. I don't have many "prized possessions" in life, but I do have a few, like the Bible my wife got me when we first started dating, which I have referenced for this book repeatedly. She really is a superstar. My wife and my oldest daughter have been with me through fifteen years of policing, and my youngest daughter for twelve years. My girls have been through the emotional ringer with me, and I am so happy to have run the race with them at my side and with their support. They have seen and heard some rough times in my career, yet they weathered the storms.

I joked earlier this was sort of like a Nicolas Sparks novel, and I wouldn't change this for anything. Has it always been easy? Of course not. Life never is, and it is not meant to be. It is meant to teach us lessons, and hopefully, we grow closer to Jesus in the process.

Anyone can say the moment they met their spouse, they *knew* they were the one, and it was a special day. The day I met my spouse was life-changing, and there were fireworks...literally and emotionally. I got to meet my spouse because I was on a terrible schedule in a place I didn't really want to be that day, doing something I loved to do, riding that nearly silent machine called a bicycle, and all because I wanted to look cool like the bike cops on TV and the show "Pacific Blue."

The Bike Patrol was disbanded shortly after that, and we were split up into various locations. The other guys were given their new assignments, and I took the role of the new School Resource Officer for our middle schools. This gave me a better schedule, and I was home at night and on the weekends with my girls. It opened up new opportunities and paths God had for me He had not yet revealed. He just needed me to get all of the support in my life before He moved me on to the next chapter. I may have had to give up the bicycle for the most part, but I gained my wife and a family. The day I grew up wasn't when I turned eighteen. It wasn't when I became a Police Officer. It was when I gained my wife and my family. That was when I grew up. That was when I knew it was time to man up.

Sounds like a win/win to me.

I love you, girls.

LOVE NOTES TO MY GIRLS

Shew! Where do I start with this one? This part is going to be sappy, and you know what? I don't care. This is my book, and I will say what I want to. These girls are the ones who lived it with me. My wife and daughters lived the craziness that is policing for over fifteen years. They heard the funny stories and loved to hear me tell them. We have laughed about my days and all the crazy antics and things I have experienced. I have watched them giggle as they let me act out the stories and events I have experienced in an animated fashion. If you know me personally, you know I love to do that. And let's just say I am not going to win any acting awards any time soon, but we sure do have fun with it.

Still more, they have been with me when I have been at my absolute lowest points in my career. They have been with me when I wanted to quit, and they have been the reason I kept going so I could better their future with a retirement residual income. They have experienced a line-of-duty death at our agency. The girls' schools were decorated to support with the Thin Blue Line and his badge number. Our youngest hugged me when I cried on the kitchen floor after losing my friend.

They were there when I got hurt or even just sad. They were there when I had a bad day or a good day. They were there when I had a stroke from a brain bleed. They have been there when I couldn't be because I had to work. They have stood with me at events I did have to work because that was the only way to get to see me on a holiday event. They pinned me when I received my promotions as I moved up through the ranks. They can't even remember my old badge numbers anymore, but they have been there the whole time. They have seen social media and the news and posts by family and friends against the police when their own Police Officer didn't do anything wrong but caught the flack for someone who did. They have noticed what the world says. They have seen the changes in our culture and had to choke down the garbage people say about police while I told them to remain silent.

My advice to anyone reading this about your family is to keep them close. They go through the trauma with you. They just experience it in a different way. Keep checking on them; the stuff we see as first responders is not normal. If you see there is something they are struggling with, help them or get them help. There is no shame in this. Don't wait. This could be one of the most important leadership decisions you make in your entire life.

To My Wife:

There is no way I could have planned how we met or how our lives would have been shaped. You have stayed by my side through it all. Even when I wanted to quit...even when you wanted me to quit, you never gave up on me and trusted me to let God lead me.

We have worked with kids and traveled for my job. We have worked opposite shifts and barely seen each other at times. We have experienced promotions, career changes, and loss within our families and friends. Still, you are there. You have stood by my side, even when it was difficult. That requires knowledge, intelligence, patience, and understanding.

"The highest form of knowledge is empathy,
for it requires us to suspend our egos and live in another's world."

Plato

We have traveled the world together and learned valuable life lessons together. You have made our house a home even when I couldn't be around to help. We have experienced pain, trauma, and victory. You have blessed other families in ways only a few understand. You have been an inspiration to me, and I have loved studying you and learning from you. No matter what has occurred, you are here. I am proud of you, and I am so thankful for your support.

You have helped to make me stronger when I have been the weakest. Thank you for the adventures, the laughs, the cries, all the fall festivals you love so much, and for doing this thing called life with me. I could go on and on about it, but ultimately, it comes down to this...my life is better with you in it. I love you.

Josh

P.S. The first mountain has been conquered, and we have seen the tops of the peaks and the valleys in our younger days. Let's climb that second mountain of life...together.

To My Daughters:

The day I grew up was not the day I turned eighteen years old. Some of the stories in this book will justify that statement. The day I became a man and grew up was the day I had you in my life. I never knew love until I had someone to teach a legacy to. You are both so loved.

From the days of book reading, the dreaded homework for school, life lessons for you and me alike, to the little things, both of you and your mother have been my world. I have loved our fishing together (even though it has never been about fishing for me; it was about watching you have fun), and I have loved watching you grow up into the young women you have become.

Thank you for trusting me even when you were mad at me for making you finish a season of soccer or archery or whatever else we did, even though you didn't want to do it anymore. You trusted me to teach you about teamwork and not leaving your people. You got mad at me, but it all worked out in the end, and you held up your end of the bargain. You took care of your team and showed up, no matter what the outcome was.

Thank you for letting me come to your schools and talking to all the kids, even though they were your friends and I know it must have been embarrassing to have your dad at school speaking in front of everyone. Thank you for letting me take you to school and pick you up. I tried not to embarrass you when you were in a police cruiser; it was kind of hard not to notice that. Thank you for all the holidays you were excited to see me and all the fun we have had no matter what.

I am so proud of you and who you are becoming. You are both so different in your personalities, but you are strong-willed and a force to be reckoned with when you put your mind to something. Keep your focus on Jesus andalways try to do the right thing, even when we fail. Everything else will work out as it is supposed to. I love you both so much.

Dad

A Prized Possession

I don't have many "prized possessions" in my life. I have nostalgic things, but not many objects I never want to lose. Towards the end of my career, a few years away from retiring, I was given one. My oldest daughter was working her first job and got me a pocket knife. This was not just any pocket knife. It is a police edition Tac-Force folding knife in blue and black with a police badge on the side in gold coloring. It has a seat belt cutter and an inscription. On the knife blade itself, there is a black line with writing on it that says, "Be safe, we love you!"

She got me in the feels on that one. My daughter worked to save her own money at her job to purchase me a knife and have an inscription put on the blade. While I was on duty, I carried it or had it with me all the way up until my retirement. I love that knife...and I love my family. To all my first responders reading this, hold them close. They go through this with you. You are not the only one.

More than Child's Play

Warning: Trigger Alert

(I am passionate about saving lives,
and some of this might step on some toes)

For several years now, I have been working with kids in schools and have been traveling the country and speaking to kids and parents about youth violence and the problems that affect our youth today. I have seen many things, and my eyes have been opened to the twisted culture that our youth are being raised by.

I am now a firm believer that our kids as a generation are being raised by cellular phone apps, the internet, and media personalities, no matter how inappropriate their role models may be. When our kids know more about what or why some rapper or celebrity got arrested than they do about *real* issues that plague this world we live in, there is an underlying problem that needs to be brought to the surface.

By the way, if you asked your children who the "popular" artists are right now, I guarantee they would know more than you do about it. Music glorifies sex, drug use, suicide, and violence. Let's face it: Miley Cyrus is not Hanna Montana from the Disney Channel anymore. That's just an example. Thanks to the 2 Live Crew and Judas Priest lawsuits of the 1990s, virtually anything is fair game to be marketed to our children under the cloak of freedom of speech. Sexual predators run rampant in our streets and on the internet. Hollywood turns its head to human trafficking or even participates, and the only way to catch someone's attention is to put it on social media or a Netflix special.

It's time to have a wake-up call if you are a parent, a grandparent, a youth leader, a school administrator, or someone who deals with kids. It is time to make a stand to save a generation. What are we going to do to stop the epidemic that is infecting the minds of our children and polluting their futures? What are we going to do to stop predators from preying on our kids on social media platforms and online games?

If you are reading this right now and you get offended and triggered easily, you might want to put down the book for a moment and take a breath or just go on to the next section. I believe from the bottom of my heart that, in general, parents are becoming apathetic to what goes on in the real world and are allowing their kids to do whatever they want, and the children run the show. I am not saying every parent, but many of the ones I dealt with while in law enforcement and public speaking. I spent much of my police career dealing with kids in some fashion and hunting the creepy people who would do them harm. But from my experience and in dealing with the youth of today and the culture they thrive in, we have now opened Pandora's box, and we can't close it back. Never.

It is our job as parents, law enforcement, teachers, and administrators to protect our children and the children we come into contact with. Instead, we have become so concerned with what people will think or being hit with a lawsuit that we look on as if there is nothing going on in our schools and in the lives of these children. We are telling kids who will not have a fully developed brain until around age twenty-five that it is okay to change into a boy or a girl or whatever you want to be that day. There are those who would allow gender surgeries and gender changes when kids cannot even decide what they want to do for a career when they grow up.

Officers are being dispatched to a home because a child refuses to get on the bus and go to school. I have gone to homes with children as young as kindergarten age. They are walking the hallways of schools and being asked to deal with discipline problems instead of watching out for weapons and predators. While the partnership is great to have Officers in schools to interact with the kids, these are not law enforcement responsibilities. It is on us, as parents, as a society, as a church, or as a school system, to play our roles.

We stand by and watch as kids disrespect parents and grandparents or any authority figure, but when I was growing up, it would have gotten you smacked back to the stone age. I am not advocating for abuse, but there must be a line drawn and a lesson taught; otherwise, we have kids who grow up to burn down cities, or as the media calls it, "peaceful protesting."

As a society, we give cell phones at too young an age, and it is my belief it alters the development of the brain, causing addiction issues. We don't spend time at the family dinner table like we used to in the *old days*, and our children have very few social skills they would have acquired if we didn't have smartphones. Kids run away, are more depressed than ever, and teen suicide is at an alarming rate. This world has lost its collective mind, and the train is on a collision course with no brakes!

I have been very blessed to have had the opportunity to speak to thousands of kids and teenagers about the real issues in life. In school assemblies that I present and parent meetings alike, we address issues like drugs, violence, bullying, school shootings, suicide, texting, and "sexting," as well as how to combat the evil that thrives in this world. Kids today are not the kids of years past. Chewing gum in class and talking are no longer the issues to handle. Murder, drugs in schools, child pornography from cell phones, and the most violent generation yet are now what we face. I have heard stories from the lives of American kids in our schools that would absolutely shock you in regard to violence and how it affects our youth. It is celebrated.

When did it become okay for violent entertainment to be allowed in the lives of our kids? When did it become socially acceptable to market the sale of movies, video games, and entertainment to children who are not adults? The questionable entertainment has to have ratings on it for adults, so why do parents and other adults think it's okay to purchase something like that for kids? I'm going to tell my age a bit here when I say that when I was a kid, we had Mario Brothers on Nintendo and Tetris.

I had a conversation at the video game store not too long ago, and even the people who worked at the store thought it was inappropriate to sell some games to kids...and they work there!

I have a theory. At some point or another in our adult lives, and because of the pressures from our culture, parents have become scared. They want to make sure that their kids have friends and have what all the other kids have and want to be the "best friend." Parents sometimes think that they have to give their child every tech gadget a week before it hits the stores. Your child does not need a "best friend mom or dad." They need you to be a parent and try. They need you to be there for them. They need you to stand up for them.

I remember in the 90s when my mom got a cell phone in a bag that plugged into the car. It was the coolest thing I had ever seen and I thought we had really made it at that point. Now, there are kids in schools that have better phones than the Apple store. I can almost guarantee you that most parents who have done this do not take the time to research the apps out there or the statistics on child predators and kids with social media.

In my career, I have had numerous cases where child predators have preyed on teenagers by making contact through social media like Facebook, Instagram, Twitter, TikTok, or Snapchat. There are so many others that I can't even describe them. If you want more information and ranting on social media, find my contact information and come to one of my talks or trainings.

I personally think that some parents give their teens and younger kids a cell phone because they don't want or know how to interact with kids anymore. A recent study I saw said the average age for a smartphone to a child is now around five years old. Come on, I know some of you just snickered or giggled or are shocked at that comment because you know it's true. We have all had our moments as parents when we just want peace and quiet. The difference between a pacifier and a cell phone or electronic device is that one doesn't have access to literally anything you can imagine via the internet. If you can imagine a way your child could get into trouble, imagine that danger in unlimited supply when you give them access to the entire planet on a device *you* are paying the monthly bill for.

I would not be naïve enough to even think there weren't some people taking offense to this right now and making excuses for their child. If that's the case, let me repeat myself: I just want you to realize that most studies I read show that the brain is not fully developed as a child and that little Johnny or little Suzie may not be the best person to lay all of your trust and reliability on for life's most trying moments. Keep in mind the worldly influences your child battles every day just going to school and dealing with other kids. Instagram, Snapchat, and filters are raising our kids. So, even if this is something you have done, be smart about how you take things from here. Educate yourself on youth culture and be involved in everything in your child's life, from text messages to dating life. It could save your child.

Now, I am not going to stand on a podium or get on my high horse and say I have done it perfectly. *I have not.* I have made a ton of mistakes as a parent and as a husband, just trying to do the right thing. As a parent, I will tell you right now that I have been hard on my daughters, probably too hard on them at times, just trying to keep them safe.

Over the years, just like I did, some of their friends have been just as incapable of making adult decisions as they are and were. I didn't even make good decisions at their ages. My daughters need parents. They have them. We have successfully raised one child to adulthood, and she still learns every day, just like I do. My wife and I are not afraid to tell our children *no* if the occasion calls for it. We have the age-old system of having to earn something and learning what true value is.

As a parent, if you are reading this, you have a duty to protect and provide for your children. Sometimes, you must protect them from themselves even if their culture has said it's okay. When you give your children everything they ever ask for, it will only make your life more difficult along the way, and someday, you will wonder why your child has no respect for you and why you can't get them to do what you want.

Stop being afraid to discipline your children if they need it. That does not mean abuse or beat your children. Spare the rod, spoil the child. There is a scripture in the Bible from the book of Proverbs in 22:15 that says, "Folly (foolishness) is bound up in the heart of a child, but the rod of discipline drives it far from him." In verse 6 of the same chapter, it says, "Train up a child in the way he should go; even when he is old he will not depart from it." If you give in to your child's every request, it will only come back to haunt you when you least expect it. It's time to put your foot down. As a Police Officer who has been both on the road and assigned to the schools, I saw on a daily basis the vicious cycle that exists between the two worlds I have worked. The kids I deal with in the schools have come from those same homes that I have answered the calls to working shift.

Prior to my retirement, I had worked three generations of families. I dealt with the parents, their kids who became adults, who had their own kids. That makes grandparents, parents, and kids. These families I refer to in this paragraph are the ones who cussed, spat at, and fought the police. And they passed that down from generation to generation. It gets worse and worse and worse. Then, I had the "helicopter parents" who would hover over their babies every moment or worse, the "lawnmower parents" who would mow over every obstacle for their kid. They did this even if their kid was in the wrong, if that meant challenging the school or the police. They were not doing their kids any favors, and a few got arrested or almost arrested in front of their kids playing that game. These parents did all that with the best intentions for their child.

That being said, I want to clarify an opinion that I have developed over the years. It was difficult for me when first working with juveniles to separate my experiences on the streets. I used to believe that when a kid messed up, he or she was just a bad kid. Now that I am a parent and deal with other people's kids on a daily basis, I know that we don't have bad kids. We have kids that come from bad backgrounds and make bad decisions. That doesn't condone their behavior, but it most certainly helps to explain it and truly attempt to save this generation that seems lost.

I have dealt with kids who have committed crimes to get put into the system because they knew no one would do anything for them at home or help them until the courts forced them to do so. I have seen courts remove kids from their homes only because the child committed the offense. I have seen a child who is in danger not meet the "qualifications" according to social services standards because even they don't have resources to help them. Why does it take so long to save one child? Why have we turned a blind eye to our decisions and expect others to handle something that we could help with? You see, I truly believe that we have it backward now.

As I say that, I told you I love sports. I love to watch sports, play sports, talk about sports, and even argue about sports when it serves no purpose. Now, with that in mind and given the chapter that you are reading, tell me why it makes sense that we spend millions and millions as a culture that pays the best athletes and coaches in all facets of sports, and yet we don't have the resources to hire more social workers or have more placements for our children when they need us. How has our culture become so perverse that we have the resources to keep that star athlete on track, but that kid who has no one to care about him or her, we fail because we turn a blind eye to reality?

Does that mean our schools are failing? Of course not, but our education system has stayed in the traditional format, or we are "teaching to test" our kids and not teaching them to learn or to survive. I've found working with the school systems that it all revolves around the almighty (or once almighty) dollar. The higher the test scores, the more funding your school can receive. We can't get our teachers more funding or salary or even supply their classroom supplies, but we can spend millions of dollars on a football field or basketball gym. It is backward. I had probably better stop right here regarding that topic, although this is one chapter I am not worried about offending anyone. I am trying to save kids' lives.

And yet, how can we expect our children to learn and test well if we cannot provide them with a safe environment free from drugs, gangs, the social media craze, and the threat of poverty? How can a child test well when they have to stress over whether or not they will eat when they get home if Mom will be high again, or if Dad is going to come home drunk and want to fight or beat them again? Our social services system is overwhelmed and overworked because they don't pay social workers enough. We are scared to search kids for weapons when they come into schools now because it might be *too invasive and traumatize them.* No, we as a society are too afraid of getting sued and won't take the necessary measures to provide safety for our children. Then, when something does happen in a town, we missed all the signs that have been as plain as spray paint on a wall and hand off the problem to the police, expecting them to solve it.

The solution much of our society has come up with is to incarcerate our youth for the low-risk offenses they commit. We don't punish the men and women who put these children in survival situations enough because our jails and prisons are overpopulated. We don't remove children from homes that are dangerous, and the toddler remains in the house where they cook and sell methamphetamine or nearly overdose on fentanyl (yes, I have seen it happen). Sometimes, it is easier to purchase and name your own star in space (and yes, you can do that) than it is to remove a child from a home.

Politicians spend thousands to millions of dollars on campaigns that talk about saving our youth, and when push comes to shove, nothing gets done. We have a severe problem in the area of legislation, both at state and national levels. I guess, to put it simply, we can ask ourselves a question. Are we doing everything (and I mean everything) we can to save our youth, or are we failing them? I think if we answer honestly, we will all agree that we are failing our youth as a society, and many people are afraid or don't know how to do anything about it.

We have to depend on our teachers and school administrators to be the gatekeepers for things they should not have to be looking out for because society has become too scared to police in the home. We have people in schools who step up and save lives all the time just by paying attention.

I once had a case in the schools where the middle school notified me that the mother's live-in boyfriend was using a cattle prod on the special needs children in the home but was too afraid to say anything because he might leave her. The kids mentioned it to their teacher, and with great due diligence, the teacher reported it to the Principal. This led to me getting called. We didn't let the kids go home on the bus, and instead, I went to the house and met with the mother, who protected the boyfriend, who called him, and he then came roaring up the driveway in his farm truck. I nearly had to fight him at first, but once we got everyone calmed down, I was able to get him to confess on body camera he had used a bull prod on the children to scare them and gain compliance.

He provided the prod from his truck, and I matched it to the children's markings on their bodies. He was arrested and charged with criminal abuse, the mother also because she had allowed it to go on. The children were placed in foster care. I seized the cattle prod and ultimately tested it on a volt meter. It was so strong it fried and broke the volt meter I used.

I was subpoenaed to Family Court on behalf of the children so they could be placed in a new home. I had to go meet with the attorney representing the Commonwealth for Family Court prior to the hearing at his office. When I arrived in my uniform, I had the cattle prod with me, and we began discussing the case. He said to me, "Josh, you know this is going to be hard to win in Criminal Court, right? There is no law against corporal punishment in the state of Kentucky."

I thought I was going to blow a gasket as my temper blew up, and I immediately screamed back at him in defense of the kids. "Well, I tell you what. How about I use this on you and you can tell me if I can win this case in court or not?!" I was already coming across the room and getting ready to come across his desk with a yellow cattle prod about three feet in length, so my reach was just long enough to be like the old AT&T commercial to "reach out and touch someone."

Thankfully for him, his boss saved him from a shocking revelation (pun intended). He told me he thought it best if I left. I took heed, and I left and told him I would be prepared and would make sure the Judge and everyone else was very aware of how dangerous this cattle prod was when I testified in both Family and Criminal Court. I kept true to my word. The Judge himself in Family Court kept cattle and stopped me in my testimony and stated he recognized it as a "significant prod." The criminal case went fine, and the man was indicted, pleaded guilty, and sentenced to prison for the abuse charges.

Let me give you another example. I have been so blessed over the years to interview numerous politicians and celebrities, even speak with Governors and those in the highest offices of our state. In 2014, thanks to a former and now retired school administrator I became very good friends with, I was able to participate in legislation making October Anti-Bullying Month in the Commonwealth of Kentucky. Bi-partisan legislation made the colors of Anti-Bullying Month purple and yellow. Purple is the color for domestic violence awareness. Yellow is the color for suicide prevention and awareness. Put those two together in an awareness ribbon, and we had the Anti-Bullying Awareness ribbon for October. It was a phenomenal plan.

The Governor at the time came to one of our schools and walked into the building, and I will never forget it. He walked into the building and saw me and said, "I know who you are. You are Josh Hale." Now, whoever his handler was, I applaud you. I had never met the Governor, or any Governor for that matter, at the time. It made me feel like a rock star and work harder than ever! I shook his hand, and we entered into the auditorium. It was packed with about 600 people, including students, teachers, Principals, Senators, Representatives, the Chief of Police, the Mayor, and other special guests.

Several people, including me, spoke at the podium that day about all we were doing to save our kids and stop bullying. Then, the big moment arrived. The Governor signed into law October being Anti-Bullying Month and announced the colors and all we would do to save the lives of our kids. I was so ecstatic I could barely contain myself standing in the background as kids and legislators stood around the Governor at the table on that stage as he signed the Bill. I thought we were going to do something together as a team. I decided we would go national with this bill and take it to every kid, and I was excited! A fire within me had been lit that I cannot explain, and I thought everyone felt the same way I did. I thought *we* were all going to do things and go forward marching the Anti-Bullying banner. I'll say this....watch out for we's.

I found out later on a trip to the Capitol it had been nothing but a dog and pony show. It had been a puff piece for the papers.

Shortly after the ceremony was over, the Governor left for another appointment, kids went back to class, the media turned off their cameras, all the guests left with little to no conversation, and eventually, they turned the lights out on the auditorium. Afterward, I sat there in the dark for a few moments, taking it all in. Little did I know, they might as well have turned the lights out on the entire plan, and it was all for nothing. The man who is my friend, who had drawn me into the battle with him and who had put so much work into this, was not going to get the backing he needed in Frankfort.

Most kids, even in our town, don't know it is Anti-Bullying Month when October rolls around because we have so many Awareness Months there is not enough to go around. Those organizations with the most money and followers are the ones who are able to put out signs and paint the town, whatever color it is for that month. Not a dig at any organization. I just wish it had all worked out for Anti-Bullying Month. People hardly even advertise it anymore, if at all.

We as a society throw around the word *bullying*, and yet we and even our own legislators, whom *we* elected throughout the Commonwealth of Kentucky at that time, could not come up with a definition to put into real law so we could put some teeth behind the movement or some punishment for those who hurt people. I know it is like that in most other states, as well.

Honestly, for most people, they believed it was a waste of their time and a ridiculous notion, although we would never want the constituents to hear us say that. I remember school Principals who shall not be named and even Superintendents from all over the state who believed the same way. I wonder how parents would feel if they knew this was the true thoughts behind some of the so-called leadership in the schools across our Commonwealth or those people we elected to be the voices for us at our Capitol.

But I didn't stop...no, I haven't stopped.

Since 2013, when it all began to gather steam in Frankfort at our Capitol but quickly dissipated through the halls and domes of the Capitol building, I began speaking publicly. As of this chapter being written, I have spoken to over 70,000 kids at the time of publishing this book (and there *will be* more). I spent my time as an Officer speaking when I could. I took days off to go speak to kids. I spent my own money to travel. And sometimes, I was blessed enough to get paid a little bit to drive all over the place and let people hear the message.

My family knows I have done this. I blast it all over Facebook and social media to get the message out there, and I show pictures of the places I go. And yet, of the thousands of people who are on my "friends lists," very few have reached out to hear what I am doing or invite me to their schools and towns. They hit that *like* and *love* button and scroll on to the next person in their feed. I appreciate that gesture, but I don't need followers. I need those who would stand with me and fight the fight to save our kids.

We must stop being afraid to discipline our children or even raise them the way we were raised. Maybe not in the same way we were raised because even that had issues. But I come from the old-school philosophy. And old school is good school. Clearly, what is being done now as a whole is not working or has provided far more complications and dangers than desired. Keep your head up if you are a parent of children in today's world. It is not going to be easy for you, and it will be a hard road to have to travel.

Many, if not most, parents will not think like you do and will likely disagree with how you are doing things. That's okay. They are not responsible for your child. You are. They will come to you as they do to me and ask questions about how to help their child out of trouble. I don't mean to be offensive to people;

however, I will not apologize when I am trying to save lives. I will learn from my mistakes as a husband and as a parent, and I will work toward being a good role model no matter if society agrees with me or not.

Most school shooters have been or were bullied. There are many other factors to determine and examine in school and mass shooters, but bullying is up there on the list. If there is nothing that scares you as a parent, this should. And I am not here to instill fear in you. I want to give you hope that you can make a difference.

Keep your faith. Keep doing good. Your children...our children...our society needs you.

This is more than child's play. This is for real.

HUNTING THE PREDATORS

The night air was cold, and I could see my breath appear in a small cloud that I exhaled rapidly. No sooner than it appeared, it would vanish without a sound. Off in the distance, there were shouts of voices, and periodically, throughout the dark, beams of light would illuminate certain places and then quickly sweep to another location.

Radios crackled through the night air, cutting the silence like a hot knife through butter. Other than that, there was nothing. *No, wait.* Somewhere close by, there was the very faint sound of horses hidden out there in the night. Darkness. Open space.

Looking up, I briefly remember thousands of stars twinkling in the sky like diamonds on a massive, black cloth. I turned around to look back and saw all of the emergency lights and vehicles in one seemingly close cluster from off in the distance. I was well away from everyone and everything. There was nothing out here except the grass that came up to my knees and the few trees seen only by a dark, black silhouette.

No. There was something out here in this silence. There were four of them, and they could be anywhere close by or far away, watching us, waiting, hiding. The thought sent a shiver down my spine to know that they were out there somewhere and could be watching my every move, ready to attack or flee at a mere whim and at any time they wanted to. Of course, those thoughts raced through my mind. How could they *not* do so?

Physical exhaustion from running was starting to set in as I felt the dull throbbing in my left knee and the aching in both my legs. My left knee was flaring up from an old injury I received during another foot pursuit two years earlier. My chest was pounding from the seeming lack of oxygen in the cold night air. My mind began to play tricks on me as I stopped and stood there in the middle of the vast field and wondered where they were. There was no doubt in my mind that we would find them out here. The only thing I wanted to know was whether it was going to be under their terms or ours.

Good versus evil, right? Good guys versus bad guys. Light versus darkness. Cops versus criminals. Oh yes, one side or the other would win tonight...but the good guys had already lost to a certain extent. A Police Officer had been hurt.

The vehicle pursuit started in our county and ended up in another county. I remember my car hitting 110 mph on the interstate as we were chasing the bad guys' car. The four men fleeing from us crashed out of their car next to a big farm in the next county over and bailed on us. Unbeknownst to me, one of the bad guys had been injured in the crash and was still lying next to the vehicle. He wasn't going anywhere.

Once the vehicles came to a halt next to the big field, the three remaining bad guys vanished out into the night, and we took off after them. Now, here I was in the middle of this field, surrounded by only darkness and the thoughts of my mind that closed in around me. We had already had one officer hurt through the events of this night; would there be more?

I hate to sound so negative and melancholy, but sometimes, our emotions do come into play. The odds, however, had shifted in our favor. There were numerous Officers, Deputies, and State Troopers out here in the dark searching for these guys. We had flashlights to find them and canines to track them, and it was only a matter of time. It was only a matter of time until...

"Show me your hands! Now! Show me your hands! Get on the ground, now!" I heard a voice to my left in front of me shout. I ran to the voice and found a Trooper lifting a male off the ground and nothing short of nearly carrying him to the car.

"You gonna run anymore?! Huh?!"

"No, sir, I'm not gonna run anymore." That was all I heard from the man as he walked away toward the flashing lights off in the distance in handcuffs. There wasn't much to be said. He wouldn't tell us where his buddies were; he was denying all involvement with everything that had happened, and therefore, it was pretty much pointless. But that's okay; we knew the truth, and we also found his buddies hiding close by in some thick brush.

Looking back now, I never realized what kind of people we deal with on a day-to-day basis. Most of the time, it is people at the worst point in their lives, and they don't care who they bring down with them in the process of it all.

It makes me wonder what this world is coming to as I get up out of bed and put my feet on the floor each morning. What will each and every day be like?

There have been many days in my career when I was not even sure if I wanted to go to work. I have wondered what it would be like in a different career, working a normal job. And let me tell you this: the job of a Police Officer is not normal. As a patrol officer, you do not work behind a desk. You do not deal with the normal job that a banker does, and I was a banker for about three years before becoming a Police Officer. It's not like any other profession out there today. That is not to belittle any other profession. It is just a complete difference of night and day.

Being a Police Officer is filled with think-fast decisions that hold the weight of someone's world in them. We are the gateway between the good and the bad, that thin blue line of protection between the good people and the predators out there. And trust me when I tell you this: the world is not some happy little place. It is a battlefield of the mind, body, and soul. There are predators out there watching us, waiting for us to make mistakes, and waiting to prey on those innocent people who do not go out and commit crimes. They wait for us to leave our homes to go to work or wait until it gets dark to break into cars. They watch from a distance as your children play in the streets and in their yards. They sell drugs on the street corners and out of cars that travel behind you and me every day. Oh yes, there are predators out there, and they are hiding in plain view.

This is not meant to scare you as you read this but merely to wake you up and let you know the truth. This world is not the "Leave It to Beaver" or "The Brady Bunch" reruns you watch on late-night television. There is a darkness that surrounds us that we do not even know is there most of the time. It is the police who separate this world from the world that everyone else lives in, even though it may not seem so.

Think about this: while you or your families have been at home opening presents on Christmas Eve or Christmas morning, there are Officers out there who are working suicides from the people who have shot themselves or taken too many pain pills or overdosed on heroin. There are Officers out there hunting for those who have broken into homes and stolen Grandma's heirloom necklace or Grandpa's old shotgun that was resting against the

Joshua Hale

wall in the corner. There are Officers out there freezing their tails off in the pouring rain, sleet, or snow as they work a fatality crash or an injury collision on the Interstate Highways, sometimes even directing traffic for hours at a time just so you can commute to where you are going. And me? I've done all of these things just like every other Officer out there.

Then there are the sexual predators. We can never leave them out. After finding out who they are and obtaining search warrants, we find all of their child pornography on computers, DVDs, and VHS tapes. Then there is the interview with the suspect, who then tries to justify to you why it is okay to have sex with a five-year-old child. They actually want you to be understanding and empathetic to the way they are. After all, it is not their fault. They were *just born this way* or *had a bad childhood*. Of course, this is only one example of a sexual predator. There are all kinds out there.

If you are sensing a tone of sarcasm in these words, it is because this has been one of my biggest battles to personally fight throughout my career. I have always had a difficult time with the way anyone perceives that this is right or justified. We have to sit down across a table from these people and do our best to get them to explain why they do this while being recorded.

Imagine it like this. Imagine that you have invited someone over to your house for a game of chess. You own the board and the location you are playing, but you do not control the moves of all the chess pieces. Any interview or interrogation is the same way. Generally, the interview will take place at the Officer's discretion or at a specific location designated by that Officer. The Officer will ask questions or make statements to the suspect, but it is the suspect who controls his or her own moves. They can choose whether or not to talk to the Officer, or they may have a lawyer present if they so choose. This definitely makes the playing board a little bit more challenging, even if the suspect is giving you the entire story as he or she said it happens. You cannot make the opponent's moves for him. You never know what is going to be said next.

It is the job of the Officer to sort through all the nonsense and lies that come out of the suspect's mouth and determine if there is, in fact, any truth to the tale that is being told. More times than not, the suspect will tell half-truths, and we have to finish the story using facts that we already know.

Sometimes, this is not as easy as it sounds, especially when the facts that we have are limited to start with. Most police work is reactionary in that there must be a crime committed first before we can investigate. Otherwise, there would be no need for any type of Detectives or investigations at all.

Sometimes, you just have to think like the bad guy in order to achieve their next move, and even then, it is still only a guess. With technology today being as advanced as it is, the bad guys are usually at least one step ahead at all times. That is where teamwork, education, and training for Police Officers come into play. Once again, it goes back to the analogy of the chessboard. We can't make the moves for the bad guys, but they can't make the moves for us, either. It is the world's biggest and most never-ending game of cat and mouse. Where we run into the problem is that there are far many more bad guys than there are police, and we, as Officers, can each only work one case at a time.

It is difficult for me to convey that to victims on the streets sometimes because the situations that they have experienced are, most of the time, the most traumatic events in their lives. Therefore, the need to solve the case and bring the bad guys to justice is the *most* important thing in their lives. It is difficult to explain to someone who has just had their home burglarized that you have no suspects and that there is no further information to go on.

Bottom line: they don't want to hear that come out of the mouth of a Police Officer. They want the bad guy to go to jail and all of their property returned. Believe me when I tell you, we do too. After all, I wouldn't have gotten into this career if I didn't want to put bad guys away.

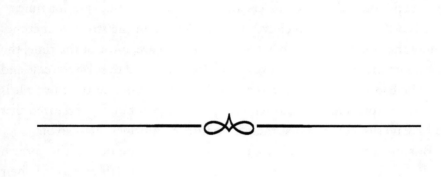

A Real Issue

In today's world, though, the plot has thickened in regard to how predators prey on children. Studies have shown data on child predators and the extreme correlation with social media. Snapchat, Instagram, TikTok, Facebook, Twitter, Instagram, Myspace, Kik, MeetMe, and so many others have become playgrounds and hunting grounds for child predators.

In today's fast-paced world and with the youth culture we have, the challenge now becomes to keep the children away from social media. Kids know things before parents do because of the internet and smartphones. Smartphones are allowed in schools, and when an incident occurs, it is often blown out of proportion from what the actual facts of the situation are due to texting and the online world.

I like to equate the issue of teenagers and smartphones to a toddler being weaned from a pacifier. Parents give their teens a phone to shut them up. Because no parent wants to deny their child something that every other kid has, right? The problem with this new philosophy of parenting is that parents of today do not understand that they are putting their children at risk by giving them this device. If you thought that predators were looking for your kids before, now you have given them a device that allows them access to anything in the world with little to no filter. Even worse than that is the fact that predators are familiar with GPS locations on phones that a child uses.

The key to helping solve the issues with our youth is to stop letting them run the show. In dealing with kids like I do in my career, I have found that this current generation as a whole does not understand what it means to have to work for something. This generation believes in the ideal of entitlement. In my experience, many kids think they should have things just because they want them and that nobody will tell them "no."

Sadly, in most cases I have dealt with, that is true. The lack of discipline from parents on their children in today's world is sickening. Even more so than that is the fact that when parents do not interact or have a leadership role in a child's life, they are more likely to have behavioral issues or even have a future of drug use.

I come from the School of Hard Knocks philosophy. My parents disciplined me, and if I had ever gotten in trouble with the police as a kid, I was safer with the police because my parents were going to take care of whatever "issue" I had as soon as we got home. But hey, old school is good school. We have tried to fix something in our society that did not need to be fixed, and instead, we have broken the system that helped keep our youth on track. We have reaped the whirlwind of those actions since that time. In short, we as parents need to stop being lazy. Understand that I am talking to all parents, so if this doesn't apply to you, just turn to the next chapter.

We need to continue our education on youth trends and pay attention to what we have seen in our own children. If you pay attention to the music or movies, you will notice that is the direction that the youth culture will go. When I speak to the large groups that I do, I typically will talk about youth trends because that is what our society at the time is dealing with.

If you are a parent, you cannot put the parenting car in neutral and push it over the hill and hope for the best. You must be engaged in your child's life, and you must be steering that car. If you let your kid drive, you will crash. Remember, nobody said we were perfect, and sometimes, we make wrong turns. When you do make mistakes, put the car in reverse and go another way. Your kids will look to you for answers in life. Keep that relationship with them strong always and understand that they are teaching you just as you are teaching them.

Let me give you a warning about the youth of today as I close. Children desire that connection with you as a parent and as an adult. If you don't believe me, go to a school assembly sometime and just watch the behavior of the students. When you have their attention or give them a task, they will follow you or listen to you. When they get bored or you lose their attention, they start touching and hitting one another because of their desire to have human contact.

If you don't stay focused on raising your child and protecting them, if you don't give them attention and just hand over nifty gadgets or toys, or if you don't give them the affection and love they need from you as a parent, I promise you that there are predators out there just watching and waiting to take the opportunity to give your child the attention that they do not want. In all of my investigations dealing with child predators and pedophiles, one thing has remained constant from the comments of the children who have been victims, and I'll summarize: "Nobody else wanted to give me attention, and he made me feel special."

LETTERS FROM PRISON

I must admit this chapter I have debated for some time about whether to include it in the book. I have had conversations with my publishing team about what to do and how to put into words what I am about to discuss. As you might have guessed from the title, I am referring to a letter I got from prison. It was a completely unexpected letter that arrived at the police department in the fall of 2021. We often get mail from little kids who support the police or from schools who do projects, but this one caught me way off guard.

In looking at the address and the envelope, I saw the letter had come from prison and had been opened and then resealed. All mail is read and resealed before leaving prisons. Now, when I read the name, I knew exactly who it was that sent it to me. I put him in the place he currently resided. I got a little nervous. Was this anthrax? Was this a threat to my life or my family? I was immediately skeptical. What possible good could come of this letter from prison?

Let me give you a little backstory. After speaking with the publisher for this book, we thought it best not to include the actual letter. Two reasons: too much detail and copyright infringement. You will just have to take my word for it, and if we ever meet in public, I can prove the documentation itself. Further, I will not tell who it is to protect the innocent and the guilty. Trust me, this man was guilty of the offenses he committed, even out of his own mouth during a confession he gave. But I guess we are all guilty somehow. I have had a lot of time to reflect on this letter and the case, so I will give him the benefit of the doubt.

I sat down at my desk and began to read the letter. The author of the letter had slanted cursive-style writing that immediately showed me he knew how to write. The letter was dated 9/27/21. To put some timeline into this for you, I arrested him in late January 2014. He had been incarcerated for nearly eight years. His sentencing would end up being twenty years.

The first line of the letter talked about how most felons wouldn't write to the last person they had anything good to say to. *Okay, so this is how the letter is going to go*, were my thoughts as I continued to read. It followed up about how nobody wanted to come to prison in their life. What I didn't expect was the following part and remainder of the letter, where he talked about soul searching and becoming a better man. He discussed having to determine what kind of man he wanted to be for the rest of his life, even while in prison.

He further continued about him working on self-help programs, obtaining his G.E.D., and was now enrolled in college (as of the time of the letter). He stated he wanted to focus on being a man with a career and eventually a family man. Here is the part that got me, though: he stated he wanted to become a man who helped the community like I did (now I was completely skeptical) rather than someone who harmed it. He wrapped up the letter telling me he wanted to one day look into the eyes of the man who saved his life, his future, and his family and then shake my hand. He extended his gratitude to me.

I was literally in shock. I expected to get cussed at. I expected to get threatened. I expected some kind of veiled or implied blame on me. I did not expect this!

Now, let's put all this into perspective for you since you can't read the letter and since I can't really tell you everything. To put it simply, this guy preyed on young girls, several of them. When there was no father figure in the home (and that is an entire book topic of its own), he swooped in and filled the role in his own way and took advantage of these children. He was violent in the relationships; he dangled these girls like a fishing line, reeling them in and out, and he groomed the girls he became involved with. He was charged as a sexual predator. I have a strong passion to put an end to human trafficking and to put a stop to those who would prey on the most innocent part of our population. If this offends anyone reading this, I don't care. I wouldn't have had a successful career if I cared about what others thought all the time.

It seems our world has turned a blind eye to this overall, and our culture glorifies sex, even at a young age. Then, the world acts shocked when someone they know who is their neighbor, someone in a position of authority, or even a celebrity would do this. But make no mistake, there is an agenda being pushed that is spiritual and evil. When Hollywood and big corporations such as big tech companies and the elite turn a blind eye to child sexual trafficking and exploitation, there is a major problem.

Big tech companies design programs to draw in children and the young generation. Filters. Emojis. How do you think I caught and charged the sexual predators to begin with? America is one of the top consumers in child trafficking. Wake up, people. It didn't start in America and has been going on for thousands of years, but we are certainly a major player in the game now.

Now, after that rant, back to the letter. After I read it, I sat back in my chair and processed it. I hate to repeat myself, but I am the Officer who put him there in prison. I had no remorse about doing so. Here is where Jesus started to move in my heart. Can people change? This man, who was also housed for a time with another sexual predator I arrested and sent to prison, was now talking about reform and about becoming a better man. He had probably, at several points in time, brought up my name and may have even been plotting my demise. Then, this letter arrives. It didn't ask for forgiveness, but it thanked me for changing his life. Of course, I changed your life!

Was this something some prison psychologist had made him do? Was this something he chose to do? Was this something he was forced to do for an early parole? There are still many questions I have. I was not the Judge in this case. It never went to a jury. My case and arrest were based on a given confession that came from this man's own mouth in an interview. He even told me in the letter I was just doing my job. This man had a messed up life, and, not surprisingly, he was sexually abused as a child. This does not give anyone the right to go and do the same acts to someone else.

You have seen a lot of raw emotions in this book. You have heard my deepest thoughts and my struggles. I must admit I still struggle with this today. There were child victims. I appreciate the letter, and I am glad the man is becoming reformed according to him, but maybe I am not the one to be sending the letter to. Maybe God should hear the confession, and the victims or their families should be the ones who hear this. There are still a lot of mixed emotions and questions about what I would say to him if we ever met. I would be cordial. I will still never condone what happened.

Our children are our most vulnerable population. When I arrested this man, the girls involved and his friends hated me and cussed at me. They took his side even as victims. I learned a lot from that case, as well as the other child sexual offense cases I worked on, mostly while I was in the schools as a School

Resource Officer. First off, you are always the bad guy in someone's mind. It doesn't matter what good you have done or how good you are. Someone believes you are bad in their story.

This book is called *Protected*. Well, what does that mean? Are our children truly protected by our society anymore? Do we truly care about what happens to them when we allow social media to dominate their lives instead of spending time with them? Do we truly care about the direction of the future and their lives when we allow society to force-feed and indoctrinate them at early stages in their lives? I don't want to teach my children to be like and think like me. I want to teach them to be better than me. Isn't that what we should all do as parents?

The last thing I learned from all these cases is this. Little children are the carriers of light and hope in our world. They have innocence until it is stolen from them or until we allow society to teach them otherwise. Never steal a child's hope. It may be all they have.

It all really comes down to this. Are we going to protect our children and our society or not?

Officer Down

For Daniel
Badge Number 457

This is only my part of the story. I can't speak for anyone else. We have all been affected by this. It changed the lives and the trajectory of an entire family forever. It changed an entire police department. It changed an entire community. Everything changed after this.

Grief. It is a terrible and joy-stealing emotion. Raw, unyielding in its time, and seemingly never-ending. Grief comes in all shapes and sizes and will resurface without warning. It can hit the young and the old, the rich and the poor, and anyone at any time. We suppress it and try to control it. We work through it the best way we know how and are taught. Even now, there are those reading this who picture a loved one you have lost, and the emotion is coming to the surface again.

This book has been written over the course of over fifteen years. Nearly eight years of that time, all work being done on the book stopped because of this chapter. As I sit here typing this now, tears begin to fill my eyes, and I want to stop writing again altogether.

November 1, 2015

It was a fairly warm day for November. We always had the event on a Sunday after church. We got ready. We stretched, ran a bit, we clowned around. The referees showed up to make sure it was a clean game. Yes, they were actual referees.

All of us participating got into a circle on the fifty-yard line. We were arm in arm, hand in hand, taking a knee to pray. Numbers on the back of jerseys told our badge numbers and the few sponsors we had since we could barely afford to get them. It was a somber moment. I said a few words, thanking everyone for being a part of the event and coming out there to have fun. The crowd, if we could call the few people in attendance a crowd, couldn't hear us. It was just us on the field, in unison. Together, the saved or unsaved, believers or unbelievers alike, took a knee and prayed. It was inspiring.

I remember the last time he and I spoke. We were standing on the sideline at the local high school football field, joking about the other Officers while I waited to go into the game for defense. We were having our annual flag football game between the police department and the fire department. Turkey Bowl, as it was called, was a charity event we put on and raised canned goods for God's Outreach Food Pantry. Admission to the game was one canned good, and we always advertised it, hoping we would get some public response. Usually, it was the police and fire families, a few city officials, and the players, all trying to relive their glory days of the game of football. I never had any time playing football in high school or college other than flag football, so this was the closest I was going to get to football greatness. Even still, I know everyone humored me to play on defense, and I got to blitz all afternoon. I loved it!

Daniel and I were standing there talking on the sideline about calls for service and poking fun at the guys playing and running around all over the place. He wasn't playing that day because he was working. We talked about home since we grew up in the same hometown. He was younger than me, but I was in the same graduating class as his oldest brother, and I knew his other brothers and him. Daniel and I also went to the same college together. I thought it was so cool, when I first met him as a rookie Officer, that he was from Campbellsville, like me. We laughed. We had fun, even if it was laughing with and at the other guys. That's okay. I am certain they did the same to me, laughing at my expense when it was my turn to play. That's what we did to each other.

In my opinion, 2015 had the neatest-looking shirts for Turkey Bowl we had ever had. This was Turkey Bowl V (like the Super Bowl numerals), and we ended up playing until Turkey Bowl IX. We never got to play to X. We had to stop because too many of us were getting hurt due to playing tackle football rather than flag football. We were all a bunch of crazies out there, but I wouldn't have had it any other way.

The police department had blue shirts with camouflage sleeves, while the fire department had red shirts with camouflage sleeves. On the shirt, we had put in memory of one of our late dispatcher's names. She had been killed in a domestic violence incident earlier in the year.

Twenty-fifteen was a rough year for me emotionally and regarding grief. I lost a dear friend who was my fraternity brother. Our family lost my great-grandmother at the age of ninety-nine...Wow, that woman was a pistol and had so much wisdom. It was a long life of blessings but difficult all the same. What I would give to be able to talk to her again for advice on life! Our county and agencies lost two dispatchers that year, and I didn't even know what was about to hit us next. We would lose another brother. The state also lost three other Police Officers. It was a terrible year.

Daniel and I talked a bit more while the offense was on the field, and then I went out there. Believe me, I am not a great football player. Thankfully, God gave me other directives and direction in my life. I love football. I am just not a guy who got to spend time playing it much. What I do know how to do, though, is blitz. And chase. For a smaller-stature guy, I am not too slow, though I have slowed a bit at my current age.

On one particular play, I caught up to the offensive player who had the ball. It was now a race to see if he could get away from me. He didn't. I made a dive for the flags and his belt and latched on. The flag belt started to fall off his waist, but not before my hand felt a sharp pain.

SNAP

My little pinky finger on my right hand snapped as it got caught between the belt and the pant line. Oh no! Broken? I grabbed my hand and immediately called for someone else to get onto the field. I talked to him and others on the sideline about it, and they laughed and were shocked, asking what I was going to do. I was worried because it was my weapon hand. No more football that day.

That was the last time I got to talk to him. I wish I could go back and talk forever instead of playing football. I splinted up my finger and the next day got it X-rayed. Yep. Broken pinky finger. I would get it taken care of, though. When everything happened, my pinky finger was no longer a priority. It healed on its own, still a little crooked to this day. Besides, all the doctors would have done was re-break the finger, set it, and put me off work again for months. Nope.

NOVEMBER 4, 2015

It started out as a normal day for me. It was the day after election day. It was a misty, cool morning. I was still working the schools at the time, so I directed traffic like I usually do. After that, I stopped by one of my middle schools briefly. I had heard we had had a robbery that morning involving a few suspects robbing someone at a gas station in town. A little while later, I remember hearing they would need someone to go with our K-9 Handler to walk the track with him. Patrol was tied up that morning, so I contacted him and told him I would go with him. I loved working with him and the dog anyway, and it was a chance to get out on patrol again for a while.

I met up with him, and he gave me the particulars of the case. He told me whose case it was, and we then got the dog out to let him start tracking. Wide sweeps, then smaller, then wide sweeps, sniffing with his nose the whole way. He would stop to urinate on something every now and then. Dogs will be dogs. The Officer and I chatted about things as we walked down railroad tracks and through woods, not expecting to find anything since so much time had lapsed, but still on the lookout all the same. We were in the daylight now, so that helped a lot. The Officer and I have been friends since college, a long time now, given that my career was twenty years and we met when I was a sophomore, I think.

The dog didn't seem to be picking anything up but would act weird from time to time. The Officer seemed to watch him closely, but nothing definite in the dog's behavior could specify what that meant, especially to me, as I was untrained with the K-9. I had done many public demonstrations and taken many bites on the bite sleeve over the years with him and his puppies, but I didn't have the slightest clue on how to read the behavior of the dog. So, I just learned every time we went out on calls or when we did a public event.

We must have walked nearly a mile when we finally got to an apartment complex in a high-crime area. It was truly one of the worst areas of town. When we showed up, the buildings had eyes, and everyone in the complex knew it. It was a horrible Officer safety layout in the back courtyard where we went. Buildings and windows and doors were all around us, along with a wooded area on the back side at the bottom of the parking lot. We walked down there, saying good morning to anyone who was awake. I think we might have gotten a few grunts to go with the stares we received.

We still smiled and carried about our business. We came to an area of the apartment complex with a vehicle outside. The dog sniffed around but didn't alert to, then he went to the front door of an apartment and did what dogs do: he marked his territory again and urinated on the front stoop. Again? Come on! He got pulled off the porch immediately and stopped. Nah. I can't give him a hard time for that. He was a great police K-9 when he was in service to us.

I knew at that point we had gotten nowhere with the track, so the Officer called it, and we started back on the long walk back to where we had come from. We didn't miss a beat in carrying on conversation and cutting up, making fun of the dog for taking a leak on the front step. He shouldn't have done that, but by the time we would have gotten up away from the porch to discipline him for it, he would have forgotten he did it and wondered why we were yelling at him.

After the track, I went back to my office at one of my middle schools. I sat down to work on a report and did some paperwork I had to do. A little while later, on the radio, I remember hearing Officers getting out on the street and the area where we had been previously that morning for the dog track, the apartment complex. They had located the robbery suspects.

I think the only way I could describe it legitimately in my mind is that all hell broke loose. That is not swearing; that is not cussing. That is just the truth of how it all went down. I remember the screaming on the radio from Officers yelling, "Shots fired! Shots fired! Officer down!" More descriptive details were given, but I will not reveal them here.

The emotional blur that happened next is still something I try to put together in my mind from time to time. I remember jumping up from my chair, and before I knew it, I was down the hall from the office, had jumped a flight of stairs, and went out a set of glass doors so hard it was a wonder I didn't break them. I didn't care if I had.

I have never tried to get somewhere with so much purpose in my life. Lights and sirens, screaming at people to get out of the way, trying to get across town, a mere three-minute drive from the school if we had been on third shift. But we weren't. It was broad daylight. I don't remember the siren, but I know it was on, and I remember punching the steering wheel to change the sound on it repeatedly as I went through intersections so people heard me.

My cell phone began ringing. It was the Principal at the Alternative School and Day Treatment School that backed up to the apartment complex I was going to. I hit *ignore*. It rang again. I hit *ignore*. It rang again, and this time, when I hit *ignore*, I threw the phone into my seat. I didn't have time to deal with some kid who didn't want to go to class or was being defiant. At least, that is what I thought was going on in my mind when I received the call. My focus was on one thing. Save our Officer, our brother. It is all I wanted.

When I got to the scene, it was chaos. I ran down the hill to the apartment complex after securing my vehicle. There was yelling and screaming, and people were everywhere. I heard an Officer inside in a fight and ran inside to help as other Officers were pulling Daniel to safety out of the apartment doorway. When I ran inside, I slipped and lost my footing on the floor briefly and remember hearing, "Watch the gun!" from the Officer still engaged with the suspect. I didn't know what I had slipped on until later.

The fight was on between two big men in comparison to me, so I didn't even think about what I could contribute, but I attacked anyway. The suspect was already almost in handcuffs but needed medical attention because he was bleeding. He was dragged outside and put down on the pavement. Hard. EMS was already on the way because he had also been shot. We had returned fire.

I remember one of the Majors yelling at another suspect as the suspect was slowly walking away from the scene. I charged after him even though he was not fleeing. I put him on his stomach on the ground and was immediately on his back, putting him into handcuffs. The Major came and assisted me to get him cuffed. He nearly had to pull me off of the guy who was just a little more my size. I was enraged. He was up and detained quickly, cussing me out and telling me he didn't do anything, knowing he had been the one to let the Officers in to be ambushed.

After the second suspect was put into a cruiser, I remember the Major yelling and saying the ambulances were not there yet and to load Daniel into a cruiser if we had to. Officers began doing that as I began moving cruisers to give EMS the capability of getting to our location.

After I had moved several cruisers out of the way, I don't even know whose. The EMS units arrived, and I saw they were loading both Daniel and the main suspect into separate ambulances. The Sergeant over the Detectives, who would later become the Chief when I retired and a great mentor to me, yelled, "Somebody has to go with Daniel!"

"I'll go!" I said without giving it a second thought. I jumped into the back of the ambulance with him, and someone slammed the door behind me. I remember the double *bam-bam* pounding on the back door, signifying to us to take off. Off we went. I rocked backward, nearly stumbling as the wagon lurched forward.

I couldn't have asked for a better EMS team in that unit with me. I had the Director of EMS in that wagon with me. I kept looking at Daniel, then looking outside and seeing all the lights and cruisers as we leap-frogged the intersections, stopping all traffic. It wasn't until we got across the county line into Lexington and I saw a Lexington Metro cruiser the weight of everything occurring started to push down on me.

I felt light-headed. I was turning gray. I felt hot. I remember the EMS Director yelling at me, "Josh, I need you to help us. Take his boots off, get him ready for the hospital, and get him comfortable." At that moment, I snapped back into it and started to help. I unlaced his boots, took them off, gently setting them on the floor as if I would hurt them. I covered his feet back up for warmth.

"Josh, get in that cabinet behind you and get me that packet of gauze."

I did.

"Get me that stuff behind you above your head right there." I did that, too.

I felt like I was doing something at the time. As I have processed these emotions over the years and as I looked back on what happened, I remember the EMS team taking what I handed them and then throwing it on the floor of the ambulance. They never did anything with it. They didn't need anything I gave them because they were doing other life-saving measures. They told me to do that and gave me those tasks to save me. They were helping me to keep it together and stay busy so I could stay focused. They were saving me from myself.

After what seemed like an eternity, we finally got to the hospital. I jumped out of the back of the ambulance like I was an escapee and immediately was preparing to grab bags and stretchers or anything else I could grab to help the EMS team get inside. At this point, there was nothing I could do except pray.

Around the same time we arrived, the suspect had arrived in his ambulance. I saw rage again. I felt hot again, this time for a different reason, not because I was about to pass out. Our Officers were held back by security and Lexington Metro Officers from interacting with the suspect, and we were stopped in our tracks as he was taken into the hospital, and the doors slammed behind them. They would take over from here. They, too, were saving us from ourselves.

Word had traveled fast, and the media already knew an Officer had been shot. I told one of my co-workers I needed to call my wife and let her know, but I could hardly talk at the moment. I then remembered I had thrown my phone into my seat in my car and left it, jumping immediately into the ambulance. I was losing it emotionally. He called her from his phone and told her we were at the hospital, but I was okay. She hadn't heard yet because she was at work.

That was not the case with everyone else. Leave it to social media. There were friends and family in other states who knew before my wife did due to social media posts, and when I finally got my phone back hours and hours later in the day, I had forty-two missed calls, my voicemail box was full, and thirty-four text messages asking what was going on. It was a friend in Missouri who asked my mom, and she couldn't get in touch with me. I still feel terrible about that.

We waited for hours and hours. Daniel was in surgery and made it through surgery. He was stable, from what we were told. I was still wearing the same uniform I had been in that morning. I was asked if I wanted to change since I had a little bit of blood on the uniform. I don't know who it was from.

I told the Chaplain from Lexington Metro, who offered me a fresh, clean polo shirt, that I was fine, but thank you. He offered again a little while later. Again, I politely declined. About fifteen minutes after that, I was called into the hallway by the Chief of Police for our agency and ordered to change my uniform. He said he wanted me to be out of that uniform and comfortable and somewhat more clean. I didn't balk. I went into the restroom, and I changed out of my uniform and put on clean clothes.

After we sat for a few more hours, we eventually were all sent home because there was really nothing we could ever do. We knew that, but that wasn't the point. It was about being there.

November 6, 2015

We got word that day Daniel was not going to pull through. There had been t-shirts made saying "Prayers for 457," and countless donations and items began coming into the police department. We had prayed and prayed. We had cried. Ultimately, we were blessed enough to have the opportunity to go back to the hospital to say our goodbyes. I was so thankful to all the family for allowing that for us.

My wife and I went to the hospital with our oldest daughter, and the halls were filled with my colleagues, co-workers, other first responders, family members, and members of the city. There were not a lot of words, a few nods, hugs from anyone who wanted to give one, and a lot of tears. Sobbing and somber cries filled and echoed in the hallway.

My wife held my hand as we approached the door. I almost couldn't go in. I felt guilty, like it should have been me who found the bad guys. *We went to the apartment! We went to the apartment! I should have done something more in the ambulance! Why didn't I do something more?!*

We went in and found him hooked up to machines, and family was all around him, showing love and solitude and a strength like I have never seen. It was small talk from everyone because what else was there to say? What could I say to make it better? Nothing. Not a thing. We hugged his family. I stood there in stunned silence for a moment. We cried, and I squeezed his hand and said, "I'm sorry." That is all I could do. That is all I could muster out of my mouth. I was looking at the family when I said it, but really, I was talking to Daniel.

I didn't want to talk to anyone when we left. We hugged a few more people, and we left the hospital right after that.

The world lost a great man, a real hero, later on that night.

Officer Daniel Ellis served faithfully from August 11, 2008, until the end of his watch on November 6, 2015. He is and will always be missed.

The next week or so was an emotional roller coaster we were all forced to ride and could not get off. There was a lot that took place. I was done with policing. I had already decided it in my mind. I wanted to quit. To be honest, I had lost my faith at that point. Admittedly, I even questioned God in all of this. I couldn't stand humanity. How could someone do something to someone he didn't even know? A man who had a family and didn't do anything to him except his job and try to provide for that family and be honorable.

I didn't want to be at work, but I didn't want to be at home. Home left me with my thoughts, and that was a dangerous place to be right now. There was no shortage of food and drinks at the station. We were always welcome. There were flowers on his cruiser, which had been turned into a memorial in front of the station. There were teddy bears, banners, cards, gifts, monetary donations, and so much more. It was such a nice gesture. Looking back now on it from a leadership standpoint, it was a logistics nightmare.

People were doing the only things they knew to do, and they helped the only way they knew to help. You don't want to turn it away with the risk of offending your community who is standing behind you, but where were we going to put all this stuff? When I said it was everywhere in the building, it seemed like it was everywhere! I am so thankful the community continues to stand behind us to this day, even though, nationally, that trend has changed in many large cities. Our community was amazing, and even though I was preparing myself mentally to hang up my career, I was thankful for them. The compassion didn't stop there.

During that week, the coverage on the news was endless about Daniel and what had happened. The Richmond, Lexington, and Louisville stations seemed to be a constant cycle of everything going on in Richmond. It went on and on, which seemed to only fuel my emotions. Even the University of Kentucky Basketball did something really great and honored Daniel at their basketball game at Rupp Arena. I wasn't sure who had set that up, but I thought it was pretty classy to do that.

In the days leading up to the visitation and the funeral, I was numb. I was going through the motions of life. I had cried to my wife, cried by myself, I vented to my stepdad about being mad at the world, the world that would do that to him, and I really questioned myself in a lot of ways. Whether this was legitimate or not to feel this way is not the point. That is how I felt. I was deciding in my own mind whether or not I would continue in policing. I was processing everything that had happened, and probably not in a way that got me anywhere at all. I just ran everything that happened on that scene around in my head over and over and over again. It was one constant movie. I barely slept at night.

The evening of the visitation came, and the funeral and visitation were to be held at the Alumni Coliseum at Eastern Kentucky University. It was probably the only place in town large enough to hold the amounts of people who would arrive from everywhere to pay their respects to a hero. Thousands came in droves to both the visitation and the funeral the next day. Thousands. There were Officers from all over the country who came to honor Daniel. I even remember a wreath sent from the New York Yankees baseball team in the hallway. I have always personally been an Atlanta Braves fan, but I have to admit I became a Yankees fan just a little bit since that time. It was a class act.

Since the election had just occurred, we now had a new Governor-elect and Lt. Governor-elect. That evening, while the Officers were downstairs in a room away from all the public, the future Lt. Governor Janine Hampton came into the room and met with us. She paid her respects and listened as we all told story upon story about Daniel and how amazing he was. She spent a significant amount of time with us and, to my recollection, never went into public view. While she was meeting with us, we were told Governor-Elect Matthew Bevin was elsewhere, meeting with the family privately in a place even we were not allowed to go. Again, this was somewhere the public did not see.

I have interviewed and spent time with both of these two people while they were in office and Governor Bevin had members of the agencies with fallen Officers to march in his inaugural parade after his installation in office. There are a lot of people who did or do not like Governor Bevin for his actions in office, but to me, there is no better way to enter into a public office than to come serve the people who elected you. These two politicians, who were not even officially installed yet, took time to clear their schedules, come to a place to meet with people who were grieving, and they did it quietly and without the public knowing about it. They kept it from being a circus or from being about them. They knew the media could hound them on that and spin that, or someone might turn it around. They did it the right way. They did it for the family and for us.

The day of the funeral arrived, and I had put together possibly the best Class A uniform I ever had up until that point in my career. When we got to the funeral, we lined up the cruisers for the procession afterward. Mine was somewhere in the middle of our group of cruisers for our agencies, but I couldn't even tell you how many hundreds of cruisers there were in that parking lot that day. This didn't include civilian vehicles in the procession. I am only talking about police cars. Motorcycles were in that, too. Lots of them. We took a photo of our entire police agency that day, which we had never done. We were missing someone. It should not have taken this to take a photo.

When we went inside the building, we went downstairs to the basketball floor. This is where EKU Basketball plays. I hadn't been down on the floor to sit since my own graduation from college. I stood up to work a few high school graduations but hadn't sat on the floor since 2003. It had been a long time. I sat with my wife, my mom, my sister, and all the other Officers from our agency.

The Honor Guard was all around and guarded the casket up front as tradition ordered. When the funeral started, I was holding it together pretty well so far. One of our Officers sang "My Old Kentucky Home" so beautifully. I never knew he could even sing. I had sniffled a little bit, and tears had swelled in my eyes some, but overall, I had held it together. It was a beautiful service and meant for a true hero. It was not until Daniel's cousin, Hannah Ellis, sang the song called "How Great Thou Art" that I and most of the other Officers finally broke. Lots of us started crying, and the emotional dams and barriers that had been holding us back all this time finally shattered.

There was no stopping the tears anymore. We knew the eulogy and closing prayer were coming next. The Chief also spoke that day and gave a wonderful speech, holding it together with more strength than I ever could have. His voice quivered at times, and he showed his human emotions, but he stood tall and honorable as he represented the agency like a true leader in a troubled time. He made me proud to have him as my Chief.

At the end of the service, the Honor Guard did as they had when they started and moved methodically into place. We were dismissed from the floor to go take our places outside in formation and get ready to receive Daniel for the procession. I hadn't eaten much that day and was hungry. As we walked outside, there were boxed lunches handed to us for when we left. I told myself I would eat in the car on the way to the cemetery.

Outside, there wasn't much talking in the group. We waited as people filed outside. Media cameras set up in the grassy area away from the building, preparing to film. We were all given instructions about where to stand and the directions of what was going to occur. Everything was planned specifically and intentionally. After a long time had passed and we had stood in silence, I heard the familiar command barked from somewhere in the distance.

"Detail...Attention!"

The hundreds of Officers in the crowd popped to attention at the same moment, and everyone froze, unwavering in motion. So many times before, I had done this. This time, it was different. I could barely stand it seemed.

No. I have to stand still and strong. For Daniel. For what seemed like an eternity, while the wind whistled around the building and through the trees in the breeze, we waited. Then we heard it. Then we saw it.

"Detail...Present arms!"

Slowly, deliberately, together, we all raised our arms in salute. It didn't matter the color of your uniform. We were all one. United. United under the flag now draped over our brother's casket as he was being carried by the Honor Guard toward the car. Crying and tears, sniffles from grown men and women cut through the silence as he was being loaded into the car for transport. Once he was inside the car, we heard the next order.

"Order arms!"

Joshua Hale

As slowly as they had been raised, arms and stiffened hands lowered in unison back down to the sides of each man or woman in uniform. Back to attention, straightened and trying to stand tall. A few moments later, the next command was given.

"Detail...Dismissed!"

At that point, the group relaxed from being at attention and began to slowly disperse to vehicles. Hugs were given and tears were shed as we headed to our cruisers. My wife and I got into my cruiser along with my sister. My mom drove separately in her car. I remember standing outside the cruiser for a moment and just taking it all in. Then, I started to see it. One by one.

One by one, it seemed each cruiser began turning on its overhead light bars and flashing lights. Hundreds of cruisers illuminated super bright lights in the colors of blues, reds, whites, yellows, and even some greens. It was mostly blue and white lights that lit up that huge parking lot. I was in awe. I was mesmerized. I knew Daniel would be looking down from heaven, thinking about how amazing this might look. Daniel was a man of faith and a Christian.

I got into my cruiser, and my wife told me to eat something. As usual, she was trying to take care of me. As usual, I was being stubborn. I told her I would eat along the way. I didn't want to eat in front of all these people and stuff my face right here. We didn't have tinted windows, and me shoving a sub sandwich in my face wasn't my idea of *professional*. Looking back on it now, nobody would have cared in the least.

Once the procession got moving, my cruiser was somewhere in the middle of all of the Richmond cruisers. We were near the front of the procession, which ended up being several miles long, from what I was told later on. I was still processing a lot of that emotion, and in my mind, this was the last thing to give me the strength I needed to quit policing altogether. I had seen enough, done enough.

We drove the procession all around town, and that is when God began to soften my heart. My hardened heart for humanity began to find light in the darkness. In the miles and blocks we traveled around town, I began to see people stopped on the side of the road, pulled over in traffic. This is customary and the law in Kentucky, but I did not expect it like this. There were children off their school buses with banners. There were people with their hands over their hearts. Our firefighters had brought together two ladder trucks and were flying a giant American flag we drove under. It didn't stop in Richmond.

As we got onto the interstate and traveled to take more backroads, at every bridge and overpass, there were firefighters, EMS workers, tow trucks, a semi-trailer, or some construction company, along with other Civilians flying the American flag and waving banners with 457 on them. I am getting chills down my spine as I struggle to put these words onto paper from thoughts.

Men, women, children, even animals, it seemed, stopped what they were doing to see us as we passed by and to pay their respects. Has anyone ever seen something like this? Why did this have to happen for the world to be united again? One particular man in a wheelchair was a veteran. He was a very old man, and I could see that from my cruiser as we were passing him. He was not sitting in his wheelchair. He had stood in his wheelchair, in his uniform, and was saluting Daniel and the procession as we drove by. I had never seen someone with so much honor in my life. Ever.

I had thought the respects would end the further we got away from Richmond. I was wrong, and I was glad to be. The people on the roadsides continued to show their love and gratitude for a hero for nearly seventy miles. I had said I would eat when no one was watching, but I eventually had to give up that idea and just eat anyway. I would take bites between bridges and between groups of people and towns. I finally finished the meal.

I had wanted to give up on humanity. I had wanted to quit policing. I wanted to avenge Daniel, and I didn't care if it was me who put the needle in the arm of the man who did this to him, an eye for an eye. I was angry at humanity for an entire week. I had wanted to quit being kind, and I wanted to lash out before now.

God had a different plan for me, and He was not done working on me yet.

When we got to the gravesite, it was considerably smaller than I thought, and I thought it was such a peaceful place. We parked our cars and walked to where we would form up again, and I mentally tried to prepare myself again. I knew the day was not through yet. The rumbling and earth-shaking sounds of the Harley-Davidson motorcycles had stopped. There wasn't much conversation. We had gotten back into formation. It was time again.

JOSHUA HALE

Then I heard that sound I loved so much, except this time I didn't love it so much. I heard the click-clack, click-clack, click-clack of horses' hooves. The horses were walking down the small road, escorting the casket. The haunting, eerie, awful, and beautiful sounds heard next drowned out the sounds of the hooves as the bagpipes began to play with their airy notes. Sometimes seemingly out of tune, yet not, they found their chords as the Officers playing them marched closer and closer, and the sounds got louder and louder.

The trance we had been put into briefly was snapped when I heard the familiar command yet again.

"Detail...Attention!"

As if we had never stopped what we were doing before, the whole detail of Officers, Troopers, Deputies, Civilians, Dispatchers, or anyone in the formation popped back to attention. The rest of the crowd watched from another area, as we could see from our peripheral vision. The family, the loved ones, in the front.

This next part is really hard for me to remember in exact order because I have suppressed my emotions and memory for so many years. I thought if I filed this away in my mind, the sadness would go away. It hasn't. The bagpipes eventually stopped. Words of honor were said about a great man, and he was a great man, husband, father, son, brother, friend, and so much more. I was caught up in the words. I was losing it in my emotions and just trying to hold it together, honestly.

"Detail...Present arms!"

I had almost missed it. I had almost missed the command. I almost never heard it. I was so caught up in my emotions, I had been lost in my thoughts. My right arm went up slowly in salute with everyone, and I was brought back quickly after that by the sound of gunfire. Gunshots from multiple weapons, the rifles, fired in unison. It startled me. I must have moved a little bit. I must have. I quickly regained composure and stood still again. Three rounds in almost perfect sequence. Doing the simple math in my head with the three rounds and trying to remember meant there were seven riflemen. Twenty-one-gun salute. After the echo of the gunshots faded into the hillsides and the woods, silence set upon us all again, but only for a moment. From off somewhere in the distance and yet not too far, that familiar song I had dreaded to hear all day long on an instrument I knew too well began to play.

I played trumpet when I first began playing music in the sixth grade. I could probably still play today, but I could not play like it was played that day, nor would I ever want to. Without missing a note and in perfect pitch, the Bugler playing the trumpet began slowly playing the melody.

Taps.

It is played at every line of duty, death, police funeral, every military funeral, and countless others I am certain I am unaware of. I had heard it so many other times. There will always be another time we have to listen to *Taps*. It is unmistakable. Yet another unmistakable sound was the sound of men and women who could no longer fight back their emotions and were tired of being strong and just needed to be human for once. Not robots, not those solving everyone else's problems, just being human beings who needed each other in a time of grieving and crisis in their lives. If only this world understood what it felt like that day to unify like we did, this world might be a better place.

The American flag was being folded during this time into the triangle by the Honor Guard with precision and accuracy and perfection. It was handed to Daniel's wife by our then-current Chief of Police. It was as *Taps* was concluded, and the world became still for only a moment again. I felt the breeze on my face as tears rolled down my cheeks. Not a note had been missed or off-pitch.

I later found out who the bugler was. He was working for a different agency at the time of the funeral but would be hired almost one year later to be our future Chief of Police. It really is strange sometimes how God will intertwine the paths of others as one and cause them to intersect at a certain point. It was as if the bugler, who then became the Chief, might have some sort of understanding about the culture he may be inheriting. Of course, there were other credentials other than bugler for Chief of Police required. It just shows the way lives come together on a collision course unknowingly.

The ceremony had been completed? Already? White flowers with a red spot on them had been placed onto the casket. The folded flags had been passed off to the family. There was a stillness now in the air after the detail returned to formation after playing our role and paying our respects. It would never be enough. Why couldn't we have done more? In the silence, those thoughts returned again.

Why couldn't I have done more that day?! God, why does it have to be this way?

I heard a voice speaking in the distance. It had come over the loudspeaker. I can't be certain who it was even today. We had stood still. The detail did not move. I heard the leaves in the trees. I heard the wind. I felt the cool. Then, the voice I heard had been the dispatcher giving the final radio call for 457. It still gets me on the memorial we have every year. I think about it often. The crying accompanied the final call and the tone drop from the radio. It is difficult to describe, but it was soul-piercing and heart-wrenching. I had heard the bagpipes and felt them in my bones. The gunshots shook me to my core. *Taps* haunted me.

Back in the silence and waiting for the next emotional moment to recover from, we stood still, and still we stood together at attention. Then, just as we had been called to it in the beginning, we heard the commands again.

"Detail...Dismissed!"

For a moment, no one moved. No one spoke. The detail remained as they were in formation. Then, slowly, Officers began to file out, giving hugs, condolences, and trying to muster as much support as we could for the family for one another. I don't know what kind of support I had to give to anyone.

My wife was wonderful and all but carried me back to the car that day. I was moving my feet, and I was trying to hide it, but she was arm in arm with me, being the support. My feet were concrete blocks, it seemed. I welcomed her support. My mom and my sister were there supporting me as well. Like it was for everyone else, I am sure, it was a long drive home. Longer days and nights without him in the future. I still see the number 457 everywhere I go, even today, it seems, and I am okay with that. Never forget.

I pray for the family to find God's peace in everything.

There is no good way to start a chapter like this, and there is no good way to end a chapter like this. I hope I have shown nothing but respect for a man we all cared about and loved. Daniel was our *brother in blue*. Daniel was a man of integrity and honor and a wonderful man for the community. There is not a day that goes by I don't think about November 4, 2015, and I miss him every day. We all do.

A few years later, I traveled on a trip with my family to meet some of our friends who live in the Washington, D.C., area. We had never gotten the opportunity to see the Law Enforcement Memorial. When we got there, I was saddened by all the names of the men and women on the wall, etched in time for as long as the monument continues to exist. I searched for Daniel's name, and I found it. I took an etching with me, which I still have. In silence and solitude, those names on the wall, those men and women, are forever guarded by enormous statues of lions who sit or crouch as sentinels, as if waiting to attack anyone who would do harm to those on the wall.

In the Bible and inscribed on the wall is the verse Proverbs 28:1, which says, "The wicked flee when no man pursueth, but the righteous are bold as a lion."

Daniel was a man of faith, in addition to all the other wonderful qualities he had. He lived a life of service to others. Of all the important things he had done in his life, he had given his life to Jesus. In the book of John in the Bible, John 15:13, Jesus says, "Greater love hath no than this, that a man would lay down his life for his friends." He made a sacrifice for others he didn't know. Daniel was not Jesus, but I will say this. That sure sounds a lot like something Jesus did for you and me.

Daniel, I can't wait to talk to you again in heaven. I hope you are talking with Jesus right now! Until then, we will hold the line down here.

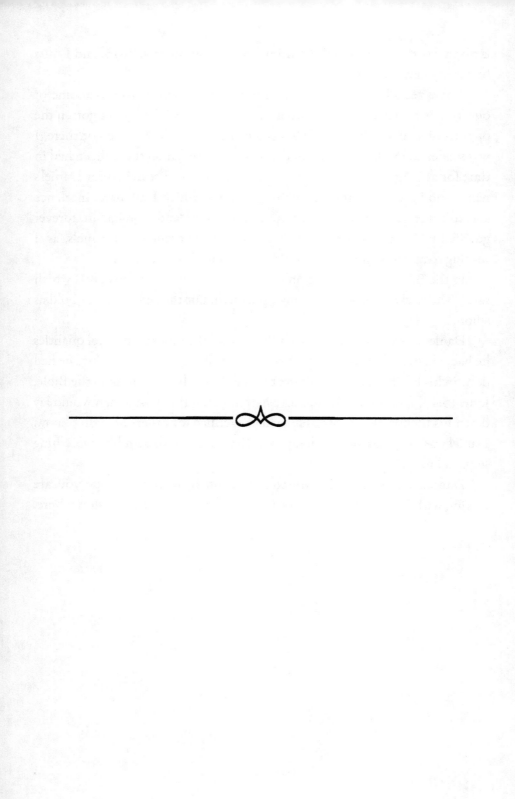

Welcome to Supervision

The last part of my career was spent in the role of supervision. I was responsible for a great number of tasks and personnel, and it was a great deal of pressure. I will be the first to tell you I could not have done this when I originally wanted to start in leadership. There is a reason you should take the escalator or the stairs up multiple floors instead of the elevator when it comes to leadership. Your mind may want to take you there, but your character has not been tested enough yet. That is why leaders fail.

When I first decided I wanted to try my hand at promoting up through the ranks, I had been assigned to the schools for about six years. I learned a lot about leadership from the people I observed every day. I was separated from the policing world and immersed in the education world. I was still an Officer, but also on staff with the schools, sort of.

I dealt with defiant students, found drugs and weapons on students at times, dealt with child pornography on cell phones and social media, and seized $1000 iPhones. This caused parents to get angry and threaten to sue me, the police department, and the school because their "baby" would *never do anything like that*. I have had to fight students to protect a Principal when the student took the first swing, only to have the Principal hang me out high and dry in front of the parents. I have learned about budgeting and fiscal responsibility from sitting through school board meetings and listening to people argue over how we should spend taxpayer dollars in the millions and on what projects.

Yep. I had seen a lot in six years about leadership. I talked to a Sergeant at the agency at the time who told me, "You will never effectively change the entire organization until you promote up." While I disagree with this to a point, there is some validity to this. So, I signed up for the next Sergeant's exam, and I started studying.

I studied for weeks for that stupid test, and the day finally arrived. I had bought a book and everything with test questions similar to the type I thought I would see. I read all the study material textbooks they gave me the best I knew how since they didn't tell you what was on the test (at all). Guess what! I bombed it! As in, *I failed it*.

The passing score had to be 70 percent. I scored 69 percent (I think). So, needless to say, I did not move on to the next stage of the process for the interview and packet with my future Sergeants and those who would then lead me. At this point, though, I learned that titles do not mean you are not a leader. They had been leading me for a long time. I had been leading others for a long time. I was already a Training Officer. I was already speaking and teaching thousands of kids. I was already leading. This was just a part of the process.

I spent the next year and a half still assigned to the schools as a School Resource Officer, but now my mindset has changed. Now, I was not only still working with the students and doing my daily tasks as usual, I was learning from every leader I could, both the good and the bad. What I mean is that I wanted to learn what I wanted to be and what I didn't want to be. I reflected back on all the incidents previously, and it lit a fire in me.

I finally got my chance to take the test again, and the next time, I passed! There was an interview board a short time after that, and I was endorsed by the board to take on the role of Sergeant. I was going to be given the chance to prove myself on a "temporary" and "probationary" status. I didn't care what they called it. I was getting promoted. I was getting the stripes on the sleeves and the collar, all that stuff. But...there was a catch.

I was taking on this new role when we had a manpower shortage. Newsflash to everyone reading this: there is always a manpower shortage in policing in America. I had to still be assigned to the schools because there was no one to fill my role (or at least no one they wanted to put in there), *and* I had to take on the role of working as a Sergeant on second shift on the weekends.

I talked to my wife about it, and the money wasn't a great amount at the time for the promotion, but it would get better; it would be overtime almost guaranteed, and we could make it work. She was really supportive. I took the offer and promotion. My days off were Thursdays and Fridays, and I had two days to learn that first weekend how to do the activity and paperwork to turn in for the shift to send up the Chain of Command for review. That's it. Two days. It was not ideal, but I made it work, and they trusted me to get it done.

I went back to the schools on Monday through Wednesday of the following week and took my Thursday/Friday days off with my family after they got out of work and school. Then, after hanging out for a bit with them on Saturday morning, my wife smiled at me when I was getting ready for work to head into roll call, gave me a kiss, and told me she loved me. She told me to keep her posted on my day, and I was in the cruiser and off to my first day in charge on my own as a Supervisor.

I asked a good friend of mine who goes to church with us and used to be my training Officer and later my Corporal and Sergeant a question once. I asked, "How do you know what to do in leadership when you don't know what to do?"

He said to me. "Josh, can I be honest with you? Sometimes, in leadership, I have no idea what to do. Sometimes, I just have to make this up as I go along. Either way, make a decision and stick to it."

My first day as a Sergeant started off really well. Everyone seemed to be very respectful and receptive. They didn't really know what to expect. You see, I had been off the road for so long, I was on an island of sorts off to myself. I had interactions with other Officers, but it was nothing negative. We gave out beat and district assignments, and I went into the office to start shift activity to get ahead of the game in case we got busy, which we always did. This was second shift. It *always* got busy.

Then it did.

The tone from dispatch came out for 10-46 on the radio. An injury accident involving a pedestrian and a vehicle, except it wasn't just any kind of injury accident. The call went something like this: "Respond to I-75 in reference to a male subject being struck by a semi-tractor-trailer. EMS and fire are also en route." I saw immediately how this day was going to go.

I responded with my shift Officers to the interstate because it was going to take several units just to get the scene shut down, let alone work it. We had to position fire trucks to block the road and shut down traffic, divert any traffic we could, have traffic direction for the people already stuck behind the accident, make sure EMS had space to work, and always provide a safe location for the first responders to be in their workspace. But I am getting ahead of myself. I wasn't even there on scene yet. This was just what was going through my mind before I got there.

When I got there, it was much worse than I expected. I expected it to be bad, given it to be a pedestrian struck by a tractor-trailer, but the circumstances made it more horrible. When we interviewed the driver of the truck, he said that he saw the pedestrian look at him from the side of the interstate, step into traffic in front of the truck, and the driver never had time to stop. The driver was beside himself. The pedestrian had committed suicide.

The accident occurred really close to an exit and a major shopping center, and the next thing I knew, the media cameras were already there. There were no Lieutenants at the time, and I was allowed to reach out to the Chief of Police and the Assistant Chief for major incidents. I reached out to the Assistant Chief first by both phone call and text and got nothing back. I was seeking guidance and also informing them of the situation. When I didn't get a response, I moved up the chain to contact the Chief. I called him first with no answer. Then, I sent a text. I still laugh about it with him to this day. He is a retired military man who takes the Chain of Command seriously. He responded to my text. I got the response I needed.

"Welcome to supervision!"

The Coroner had arrived on scene, and in the Commonwealth of Kentucky, the Coroner is in charge on a death scene. I took my cues from him as far as I needed to until he gave me the reigns. I took control from that point on. We already had the interstate shut down. I lined up cruisers, the EMS trucks, tow trucks, and the Coroner's van so the media and the public could not see what was going on at the scene where the body was and no one could take pictures. We had the fire trucks completely block all lanes, and two Officers were posted to hold traffic. Accident reconstruction was called to the scene. We began taking photos of the victim, who was over the guardrail, now somewhat down the hillside.

I listened as the Coroner gave me instruction methodically. Slowly. Never rush a scene. Now, it was not just me I was responsible for. Now, I was responsible for everyone on the scene. *Tell me why I signed up for this again.* Hours went by as we worked the scene, being respectful to the victim, and eventually, we opened up the roadway again, allowing motorists to pass by in the far lane. The interstate was opened again with one lane, but it was just as many rubber-neckers trying to look as if it was a traffic bottleneck that was stopping it. I am surprised we didn't have more accidents because we almost did.

It wasn't until several years after this I realized who the victim's family was. I saw his father in a hardware store, and he did not remember me. He didn't remember me because every time we saw each other, he had been drunk or high, and he was fighting me and running away or spitting on me and the other Officers. I know of crimes this man has been involved with, and the many, many times we have dealt with him. We have had to arrest him, fight him, chase him, had to use a taser on him. He was not a pillar of society when I had to deal with him, and honestly, he was quite dangerous at times.

I wasn't in uniform that day, and I addressed him by his name. He asked me who I was, and I told him. I questioned in my own mind whether or not I should have done this. I asked him how he was, and he told me he had been sober for several years. He apologized to me for anything he had done to me and my Officers. When I asked him what made him go sober, he said it was when his boy had stepped in front of the truck on the interstate. He told me he didn't want to live his life like he had been anymore and was trying to be close to Jesus. I asked him if I could pray for him. We prayed right there in that store in the aisle full of table saws and drills.

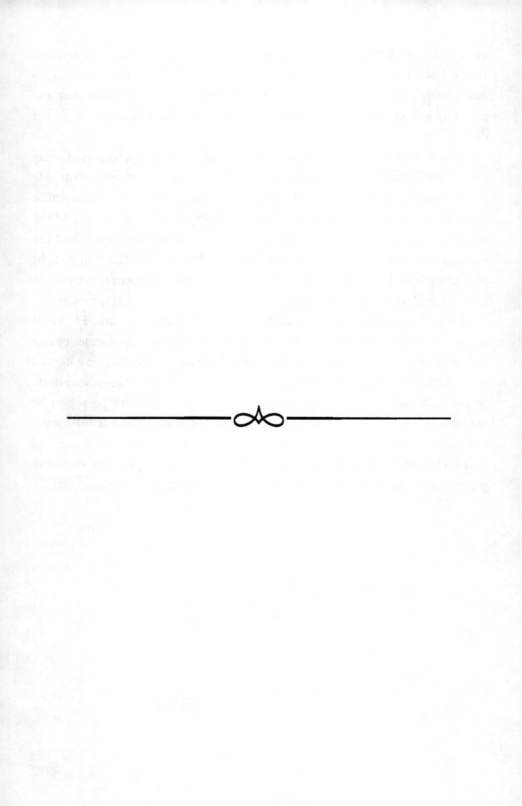

CRAZY SUPERVISOR MOMENTS

I guess by this point in the book, everything in my whole career or the career of any other first responder could seem crazy. I have had some wild, and I mean *wild*, incidents that I am probably leaving out and don't even remember because my brain became so accustomed to them. I have had the opportunity to supervise and work with some of the greatest men and women in law enforcement, and I miss working with them. They kept me on my toes and sharpened my skills as a Supervisor and drove me insane at times, but all in a good way. I have had some great teams of people, whatever shift or assignment I was given. I am so thankful for those people who taught me so much. I hope I was able to teach a little bit to them.

I learned early as a Supervisor three things about people. Never mess with people's family, their time, or their money. Once you get people to do the mundane tasks like timesheets and status forms or vacation requests and paperwork like they need to, the rest of the job is really fun.

Some of the biggest pucker moments for me as an Officer have not been when it was me directly involved. It was when my people were involved. There is something that is very stressful when you are responsible for making sure everyone else does what they are supposed to do and goes home safe to their families. Sometimes, that means discipline when they don't do what they are supposed to do, but it should always mean you are there for your people when they need you to be. Get out of the chair in the office and get out there for your people.

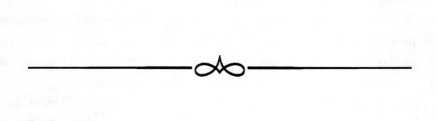

THE BABY ON A DOORSTEP

I remember one day on shift when dispatch came out with a call about a female in labor. Two of our female Officers responded to the scene to assist EMS, but they beat them to the scene. When the female Officers got to the scene, the woman had been actively in labor for a long time but had been passed out due to being on drugs. She had not known she was in labor until she woke up. Now, it was go time. The baby was crowning, and she was having the baby on the front doorstep of a house she didn't live in. She had been in the drug dealer's apartment next door, and he acted later like he didn't even know her. But for now, our Officers had to deliver the baby. Immediately. I remember the frantic radio traffic, and I was just down the road at the station, so I got up from the office and went to the scene. I also beat EMS to the scene. It was not their fault. I was just closer. We have always been very blessed in our community with having EMS close by almost always.

When I got to the scene, I saw the look of terror on both the Officers' faces as one of them held a newborn baby and the other assisted the mother of the child. They were trying to show the mother some dignity as she had pulled her pants down in street view and broad daylight for the world to see everything. The Officer holding the baby was holding the newborn like a tiny, extremely breakable object and exercising the most precise care not to drop the baby in a semi-crouched position like a catcher behind the plate of a baseball game.

The looks on their faces said it all. I am certain the look on my face said it all, too. How in the world did we escalate to this? And EMS was still not on scene. In all actuality, this all took place in a matter of minutes. It seemed like an hour. A third Officer came to the scene, who had been on EMS prior to working with the agency. Amongst all of us, we worked our way through it as EMS arrived.

When they arrived, they strolled up very unamused and not in a rush...at all. One of them just slowly walked up and was like, "Oh, you all delivered a baby. Good job." Then, he walked back to his truck and got his stretcher and told the other EMS crew to get their stretcher as they got out of their truck because the mother and baby would have to go separately. He walked back up, dug around slowly into his bag, got out some shears, and they prepared to cut the umbilical cord. I have to openly be honest here: if there was ever a time I was questioning what we were doing, it was right now, and I think I even vocalized that question. We were on the sidewalk of someone's front doorstep where this woman had just bled all over the rug, and it was clearly not sanitary and safe for the baby or the woman, drug addict or not.

I got overruled, and the cord got cut anyway. The baby was safely put into the ambulance, and the mother was put into the other one. The ambulances drove away, and thankfully, the premature baby survived, although we were checking on the baby daily for several weeks after that. After the EMS units left, we had more work to do. But first, let's catch a breath. I told the Officers how great they did and how proud I was. They just delivered a baby on a doorstep (which they later won an award for at an awards banquet)!

Then, we had work to do. One Officer went to the hospital. We notified social services because the baby was going to be taken from the mother, the baby would not have been safe. We had to find and interview witnesses and see if we could get a confession and a search of the house of the drug dealer. We didn't get the latter. Oh well, the baby was safe. This is one of the stories I couldn't make up even if I tried.

"Merry Christmas to All," Said the Grinch

If you are a first responder, you go into the job with the understanding you will work holidays. If that doesn't work for you, don't sign up. Save the job for someone who will. I have sat through many interviews where the last question is, "Do you agree and understand you will have to sometimes have to work nights, weekends, and holidays throughout your career (or something like that)?"

Of course, without question, each applicant will answer with a "yes" because they want to get the approval of the hiring board and get the job. Then, later on down the road, I can't tell you how many times I have had to listen to Officers complain about having to work on holidays and different shifts as a Supervisor. It is cut-throat when it comes to taking days off half the time because everyone wants to be off with their family on the holidays. I have worked them all. Repeatedly.

In this particular year, I was the Sergeant on the lower end of the totem pole of seniority, and it was my first year as a Sergeant, so it was my turn. Christmas morning rolled around, and I wanted nothing more than to be at home with my girls when they woke up, and I was going to try my best to make that happen. Now...generally speaking, Christmas is the *one* day of the year people behave themselves for the most part, and we do not usually have a lot of calls. All the stores and restaurants are closed except for the gas stations, and our calls for services plummet. It is usually a quiet day. Usually.

And for the record, we forbid anyone to use the words, "It sure is quiet today." All you are doing is calling down the thunder upon yourself when you say those words. Never use those words on a shift. Trust me.

So it was Christmas morning and still dark outside. I sleeked out of bed and got ready in another room so I didn't wake my wife. I was able to get out of the house without waking even the dogs, and I drove off to work. I went into roll call and sat down at the Supervisor's desk. I was a Sergeant at the time. I wished everyone good morning and Merry Christmas. No one wanted to be there, but all seemed to be fairly jovial, at least. I got the question.

"Hey, Sarge. Would it be okay if we went to our houses to open presents with our families this morning?"

"I don't see a problem with that. I will be doing the same thing. Call out on the radio and don't be out there for too long, but yes," I responded.

A rookie Officer spoke up and said, "Sarge, I don't live in the city limits, and my house is out of my district. Is it okay if I go..."

I held up my hand and stopped him. "Is your home in the county?"

"Yes," he said.

"Is the city within this county?"

"Yes," he said, this time with a sly grin.

I responded to him, but I looked around the room at the shift when I said this next part, and I smiled back. "Answer your calls. Take care of one another on each other's calls. Let's not all get out to open presents at the same time so the city is left unattended, and I want to know where you are. Answer your calls. Am I clear?"

The group responded with understanding, and the morning went off without a hitch...at first. Everyone got to open presents with their families. I got to spend time with my girls. We had breakfast together, and they all were happy and content with their gifts and snuggled up in their pajamas on the couches and chairs. I only had a few more hours to go until the end of the shift. It was almost a textbook Christmas morning until it wasn't.

The radio had been silent for a long time, and the guys had been out patrolling the city when the tone drop came from dispatch for a domestic. Two of the Officers responded to the scene—good Officers and very competent in their duties. The next thing I heard on the radio was that they were in a major fight on Christmas morning. The man inside the house had assaulted the woman at the house and was refusing to go to jail. Now, he was fighting my Officers. He had refused to give any kind of compliance to the Officers and was attempting to grab household items as weapons.

The fight was on with them. There was a glass coffee table that got broken, and the man kept fighting and trying to hurt the Officers. They were in danger of getting sliced up by glass shards or hit in the head with something as he was still fighting. Finally, they were able to get him into custody. I flipped on the lights and siren and got there as soon and safely as I could. When I got there, the guy was still fighting and kicking, bleeding all over the place from the glass table he broke. Looking at the living room of the house, there had definitely been a fight, and glass was everywhere!

The Officers called EMS immediately to get the man medical attention. They were updating me on what had happened, and other Officers had already arrived on scene to take the suspect away from the two Officers he had fought. They were worked up, and it was what needed to happen so another fight didn't happen. I looked at him as the other Officers were talking to him and nearly puked.

This guy, on Christmas morning, had fought my Officers, nearly hurt them, gotten himself hurt, and he did it all with a nasty, gangrene foot. It was green and black like the Grinch himself, and I could not believe my eyes. This guy didn't even look like he should be walking or his toes would fall off in the snow, but here we were trying to keep him and his feet warm and get him bandaged up before he got to go spend Christmas Day in jail.

I have seen lots of dead bodies in my career and lots of really, really gross things, but never in the history of my career had I seen a man with his foot probably needing to be amputated, drunk and fighting, on Christmas morning. Thankfully, no one was severely hurt, not even the man with the messed up foot. Again, this is the kind of stuff you just can't make up. Merry Christmas to all, even the man who was a real-life Grinch on Christmas.

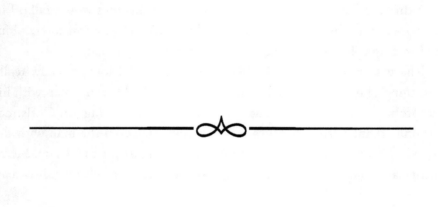

There Is So Much More to Say

There are books upon books about leadership, and I have had to learn so much in my growing as a leader, I still learn every day. I have stories upon stories to make you laugh, cry, and probably scream with rage about the things I dealt with in my career. I could talk about personnel issues, dealing with problem employees, trying to lead when you are not supported in your cause, or even employee discipline. There is so much information about leadership that could be a book I write within itself.

Suffice it to say one of the most valuable lessons I have had to learn in supervision and leadership is that I am only human, too. My people are human, and we all fall short. I have had to learn how to redirect my own emotions, though admittedly, I don't always do that well. But I always want to be a man of honor who supports what is right and supports people. I don't always agree with people or what they bring to me, but I really do try not to minimize how someone feels about a particular issue. I try to remember that even though it is not a priority to me, it may be a priority to them.

If you truly care about people, you must put aside your own needs sometimes and work toward the good of others or the organization. In time, this is how we can effectively grow closer together and how teams can be formed. I haven't always done it correctly, but I have tried to do what is right by my people and what is fair. That is a reasonable request anyone should ask anyone who wants to step into leadership and lead others.

"Talk to Me": Stories from a Police Negotiator

Wow. That is all I can say as I start this chapter and reflect on these moments. There have been some wild ones. And this chapter just covers a few of them very briefly. One word sums up working as a police negotiator. *Pressure.*

Pressure from all sides and the stress that comes with it is unseen and rarely discussed. Pressure from the person in crisis you are trying to build a relationship and negotiate with. Pressure from the Command Staff who want a safe resolution to an event without costing hundreds of hours in a budget for manpower. Pressure from your team of Emergency Response Unit members who are in the elements and are ready to go tactical to do their thing and really are not concerned about what I am saying, nor any other negotiator, on the phone or face to face with a subject or suspect. Pressure from family members who don't want us to hurt their loved one in crisis. Pressure from the community who have been displaced from their homes because bullets can travel through walls, and they must be kept safe. Pressure from the real fact that my words truly have the power of life and death based upon what I say to someone or my tone and voice inflection. Pressure.

Everything in life can be viewed as a negotiation. Your marriage is a negotiation. Dealing with your children and your family is a negotiation. Going to your job and working with people can be a negotiation. Winning souls for Jesus can be a negotiation in its own way. For me, sometimes, even finding the strength within myself to keep fighting the fight is its own negotiation.

I will never forget going to a training for becoming a negotiator when the police department flew me to Las Vegas for the class. The class was great, but the trip was overall terrible. I flew into Las Vegas by myself and stayed at Palace Station Hotel and Casino. It is an older hotel, not on the strip. That is where the training was located, and all we had to do was walk downstairs and we would be there. That was a good thing.

The first two days of class were good on Monday and Tuesday. On Tuesday night, I went to a mall to do some Christmas shopping for the girls since Christmas was only a few weeks away. While there at the mall, I got hungry. I went to this wrap place to get food. I got a chicken wrap, but I won't tell you the name of the place because of what happened later. On Wednesday, December 10 (my birthday), we finished class that day, and I went back to the mall to finish up the shopping. I didn't have anyone I knew with me, so really, it was just killing time rather than going to waste money in a casino. I got hungry again, so I went back to that wrap place in the mall while shopping. This time, the experience was not the same.

That night, on my birthday, alone in Las Vegas, I got the worst food poisoning I have ever had in my entire life. I felt like I wanted to die. I was hovering over the toilet all night long just to survive. It was awful.

I am telling you all this because the next day is when we were assigned to do scenarios training during the class. They brought in actors and extras, cool equipment to use and test, role players, and coaches, and we were evaluated on how we did as a team and individually as a negotiator. I didn't care. My body felt like it was dying from being sick the night before. I had nothing to give anyone. I remember one of the actors who was playing a suspect on the other end of the phone saying, "I'm gonna kill her! I'm gonna _____ kill her!"

In my mind, I am thinking, *Well, if you could stop talking about it and just do it, we could all be done with this training, and I can go back to my hotel room and die or puke or both.* I didn't say that, though. I wanted to, but I didn't. Hey, I am just being transparent here about this. This is that part they don't talk about in policing.

We come to work sick. We come to work hurt. We come to work with no sleep. We miss birthday parties and family events and holidays. We have issues just like everyone else. That day was a hard lesson for me, and it was a long day, but I had to find the words to say and do my job, even if it was just training. The night before, when I needed someone to care for me and even pamper me a bit, was even longer. It was miserable.

I have had encounters with several people over the years on repeated occasions. When people are in a mental crisis, it is difficult to get them to cooperate with what you want them to do. The first occasion dealing with this female, who was a juvenile at the time, she was going to kill herself over her boyfriend breaking up with her. She had climbed onto the roof of her house and was going to grab the power line, running to her home to electrocute herself.

She knew I was stalling in what I was saying to her on the ground, and meanwhile, firefighters and Police Officers were putting up ladders and trying to get up onto the roof with her to make the situation manageable and act quickly if needed. This was only agitating her further as she saw people on the roof coming toward her. The intense situation only ended when she had to be tackled while on the roof by one of the Officers because she was making a dive for the power line. Now picture this: a slanted roof, a distraught female juvenile who was non-compliant and in mental crisis, and then having to make a decision in a split second to do this and risk further getting people hurt from falling off the roof. This time, the gamble worked. She had become distracted by so many people around her and talking to her that she couldn't focus on everything at once. When she made the move, we were ready. That day was a great job by all the people involved in the incident.

On another occasion with this same female, she was standing on a railroad bridge that was an overpass to the main ByPass in town. She was about two-and-a-half to three stories up from the ByPass, and traffic had to be shut down from both directions. She was in a mental crisis, this time again about the boyfriend, and was threatening to jump. If she had jumped, the fall *might* not have killed her as long as she didn't dive head-first over, which was a possibility. But if traffic had been flowing, she would have definitely been hit by a car as she jumped.

We were in a standoff. She had no weapon that I knew of, but she definitely had the advantage in the situation. You see, she had the aerial viewpoint of the scene, and she was on the railroad tracks. Railroad tracks are cleared, and you have a 360 view around you when you are on the bridge. By my estimate, the bridge is about thirty to forty yards long and across the ByPass. She knew traffic was shut down because she kept commenting on all the lights. She was asking to talk to her boyfriend and have him come to the scene so he could watch her jump off and kill herself (this is a common thing said among people I have dealt with who are suicidal or in a standoff).

Officers had gone to both sides of the bridge, and when they would try to get closer to her, she would begin to hang off the side of the bridge, at one point even dangling with her arms. I ordered the Officers back as she and I yelled back and forth to each other. One of the other negotiators arrived on scene and assisted me with intel as we continued to work through the situation. I had known this girl since she was eleven years old when I first started working in the schools as a School Resource Officer. This was the same girl we had to tackle on the roof. She was serious and not to be tested.

I learned another valuable lesson that day about negotiations and myself. There is a reason this chapter is called "Talk to Me" and not "Listen to Me." In all the training we had, and even with the motto being "Talk to Me," I should learn to shut my mouth more. I am a fixer by nature, and sometimes, I need to let things play out and just listen to someone rather than fix them. I admit this fault in myself; I am a fixer, but that day in particular stands out to me because I got called out on it.

I remember her screaming at me from the bridge while I was down below on the street, and she was talking about how all we wanted to do was take her to jail and open the road again. We didn't care anything about her, and she told me I was trying to fix her instead of listening to what she was saying. Now, to her credit, she was right about us needing to open the road again, but not at the expense of someone's life. She was not right in the fact that we didn't care about her. She was right about me needing to listen better and stop trying to find a solution to her life. What we needed was a resolution... for that moment, then we would take one step at a time from there.

So, we talked. And by we talked, I mean she did most of the talking instead of me. She talked about many things I already knew, but I listened anyway. She talked about her family and her home life. She talked about her problems with her boyfriend. She talked about how she felt unloved. Eventually, after some time talking, I thought I would try to bring a resolution to this situation. Remember the pressure I was talking about? There is always pressure to hurry up and solve the problem and resolve the situation. Always.

I called the audible (at least in my own mind, I did) like a quarterback. I changed how we were running the play. I started talking about ice cream.

Then, when we started talking about ice cream, the conversation went to milkshakes. We talked about our favorite milkshakes. Officers moved inward on the bridge one step at a time and not all at the same time. She saw it. She was back on her feet and up and agitated again. And we were back in the same situation we had been in before, except this time, we had something to build on.

I started walking on the street toward the side of the bridge I wanted her to go to. We had jumped over the concrete barrier on the ByPass enough. We had the Officer on that side of the bridge back off. And we started talking about milkshakes again. Then, here it was. I threw the *Hail Mary* play as a last-ditch effort before we had to do something else. I offered a milkshake to her. This threw her off a bit, but there was some trust built there. I kept asking her about milkshakes and if she wanted one. The Officer on the other side of the bridge was now on the bridge fully, and she knew the walking area of the bridge had been closed in.

She was now pushed to one side of the bridge rather than two; she could not run back and forth across. She seemed to be agitated by this but had stopped cussing at me. I focused on the milkshake. I told her if she would come down safely and get some help and allow us to get her checked out at a hospital, I would personally deliver the milkshake in whatever flavor she wanted. I remember her asking, "You're not going to take me to jail?"

"Of course not!" I said. "We are going to get you help at the hospital, and I am going to bring you a milkshake like I told you I would."

What happened next happened really quickly and did not go how I would have wanted it to, but we adapted all the same. It never goes exactly how you plan it. People are unpredictable. She walked over to the ledge where the bridge ended. The Officer on that side had backed off as instructed. She went around to the rocks and started to climb herself down. Unfortunately, the slate rocks and the small cliff gave out underneath her feet, and she ultimately ended up doing more of a slide down from rocks. This caused some minor cuts and scrapes and abrasions, but it was not a suicide or her jumping off the bridge.

She was met by myself and the other negotiator, and other Officers and emergency personnel joined us quickly. We brought the ambulance to the scene, and she was transported to the hospital, which was only about a block away and close to the bridge. Success.

After an almost three-hour standoff and shutting down traffic while she stood on a railroad bridge and we stood in the middle of the road, the girl came down from the bridge over the most random thing ever: a milkshake. I delivered the milkshake to the emergency room, and she got the help she needed. The last time I spoke to her before I retired, she was an adult and was having a very successful career. We didn't talk about that day anymore. It was in the past. God used a milkshake that day to change someone's life. And in case you are wondering, it was a strawberry milkshake.

It has not always been successful. People I have talked to at one time would later go and commit suicide. People I have tried to negotiate with have many times forced our hand and had all intentions of making us go tactical on them in the beginning.

I have had suspects set fire to an entire apartment complex building while he was still inside after I thought we were making progress. As I mentioned elsewhere in the book, I was trying to take care of my team and try something different and negotiate in a new way since he had been talking to me for two and a half hours. We were going round and round and round and not making much progress, but he was still talking and had stopped shooting at us. He was popping off rounds inside the apartment, but not at the police or his kids and girlfriend anymore. I was briefing the Chief and Assistant Chief about the options and what was going on when the whole scene changed, and the building became engulfed very quickly. Firefighters couldn't approach the building to put out the fire because he could shoot at them.

What transpired from my team of Officers in the next few minutes, not me, was something only heroes do. They stood there next to the building as he was in the window with a gun, and the building was fully engulfed in flames. I was there with them, but it was no longer me on the phone. This situation had gone tactical because the suspect forced it to. He had the gun in his hand and was screaming back and forth with the Officers on the ground. He ultimately fell out of the second-story window a few minutes later as a bailout effort due to the fire.

On the ground, he still refused to put the gun down for several minutes. They finally convinced him to as the flames licked the night sky, and snow and rain fell lightly. They had stood within ten yards of the building while it was on fire and stood their ground while the heat continued to blast even on the winter night until the suspect surrendered safely and put the gun down. I am so thankful he did not point that gun at them.

After talking with him for so long while he was in crisis and knowing him as a person, I found a comparison to give you to that night. After hours of talking and negotiating, this is how I felt. Bruce Wayne's butler, Alfred Pennyworth, said it best about the Joker, played by Heath Ledger in Christopher Nolan's movie "The Dark Knight." "...some men can't be reasoned or negotiated with. Some men just want to watch the world burn."

I have had domestic abusers and would-be murderers on the phone with hostages while we listened to him cocking the pistol over and over and over again, the victims next to him. This one resulted in a fourteen-hour standoff where our agency was not the lead agency. We were only called in as negotiators. We were ordered to stand down when Kentucky State Police came and took command because they have their own team, but their negotiators heard the same thing.

Sometimes, it doesn't matter what you say or do. People just want to watch the chaos happen, and you, as an Officer, just became part of the equation and the game. The pressure and stress are astronomical.

We have come a long way in law enforcement regarding mental health. Officers in Kentucky and even across the country are now trained in Crisis Intervention, and it is much of the same material as Crisis/Hostage Negotiations. Every Officer negotiates on nearly every call, whether it is with a suspect or even two people involved in a non-injury collision.

The field of law enforcement and dealing with the general public is a privilege and an honor to serve. However, it is not all puppies and rainbows and very often deals with people at the worst times of their lives, in their moments of crisis. We have a duty as a society to provide first responders with the mental health resources they need to survive their careers and after as they serve others to help them survive their times of crisis. Not all negotiations end badly, but every one of them takes a toll on the Officers and first responders involved. Keep that in mind.

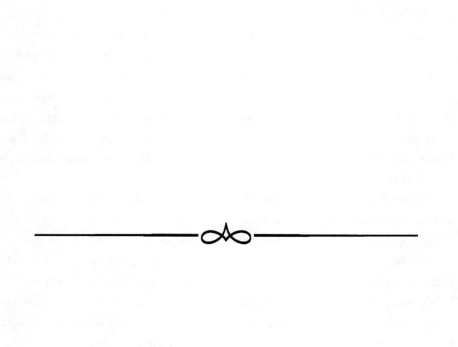

Operation: Save Bambi

I have worked with so many great Officers on search warrants I cannot even count them. I have worked some wild cases, just like every other Officer has as well. The last few years before I retired were the most stressful and yet some of the most fun years for big cases I worked or assisted with throughout my whole career.

One such case I assisted with that comes to mind was one of drug traffickers who were also in possession of stolen property, cut-off catalytic converters, and most importantly...one little baby deer they were keeping. We had gotten intelligence through the investigation that the drug dealers were feeding the baby deer methamphetamine. Now listen, I have heard of some jacked-up things in my life, but feeding a baby deer meth?! Come on!

Well, anyway, as we were all discussing it in the office, the Detectives came up with the idea to get a search warrant for the residence based on the "cruelty to animals" statute in the KRS. I was skeptical with them, and I told them it would never work and that it was way too much of a stretch to get a Judge to sign a search warrant over a baby deer. We all laughed about it, and they said they were going to try it anyway.

I have never been so excited to be proven wrong on a case in my life! I can't decide if they were lucky or genius in that ploy, but they got the search warrant signed by a Judge for the residence and the property based upon cruelty to animals charge and the fact that it shocks the conscience. Who in their normal or right mind would do that?!

Now that they had the search warrant, they started the planning and operations for the execution of the warrant. The team was assembled, and everyone was briefed on the OPS plan. Everyone was given their role, and I contacted dispatch to notify the ambulance to be on standby and make dispatch aware of our location. Here we go!

We went around a curve on a country road and saw the mobile home. Everyone bailed out of their vehicles, and we hit the house. You are not going to believe this. Inside the house was a little baby deer! We served the search warrant for the house and found some stolen property and some narcotics, and the people were also charged with their arrest warrants.

In addition to that, we seized the baby deer and had to transport it in the back of our crime scene van. We got to the station and contacted Fish & Wildlife Management, and they were on the way to get the deer to take it somewhere safe. In the meantime, we told some of the patrol Officers at the station there was a deer in the back of the van. They didn't believe us. That is not something that seems rational, of course.

Finally, one of them went over to the van and opened the door. He looked inside and closed the door really quickly. "There really is a baby deer in the back of the crime scene van." Everyone went over to see it, and smiles were seen all around.

We went over our debrief of what went well on the OPS plan and execution and what didn't, as well as what we could do better. Long story short, though, here are my thoughts on it:

Everyone went home safe, and no one got hurt. Bad guys got arrested. We got some drugs off the street. We got some stolen property. I got to work with great Officers and Detectives and tell this story for a book. And, the coolest part: we rescued a baby deer during a search warrant.

OPERATION: SAVE BAMBI
Mission Status: **SUCCESS**

WORKING DURING THE COVID-19 PANDEMIC

I have a friend of mine who uses the expression, "I've got one nerve left, and you are standing on it." Now, I *know* this is going to strike a nerve with some people, and there could be the possibility you burn this book or, at the very least, throw it across the room when you reach this chapter. I prepared myself for that reaction. However, this is my experience while dealing with the COVID-19 pandemic and working as a Police Officer.

I must openly admit: when it all happened, and now, looking back, it is a blur of how we shut an entire world down. I won't go into conspiracy theories or thoughts I have of political ideology regarding the entire thing, but what I will do is tell you my experience from my family's perspective and give you a grasp of what it was like to work through the pandemic. At first, I didn't believe it was going to be real, and everything was going to be fine—just the media blowing things out of proportion (which they did). I was skeptical. Then, they canceled sports. March Madness, the NBA, and so many others. No more UK Basketball? What?

Then came the masks and the protocol and procedures from what the CDC *thought* we should do. From the recommendations of the CDC, the local health departments and the government stepped in and decided what we were all going to do. This is when the nonsense began. I get it. People did the best they could as they were ordered by the government and the Center for Disease Control (CDC). We were in uncharted waters and had to navigate through what we believed was best, but as a Supervisor, I don't think I have ever been as mad as I was during the initial stages of shutting the world down.

Every day, it seemed, a new procedure would come down from the CDC to the health departments to the community and orders to the police department. Every day, something different to adjust to in leadership and having to find a way to motivate our people while having to work short-staffed. If we got exposed, we got sent to the house for a period of time. Ten days, five days, three days, or whatever the number was for that specific week of the pandemic. First, it was the government saying, "Just a few weeks," we would be making sure everyone was *safe*. The word *immunity* got thrown around a lot. Next thing I knew, almost an entire year had passed.

Anyway, we had daily reminders from the media, and America glued itself to what the media said. Politicians went on the air daily to give us a death count of how many people had died.

Let me be clear on something.

I have been sick with COVID, and it was terrible. My family has been sick with COVID. I have lost dear friends to COVID. But leadership should give hope during a time of crisis, not instill fear in daily media releases. Leadership should always provide hope.

Then, it was decided for us that we would pull the kids out of school. For my family, this was very challenging, just like it was for other families. Our oldest was in high school at the time. Our youngest in elementary school. My wife was working in healthcare at the time, and I was in law enforcement. There was no capability to stay at home and work via Zoom (although I did really enjoy the implementation of Zoom meetings and still do) to help our children succeed in their work for school during the day. There was no childcare. Our childcare became a home surveillance system and communication through electronics. We had no choice.

Our oldest daughter is more of an introvert, so at first, she really loved doing the homeschool thing. Our youngest daughter is an extrovert, so she immediately hated it. The kids missed classes, assignments, couldn't get logged on, lost connection with the WiFi, and had all sorts of issues. They cried about not understanding math, and we, as parents, were not able to help them very much because they have changed the way they do math in schools since we were young. We could find the answer, but it would be wrong because it was not the way they do it now. After a few weeks of this, even our oldest was ready to go back to school.

To break up the frustration and sadness of this time period, there were one or two funny moments. I remember on one occasion, our youngest got on the Zoom class from our living room. She had her mask on. The teacher giggled and told her she did not have to wear her mask at home while in class.

God bless our teachers for working through these troubling waters and times. I know you didn't sign up for that on Zoom.

But in all seriousness, that is how conditioned we made our kids during this time. And if we are really being honest about it as a society, we are still reaping the whirlwind of what it was like to send our kids home over an entire year without normal human interaction. We sent some kids home to places where it was unsafe when they had safety and meals and shelter for at least eight hours out of the day while they were in school.

Calls for service to the police went down drastically at first. Then, commercial burglaries went up for businesses because we had shut everything down, it seemed, except for the major grocery stores that probably made billions of dollars during this time while the small home businesses were forced to hang on for dear life, go into debt, and many eventually close their doors permanently. Then, everyone was cooped up at home with their families, and the domestics started to rise again. Then, the criminals stopped caring about COVID and what the government told them to do (big shock), and the crime began to rise again. To add to the icing on that cake, the government started giving benefits to everyone to offset the financial burden.

Drug users used this money and benefits to pay the drug dealers, and business was booming again! This is also the time our state and much of the nation began to have a crisis with heroin and fentanyl, and the overdose cases hit an all-time high. The death investigations and bodies were literally piling up between COVID and the overdoses.

The frustration continued for me when I got exposed to who knows who with COVID, and the health department was keeping their running list of who could be "infected." I will not apologize for this next statement. I have a real problem with that. This is an overreach of power by the government. Period.

I got contacted by the health department that day after I went home from working out amongst the world and while my wife worked front line in health care because we were known as "essential." I was told that day on the phone I would have to go to work, wear a mask, and continue to make sure I was providing for society since I was essential as a worker. Then, when I got home, I was told I had to stay in my home and was not allowed to leave.

Now listen, I have been told some stupid things before in my life, but this one might take the award for it. I hope you will see my frustration. If I need to stay home, fine. If I need to go to work, fine. But do not tell me that I, nor my wife, have to go to work and deal with literally anyone and everyone who could have anything, then come home and stay in my home and not be allowed to leave.

That was not a very nice conversation by the end of those instructions. The person on the other end of the line told me to "do my best" to abide by that, and I said, "Sure, I will do what I can." I hung up the phone and steamed for a while after that. To the health department worker, it is not your fault. You were just doing as you were told. I'm sorry.

But wait! There's more!

The maddest I have ever been as a Supervisor was during the pandemic. It really does take a lot to get me fired up, and if I do get really angry, I usually blow up, and then it is over. This was not the case.

Numerous employees from my shift had been exposed to someone with COVID. We were working short-staffed and dangerously close to being in emergency mandatory overtime as a department and not having enough police on the street. On this particular day, three of my employees got exposed on the same call for service. They had to be decontaminated, along with their clothes, their cruiser, and then we had to get them home because now they were not allowed to be at work. When you are only running with six to seven people for the day on that shift, this is a major hit.

All of them met at our Training Center and had to leave their cruisers. Then, in an open parking lot, because we had nowhere for them to go, they had to strip down to underwear and T-shirts and be decontaminated while someone in a HAZMAT suit sprayed them down. I was tasked as the Supervisor to clean their gear with some special spray to kill the virus, and their uniforms were to be heat treated with really hot heat by the fire department guys who were on scene. I will never, and I mean *never*, forget standing out there doing all this in the absolute pouring rain and thunderstorms as the fire department guys laughed at me getting mad while standing in a covered garage. There was no other place to decontaminate this stuff due to the safety hazard according to the CDC regulations for that week.

The rain made me mad because it was like I had buckets poured on me. Eventually, I gave in and just realized I was going to be wet that day. But the thing that made me the maddest, I think, was the embarrassment I had to put my Officers through by making them strip down and take away their dignity for this nonsensical procedure given to us by an organization that also thought it was okay for us to go to work and then try to force us to stay at home after work.

Another part of this story during the time of the pandemic was when we had people rioting all over the country about police brutality while the national media spewed half-truths to fit their particular narrative and cities burned. Nobody has a bigger problem with bad cops than the good cops. We don't get to have our voices heard, or at least no one cares to ask. The media continued to show footage of rioting in cities and never said anything about COVID risks while people were looting and destroying and wearing their COVID medical masks so no one could see their identity. Worse still, they remained silent when most weren't wearing any masks at all. I even heard it called "peaceful protesting" at one point. It made me sick.

Jim Morrison of The Doors once said, "Whoever controls the media controls the mind." If you don't believe me, why do news stations run the same stories over and over? Why do social media platforms target the younger audience?

The country became divided over those who were vaccinated and those who weren't. Churches were shut down along with everything else. There were those who chose to go against the government and CDC orders. That's when law enforcement became used to enforce what we had no business being involved in, and people got arrested for violating what the CDC said.

Then, there was a toilet paper shortage for some reason as people hoarded it away, and along came the formula shortage for babies. The list goes on and on. In the meantime, big executives from pharmaceutical companies made billions off the backs of the people and the pandemic. Small businesses were forced to close their doors, while the larger stores were allowed to stay open because they were deemed "essential."

My wife and all the other healthcare workers continued to do amazing things and treat sick people while the world focused on COVID. To those of you who served during this time, I know it was difficult. First responders continued to respond to calls for service. COVID or no COVID. I know it was frustrating. You don't have to tell me. Thank you. To the teachers who continued to create new ways of learning despite the constant challenges, thank you. To all the first responders, thank you. To the store clerks and those who stocked the shelves, thank you. To the churches who went virtual and those who stayed in the pulpit to give us hope during a dark time, thank you.

To those who never gave up and made it through, thank you. Those who lost loved ones, my heart breaks for you, and I am with you. You are essential.

No one should be told they are not essential. You are all essential.

Bodies All Around Us

I was so sick of death when I retired. I still am. I really don't think people realize, unless you are a first responder, Coroner, funeral home staff, or one of their family members, just how much death we see on a weekly basis. I honestly don't know how our Coroner, a man I deeply respect, does it all the time.

When I retired as Support Services Major and worked with the Criminal Investigations Unit, our Detectives for our agency of just over sixty Officers investigated over fifty overdose death investigations within one year. Just a little lower than the previous year. Just so you know, this might be another one of those chapters to strike some nerves with some people, but that's okay. If this offends anyone, you are welcome to come work the world we work and see what we see, try to view it from a different perspective, and perhaps we will find common ground.

To put it bluntly, America as a society has a consumption problem. We have an addiction problem. We have a drug problem, we have a drinking problem, we consume too much food and don't exercise enough, we watch too much television, we shop too much, and more. That is why other countries provide us with the things we need or want. It could be legal or illegal.

There are those on the side of the legalization of marijuana. I have fought against it because that was the law my entire career. It was never legalized in Kentucky for recreational use while I was an Officer. It was legalized in other states. The politicians and the advocates for it stated it would bring revenue to the states where it was legalized, and it may have just done that.

But what it also did was increase the amount of drugged driving arrests and deliver a financial hit to the drug cartels for one of their biggest profit margins. When this happened, the drug cartels were not to be outdone. They were not going to lose money. They flooded the streets of the United States with crystal meth and heroin, then eventually fentanyl and cara-fentanyl.

Now, put into perspective, this was about the time the COVID-19 pandemic hit. Bodies were popping up everywhere in our town and every single week. We found them in homes, in hotels, in the woods decomposed, in cars slumped over the wheel in the school pick-up lines. Everywhere. Was any of this uttered in the national media? Not that I can remember. Now add to that all of the deaths from suicides, natural deaths, a few homicide investigations, and everything considered COVID-related. There were bodies seemingly all around us. Stacks and stacks of case files from death investigations piled up on my desk and the desk of my Sergeant, just waiting to be divided up amongst the Detectives. They still had all their other cases of sexual assaults, thefts, robberies, and so many more to work. My team was getting overwhelmed and tired, and there wasn't any relief in sight.

We were in a Command Staff meeting one morning, and my friend, who retired as the Assistant Chief and had the same amount of time as me, had been a Detective for many years. He asked me about an investigation and was giving me a hard time in jest. He said, "When I was in CID, we had this many investigations and solved our cases a lot faster," smiling as he said it.

I didn't miss a beat. I responded, "When you were in CID, you had more Detectives, and you didn't have bodies falling from the sky every single day." He didn't say anything else. I smiled back and looked at the Chief. He was smiling, too.

We would track down where the drugs came from, find out it was fentanyl, find out it was given by whatever drug dealer, and even get search warrants. Lots and lots of police work went into what seemed like the only things we worked on: death investigations. Then, we would charge someone with the offense of manslaughter, only for it to get dismissed through the courts for whatever reason. How, as a leader, could I motivate my people to keep fighting the good fight for the families of the victims when the courts or even half the general public believe it was the victim's fault for taking the drugs? Why should we care?

I heard so much during that time about Black Lives Matter, Blue Lives Matter, and All Lives Matter. It was all races and genders who were dying. How could we truly say All Lives Matter if we have people dying in multiple races, people rotting in prisons when they shouldn't be there, or people getting let out of prison when they shouldn't be? Our system and our mindset are flawed all around.

I remember specifically going to a call at a hotel. A little girl was outside in the hallway with EMS. She couldn't have been more than four or five years old. Her father had not checked out on time, so housekeeping and management came to check the room. There was no mom. The little blonde-haired girl in the blue and pink pajamas did not answer the door and was watching the Mickey Mouse Clubhouse on her iPad when the hotel staff entered the room.

When I entered the room, I immediately saw the drug paraphernalia on the nightstand next to the man's head, who was very clearly deceased for a significant amount of time. On the fold-out couch was a makeshift bed of little blankets and a teddy bear with one little pink pillow.

They found the little girl sitting in the chair, trying to be quiet and not wake Daddy, who was sleeping. When I interviewed her a few minutes later in the lobby, she told me she had seen Daddy's lips and skin turn blue, and he was cold when she touched him, so she covered him up with a blanket, trying to make him warm. She went back to playing on her iPad and let Daddy sleep. She didn't have anything to eat and had gotten really hungry. She hadn't eaten since last night, she said. It was almost seven o'clock the next evening.

This is just one of the many stories I could tell from all of the overdoses we worked while I was an Officer. They haven't stopped. We are losing entire generations of people of all ages, young and old, to drugs that are no respecter of persons. How do we stop it? It is sad to say, I don't believe there is any stopping it.

There is a way to give comfort to the broken, support those who are grieving, and help guide the ones who are lost. There is a way to change your perspective and open your eyes to the fact the world doesn't revolve around one individual or one cause or one single thing. We are all tied together, no matter whether we choose to believe it or not. The death investigations my team worked so hard to solve affect the general public. The children of the parents who die are affected by the loss of their parent and may even interact with my own daughter or your own child. We are all affected. Should we turn a blind eye to those in need? Should we allow people to deal poisons in our streets and in our schools? Should we allow mental health to go unaddressed? Should Christians remain silent as the church is so great at doing or persecute when it should love, which it is also so great at doing? Or should we come together in love and push back the darkness?

I know what my answer is. Give me the torch. The darkness has to go.

THE DAY GOD MADE ME LAY DOWN

God has a way of slowing you down if you don't listen to Him. I had so many people telling me that if I didn't slow down, it would catch up to me. My wife, especially, kept telling me to slow down and stop doing so much for everyone else. I was drinking several energy drinks a day at about 300 mg of caffeine each, running on very little sleep (probably because of the caffeine), working long hours, and doing anything I could to serve others... because that is who I am (look up what Enneagram 2 is).

It wasn't just my wife, though. It was my mom, my oldest daughter, my best friends, coworkers, and even people in my LifeGroup at church. Most of these people are those closest to me. Out of this list of people, though, even those who were not the closest to me were telling me to slow down from the pace I was moving at. Looking back now, this was probably God speaking through other people trying to get my attention. As usual, I was too stubborn or moving too fast to pay attention.

At the time, I had recently been moved into the role of Support Services Commander and had been there a little over a year. My rank was Lieutenant, and I had turned in my Major's promotion packet, which is the equivalent of a giant resume in book format about my whole professional life. My role as Support Services Commander included being responsible for the Criminal Investigations Division (Detectives), several grants for money and the agency, Parking Enforcement for the City of Richmond, park security, the internship program, Hostage/Crisis Negotiations Unit, Evidence Technicians and all evidence for the agency (over 100,000 pieces of evidence), Honor Guard, and the UAS (Drone) Unit. I was also still responsible for helping to plan our RPD Summer Camp, which is five weeks of fun-filled adventure for between twenty-five and fifty kids. For the administrators and Officers running the camp, it is a logistics nightmare that involves money from the budget and planning to the Nth degree. I am quite certain there was something else thrown in there I am forgetting, but I am building the suspense for the day my career could have been over and the extreme stress compounding on my body.

If you made it through that entire paragraph above without skipping it or falling asleep, you will at least see the amount of responsibility I was given for the Richmond Police Department in that role, and you will probably recognize the stress I was under. That being said, I have worked with some of the most amazing people in law enforcement in my career. At times in CID, they have needed help because of the schedule. I even took part in the on-call schedule for the Detectives. So, for the role of Support Services Commander, I was basically on call constantly for one thing or another. This did not always sit well with my family, especially getting called out in the middle of the night or to major crime scenes or stand-offs requiring our Emergency Response Unit (SWAT Team, to put it in a recognizable term).

There was one incident in December when I got called out for a hostage negotiation with the ERU Team for a barricaded male who had hostages. I spoke about it in the chapter about some of my stories from a negotiator. Here is even more context and detail to that story. While I was getting ready in our bedroom, my wife and two daughters were in the room, and I turned on the radio. When we listened on the radio, we heard gunshots as the Officers were screaming through transmissions and being shot at. This is what I was going out to, and my family heard it. I was out all night, and they hardly slept from crying and worrying about me and the other Officers.

The man at first had hostages, who were his ex-girlfriend and their small children. He let them leave, but then we got into an hours-long stand-off with him, and I negotiated over the phone with him for several hours. I had our Officers standing outside in the snow and rain while I was trying to talk to this guy, who continued to pop off rounds even while I was on the phone with him. I made the decision to try something different because we could not win while the suspect was warm inside the apartment while we were fighting the elements. When he hung up because we were getting nowhere and I was mentally exhausted from going round and round with him while he was drunk and high, I was on the phone with his mother trying to convince her to be what we call in negotiations training as a TPI, Third Party Intermediary. It is something I always tried never to utilize except as a last resort because it really could go either way with the bad guy. But his mother had a good relationship with him, so I thought it could work. Our people were cold, wet, and something had to give. I truly was trying to think of our officers with my plan.

Meanwhile, as I am on the phone with his mother, the suspect decided (I guess) he was bored and thought we needed another challenge. Now, at this point, you feel free to read the undertone of sarcasm that I am completely throwing in here. A few moments later, I heard on the radio one of the ERU members state they observed smoke from the building the suspect was in. Then, the smoke turned into visible fire. From there, the entire building caught ablaze, and flames rolled out of the windows and the rooftop while black smoke billowed into the night. That idiot had set the building on fire while he was in there. My assumption is he believed we would come rescue him, or he could funnel us into the home while it was on fire and shoot at us.

Let me further paint the picture by saying the building is halfway engulfed in flames as smoke and fire licked the night sky. The firefighters on scene were not going anywhere near that building because of the gunfire, and neither were we...at first. On the off chance that some of my coworkers hopefully read this book, I don't want to give them too much credit and let it go to their heads, but those guys were heroes for real that night.

The suspect was then spotted on the second floor of the apartment building window while the building was engulfed. He still had a gun in his hand, and he had not given it up. The guys on the ERU Team did what they do best: they saved lives. They continued the stand-off with the suspect from the ground next to a burning building and talked him out of the building while he was still screaming at me and trying to talk to me. I was around the corner and ordered to stay there at that time with some equipment. The suspect fell out of the window with the gun in his hand and continued to ignore Officer commands to drop the weapon. When he finally threw the gun away from him, he was taken into custody. I know any of the guys reading this who had been there can probably still feel the heat from the building.

As I was walking with another Officer, we were taking the suspect to EMS for medical attention and sat him down in the ambulance. One of my Detectives, who is currently (at least as of this book being written) the ERU

Team Leader, had taken his helmet off since we believed we were away from the scene enough to do so. At that moment, some man came from around the corner of the ambulance and tried to attack the suspect by hitting him in the head with a large, heavy-duty thermos. He nearly struck the Officer, and we ended up having to fight this unknown male on the ground and arrest him, too. This was the night that kept on giving.

I was beating myself up mentally because I had not been able to get the suspect to surrender. And then, he decided to set an entire apartment complex on fire, displace several families from their homes, and cause almost a million dollars in damages. And you know just as well as I do he was not going to have to pay for that. As the ERU Team was debriefing and I was listening to what went well and what went bad (I was one of the bad parts even though I know I can never predict what someone will do), I was gearing down mentally from that role in order to transition to another role. My Detectives were on scene, and several of them were on the ERU Team. Now that the major incident was completed, we had to do what we do at a crime scene and collect whatever evidence we could that had not been destroyed by the suspect, the fire, or the fire department as they had put out the fire. It was time to work through the remainder of the night and help our outstanding Detectives preserve what we could.

I remember our Detectives and I leaving that scene very early in the morning hours. They were exhausted. I was exhausted. And when I got home, I remember finding the lights on in the house and my wife asleep in the bed with the lights on. My youngest daughter was asleep on the couch because she had tried to stay up to wait for me. Actually, both my girls tried to stay up all night and wait for me. My wife said she was worried about me all night long until exhaustion finally kicked in for her, too.

I said all of that story (and there is even more to it) to say this: these are the kinds of things they didn't talk much about in the academy. These are the constant stressors put on a Police Officer daily. Perhaps not to the extreme as the call I just spoke about, but the daily grind of patrol. Take into account the schedule, also. Second shift, third shift? These are not normal hours for the human body overall. What about the consistent negativity and dealing with people's problems every day? Sure, there are those who would say we sign up for it, and that is true, but the body is never truly ready for that kind of wear and tear. That is why Police Officers have back problems from the heavy gear. We have heart attacks, high blood pressure, diabetes, and a number of other things. In my situation, something else entirely.

Sure, they have you read a book about it, but what if your family isn't a bunch of readers overall? Does that mean they shouldn't get the information? And besides, my youngest was ten years old at the time, and my oldest eighteen...they are likely not going to grasp that kind of book dealing with trauma and law enforcement. But I will tell you this: they were sure affected by something that happened to me a few months later.

My dear friend Aaron, whom I had worked with for many years, had been battling cancer for several years. He had passed away and is now with Jesus. My heart had been very heavy for this loss. However, his family and the Chief requested we honor him in the proper way we should. I would have done anything to accommodate that request for Aaron. The request was to assist the Kentucky State Police Honor Guard with the funeral detail. I was in charge of getting the Honor Guard squared away at the charge for the Richmond Police Department, making sure they had the supplies they needed, were fed, and changed out with KSP so the Troopers and Officers did not become exhausted for the visitation and the funeral. The visitation was on April 24, 2022, in the evening. The funeral was on Monday, April 25, 2022, during the day.

I remember the night before and all the many people I knew coming to the Visitation for Aaron. I still feel selfish for saying this, but pure exhaustion from stress and work had finally set in. I remember the weight of the gun belt around my waist. After the visitation, I went home and hung out with my wife and daughters. The next day, I went to work like any other day. It was Monday, April 25.

While the Chief of Police was giving a great eulogy for Aaron, I listened as the Chief spoke of memories that made me happy, and I could just see Aaron smiling and telling stories like he was right there beside us again. I couldn't believe he was gone. I never expected what would happen next.

I had been feeling funny the last day or so, more tired than usual. I guess it really doesn't matter how I say this now since Worker's Compensation didn't cover anything from the incident. The city was wonderful to me. Them? Not so much. During Aaron's funeral, while the Chief was speaking, I started to feel weird. I really can't explain it any other way. I felt the left side of my face go numb. My left eye began to lose vision and become blurry. I knew at that moment what was happening. I was having a stroke. The left side of my body started seizing and twitching as I began to have seizures. I had six seizures during the time the Chief was speaking. I was sitting in the middle of the pew with people around me. I remember an entire pew of Kentucky State Troopers behind me that I thought would see me during this time. I must have hidden it well because I had to sit on my left arm because my body was trying to raise it like I was asking a question in school. This happened at least six times during the course of the funeral.

I knew when the onset of an episode was coming because my vision would become blurry, and my left eye would start shifting focus all over the place. Within a few seconds, my body would start seizing and convulsing, and there was nothing I could do about it except ride it out. I was completely helpless. I remember my wife being at work in another town and not being able to be there. It was right in the middle of the funeral, and the only person I wanted to talk to was her. I started praying immediately about my body and for Jesus to just get me through whatever this was, although I suspected I knew.

When I was in college, I took several years of psychology and picked up a minor from all those courses. During this time, I remembered that the right hemisphere of the brain controls the left side of the body. The left hemisphere controls the right side of the body. My seizures were happening on the left side of my body, and that is where my vision was going blurry. For almost twenty years, I had been certified in CPR, and I remembered from those short courses we always had to take the symptoms of a stroke. I was having a stroke.

As I had prayed, my symptoms subsided, for a time at least. The funeral ended, and, like many of the other police funerals I had attended, all the Officers lined up outside the church to pay our respects. I stood up in formation at the back in case I had another episode, and I did. While I was in formation, my vision blurred, and my arm started to seize up again. I fought through it, and as we were all getting into our vehicles, I told my immediate

Supervisor, the Assistant Chief, "I need to go to the hospital to get checked out." He asked me if I was okay. I told him, "I don't know."

So, right or wrong decision, I got in my unmarked Chevrolet Tahoe cruiser and tried to leave the parking lot to drive to the hospital. Here was the issue. I got caught in the processional. I would not *ever* get out of a procession for my dear friend, so I drove around town, and I mean all around town, until we reached the front gate to the cemetery. When everyone else turned into the gate, I went straight on to the hospital.

Now, to paint this picture for you, when I arrived at the hospital waiting room, I was in full uniform, and the entire emergency room was full of people waiting to be seen. I asked the front desk staff if I could speak with them privately so I didn't have to let everyone and their brother hear my business. They brought me back, and I explained what I had going on. The charge nurse just happened to be passing by and heard me speaking. She grabbed the PA in the hallway who was nearby, who shook his head firmly and said, "Uh-uh. No! Bed 16! Right now. Check him in!"

They tried to usher me back to the ER rooms, but I explained I still had to take off my weapon since I knew they were going to have me admitted in a robe. I couldn't very well run around with a hospital gown on and nothing else with my gun belt. So, the PA escorted me to my cruiser, and I secured it in my weapon vault, and back into the hospital I went! Bed 16 it was!

I still chuckle to this day, thinking back on getting into trouble with the hospital staff for driving myself to the hospital. Before you go judging me if you are reading this, I was not having an episode at the time, and I would pay for that when the doctors found out. They got really mad at me for that. Also, at the time, I had been a cop for nineteen years, so I did not know there was a law about seizures specifically. If you have a seizure, you are automatically not allowed to drive for three months. I didn't find that out until later on that night when I spoke with a neurologist via Zoom after all my testing.

I notified my wife, and so began all the IVs and testing. My wife and my oldest daughter all came to the hospital while they were doing testing, as I had not been officially admitted yet. That was forthcoming, though. They all watched as I had seizure after seizure until my wife went out in the hallway and not-so-gently told someone to give me something for this so it did not continue to happen. It had gone on for long enough, and they could have done something about it. Since they started that medication, I have only had one seizure since April 25, 2022.

After this, they began running test after test...after test on me. I hope you can sense the aggravation as I dragged out that statement. They could not find anything wrong with me at first. Then, we did a CT Scan. I kept a positive attitude with the staff, some of whom I knew from working in town on patrol. I made jokes and light of the situation and wasn't worried about anything.

I was feeling fine, being stubborn as always, and ready to go home. I had a promotion interview coming up on Monday of the following week. I was ready to get back to work. My wife put me in my place (where I should have been put) so I would sit still and we could figure out what was going on with my body). The emergency room doctor comes back in the room after an hour or so and tells me in front of my wife and my daughter this..."We have found a mass on your brain. We are going to have to run some more tests."

Now listen, I really am trying to be like Jesus here, but in that moment and the bedside manner that was just delivered in front of my family, I did not feel like *acting* like Jesus. If I am being very candid about things, I was thinking I wanted to go *Fight Club* on him and not talk about Fight Club. Why would you say it like that in front of my family?! My wife and daughter started crying, and even I teared up.

It then became real and stopped being funny anymore, and I was not light-spirited. I realized I had needles in my arms, had my brain scanned, and was cold in a hospital bed with my family around me crying.

I was mad. I was confused. I was helpless. I had nothing to do but what I should have been doing all this time: pray and turn to Jesus.

I was admitted to the hospital that night, and no one was allowed to stay with me. I had to FaceTime with my youngest daughter, and she immediately started crying because she saw me in a hospital bed and gown. She was so upset and scared she hung up on me when I told her I had to spend the night in the hospital. She didn't understand what was going on and why Daddy wasn't coming home.

I remember FaceTiming the Assistant Chief, which I had never done before, nor since that time. He answered from his kitchen table, and his wife was behind him in the background. I remember him asking, "Why are you FaceTiming me from a hospital bed in a gown?"

My response was jovial as best I could when I said, "Do you want the good news or the bad news?" His response was as I expected. "Is there any good news?" I laughed at him and told him the good news was I was still with him and that God saved me to annoy people a little longer. Then, I went on to tell him I had a stroke from a brain bleed that caused multiple seizures during the funeral of our friend. The color drained from his face on the phone as we talked about it, and he was shocked since he was about a year younger than me.

The night was difficult for me and my family as we awaited the results of whatever was going on. I was forced to stay in the hospital that night alone since they would not allow anyone to stay. We were coming out of the COVID-19 pandemic, and there were still weird policies in place, whether or not they made sense being a whole different matter. My wife didn't sleep much that night because she was worried about me. I did not sleep much that night because of the stupid monitors that kept going off every time my heart rate would go down to resting heart rate. I had such a good heart rate that when I fell asleep, the machine would start going crazy because it was set at a certain level for the heart rate. They would come racing into the room after freaking out and wake me up again by making a bunch of noise and checking all my vitals. It was ridiculous after a while. I didn't sleep hardly any. I finally just asked them to turn off the sound in my room and they could watch it from the nurse's station in the hallway so I could get a little bit of sleep. They agreed. That didn't last long. Shift change was at 0600 hours, and it was right back to waking me up again.

My rest was short-lived the next morning when construction began in the room next door to me. My brain was pounding, and looking back now, it is quite comical. My wife not-so-gently finally asked them to stop drilling and pounding in the room next door to me or have me moved to another location due to the major headaches I had from the episodes. Shortly after this, the construction crew took an extended lunch break. When they returned, it was only short bursts of the drill as quietly as they could do it. Again, it's quite entertaining looking back on the whole situation.

The day was filled with lots more testing, like CT Scans and MRIs, to find out what in the world was going on in my brain. During the MRIs, I became acquainted with the techs and one specific person in general. Dave ran my MRI tests several times. If you are not familiar with an MRI machine, they put you in this big, giant, magnetic tube, and it makes a lot of noise and has lots of lights. Then, they give you headphones and let you listen to music. The first time I listened to classical and fell asleep. It was a great nap. The second one, they woke me up, put some stuff in my IV, and told me it was going to feel like I had peed myself (which I didn't) and I should probably try to stay awake.

For this one, I chose country music as a different genre. The contrast went into my IV. I did feel like I was about to pee myself, and the song "Fancy Like" came on the radio in my headphones. "Got me fancy like Applebees on a date night…" I was jammin'. This was the song made famous on TikTok, and then Applebees took it and made it into a commercial. I loved it! Dave told me I was moving my foot and I had to sit still. If there is a favorite memory from the whole hospital encounter, that was probably it. I still laugh about that to this day. And if you know that song, you're welcome. Now you will be singing it all day.

A calcified cavernoma is what I was told I had. I didn't want to accept it, but it is what it is. That was my diagnosis. The city of Richmond was wonderful to me, even though I had to be put off work for a period of time. Worker's Compensation denied my claims, stating it could have been congenital. My wife was my rock during this time. She drove me around and took care of me. My children stepped up to take care of me. My mom and some of my other family took care of me. My LifeGroup from church took care of me, driving me places and even mowing our yard when I was not allowed to. Other people took care of me. This is something I was not used to at all.

I was not allowed to work for quite a while, and we kept it pretty quiet overall about what happened to me, so I had the chance to heal and be left alone. This was fine at first and made sense, but this was a hard transition for me. I went from being someone who goes after it every single day to being forced to stay at home, and I basically felt like a prisoner in my own home. Now, mind you, this is not the case. I could have called anyone, and they would have come and gotten me to take me places, but I felt less than a father and a husband at this point because even though the money had not stopped due to my insurance and sick time, I felt like I was not providing as I should be because my wife was the one at work while I was sitting at home. This was not what I wanted. Depression set in within my own mind. It began to work on me in the silence. This was not, however, what God had for me at the time. He rescued me.

I have read over Psalm chapter 23 so many times I cannot even count. Next to John 3:16, it is probably one of the more well-known sets of Bible verses in the entire Bible. How had I missed this thus far? So many people had been telling me to slow down in my life. I would not listen. My wife, especially, and repeatedly. Finally, on April 25, 2022, God got my attention.

Psalm 23:2–3 says, "He *makes* me lie down in green pastures. He leads me beside still waters. He restores my soul. He leads me in paths of righteousness for his name's same."

I hadn't been listening. Not for a long time. God is always calling us to draw closer to Him. He is leading you into places of solitude and will feed you on His word and His love if we will just listen to the *still* voice of the Holy Spirit. I have never had God shout at me. I have only had Him redirect my paths when I was messing things up. God will always chase you. He will just chase you gently. That day changed my outlook on life. I realized my own mortality. I want to work toward saving the lives of others from my experience and drawing them closer to Jesus because of what I went through.

This was not the end of my battle, of course. I had a lot to come back from, most of which I did to myself emotionally and mentally and allowed to happen to me spiritually. I did not stand on the promises of God at first like I should have. I was put off work for several months, with my wife and children having to drive me around. Others from my LifeGroup at church stepped up and brought us meals and continued to pray for us, and the men even mowed my yard.

As grateful as I am to those people closest to me, I must admit this was very difficult for me. I am not built to let people wait on me and take care of me. I absolutely and utterly hated it. I hated to have to ask my friends when I needed help mowing my yard. I was so high on medicine they gave me for my brain and the seizures I couldn't operate my own mower. Couple this with the fact that legally, I was not allowed to due to having a seizure. It became frustrating, I know, for my wife and children because I became irritable and aggravated frequently and often. I felt like I had lost my purpose.

God never stopped working on my heart. He kept speaking to me in the quiet of my house, which was empty, all but myself and our pets. My wife and children returned to work and school, and I remember the dogs and cats being the only ones in the house with me. Again, God used others to keep working on me because I went to a dark place for a period of time. I never became suicidal, but I felt everything had been taken from me since I had been forced to stay home from what had been my calling for nineteen years at the time. God kept using our LifeGroup men to come pick me up and take me to the grocery to get me out of the house. My barber would come to the house and pick me up to get my haircut or cut it right there at the house. These are the things I have not forgotten. This was God's mercy being shown through others on me in my time of need.

I eventually gave in to the realization I would be home for some time and started to find some acceptance. I didn't really do anything productive, though. I played PlayStation some. I slept. I read when I felt like it. I cleaned the house some, but not nearly like I should have to help my wife. It was during this time God began speaking to me the most. Enough was enough.

Vacation Brought Motivation

We had gone on vacation during the time I was off from the stroke. We went to my niece's wedding and then left that next morning to drive to Florida to go to Disney World for a week. Someone in our church had blessed us with a VIP service on one of the days. It was fantastic. The guide was very knowledgeable, and he took us everywhere we wanted to go. The problem was, many of the things we could all now go on together since both the girls were old enough and tall enough, but now I could not.

Sure, there were lots of rides we could ride on together. This was Disney World! But, anything similar to a roller coaster, nope. Not happening. I will never forget sitting in the middle of the loading area, waiting for the girls to get off the ride Guardians of the Galaxy, and hearing them say it was one of the best roller coasters they had ever been on, if not *the* best. I had been told it probably wasn't a good idea to ride it due to all the strobes, loud music, and jarring of the ride. I had sat there by myself, pouting for lack of better terms. It had really hurt me. Now, since I want to be honest about this whole experience, I became a real jerk. I was processing so many emotions, and I really didn't know how to do so. So, to my wife and daughters, when you read this, I am sorry. I know we have discussed it before, but I felt like it needed to be said. This was a really difficult time for me, and I was being selfish when God gave me a second chance.

We spent a few more days at Disney World throughout the various parks, and I wasn't awful all the time. We did have fun. I just didn't do as well at keeping up as I normally would. We slowed the pace down a great deal when we went to the beach for a few days. That was nice. I was really glad to take the girls to a new place they had never been. The ocean always does something magical for me. It allows me to let go.

That is what I had to do. I had to let go and let God do whatever He wanted to do in my life. I remember asking in prayer during this time that if God would allow me to retire on my own with my time and get full benefits for my family, I would do it as soon as possible. That is exactly what is going to happen when I retire on August 1, 2023. Praise God.

RETURN TO WORK

As Support Services Commander at the time I was put off work and the rank of Lieutenant, we had to cancel the Major promotion interviews because of my illness. I returned to work when they honestly didn't have to let me. I had two Supervisors, the Assistant Chief of Police, and the Chief of Police. They continued to check on me, and I asked them repeatedly to let me work from home and was denied. They wanted me to rest. Finally, after several months, they and the city of Richmond allowed me to come back to work on modified duty. I was still not allowed to drive, so my wife, my oldest daughter, and even my Detectives picked me up at home and took me to work. This would not have been possible without them. I am so grateful and blessed.

If I am being real about all this, for a while, I did not accomplish a lot, at least in my mind and likely in my department. I did paperwork and probably got in the way more than anything because I was not allowed to be out on the street or on calls. I know I was slow in reacting to anything due to my medicine, and I know I was frustrating to those around me. But I was starting to get my purpose back. Serving. Helping others. There was a lot of patience and grace others showed me during this time. They could have given up on me.

I finally had the Major promotion interview that had been postponed due to my illness. There were several great candidates interviewed who had also waited long enough, and I told them I was ready to do the interview, whether on modified duty or not. I was blessed to be one of those selected to Major, and I was promoted not long after. I was pinned by my daughters at the City Commission Meeting.

I cannot lie to you; the struggles during that time seemed like God had abandoned me at times, but He was preparing me for other things. I had lost a lot of weight due to my depression and the medication curbing my appetite. People would tell me I looked sick, as if I didn't already know this. People told me I should eat more to keep me healthy. I have always had an *extremely* high metabolism, and the weight just fell off me. I didn't have it to lose at five feet eight and 135 pounds. Total weight lost during that time was twenty pounds. So, I got down to one hundred and fifteen pounds. I finally had to admit it: I was sick. This was not good for me. I had mentally and physically tried to be strong my entire career. People told me over and over and over: "You should eat." "You look thin." "Don't you ever eat?" People I don't even know! Mind your own business. Did you know my brain medication causes weight loss? Did you think men can be body-shamed like women can? Do you think your comments help me?

I finally hired a trainer/nutritionist to start getting me back to at least my former self. I had a consultation with him after I was allowed to drive again. I thought I would be allowed to go in and start working out immediately. This was not the case. I was not even allowed to touch the weights until I got my nutrition under control and started eating correctly again. It was basically double portions, if you will, because I had to get the macro-nutrients down before I could do anything. When we did begin working out, I must say this: we worked. We alternate between strength week and hypertrophy week. I am happy to say that well over a year and a half later, after finishing writing the book, from beginning my training, I am stronger and eating better at least. There is still work to do, but the improvement is there.

A Lot to Be Thankful For, and People Who Have Gotten Me There

I guess to wrap this up, I want to do two things. First, I want to go through the lessons I have learned in this process and when God made me stop and change my course. I have many more lessons to learn, but here are just a few I have studied repeatedly since April 25, 2022, and some highlights and learning points.

"One day" or "Day one"? You decide. You must learn to decide whether or not this is just one day in your life or the first day of a journey God has you on. How you handle a situation is up to you and you alone. You have to decide what you are going to do. "Life is 10 percent what happens to you and 90 percent how you react to it" (Charles R. Swindoll).

We are all a little or a lot broken. But last I checked, broken crayons still color the same as whole crayons. I have no idea where I read this or heard this, but I put it in my journal because it captured my heart and mind in a way that made me think about my circumstances and the fact if I'm not dead, then God is not done with me.

The quieter you become, the more you hear. This is very difficult for me. Anyone who knows me knows this. When I had to stay home and couldn't leave or go anywhere, or I was laying in a hospital bed, I started to listen to what God was telling me and had been trying to tell me quietly for a long time.

You will become what you constantly think about and say. Watch yourself. This one stings a bit for me. I had to get out of the pit and stop whining and pitying myself for God to work in my life. He has a plan for me and for my family. I need to listen and stop trying to be something I am not. I also had to learn how to use God's word to uplift my heart and how to bring me closer to Him.

"As thy days are, so shall thy strength be" (Deuteronomy 26:25). No matter how tough your battle is, God will give you enough strength to get through it. He will give you provisions for your purpose.

"Whenever God means to make a man great, He always breaks him in pieces first" (Charles Spurgeon). The teacher is always silent during the test. We are tested throughout life. This is where faith comes into play.

In life, you are always going into a storm, through a storm, or coming out of a storm. How are you going to handle that? I had a lot of time to think about this. I tried. I failed. I fell. Others picked me up. I intend to do the same for them when they are in need. We are all just navigating through storms.

I don't care who is doing better than me. I am doing better than I was last year. It is me vs. me! If there is one thing I have learned throughout the recovery, it is to stop trying to compare myself to others. We live in a world of comparison that is based on the lies from social media and the small sliver of people's lives we see. This is still a struggle for me. I will never be the biggest guy, strongest, best looking, smartest, on and on and on. However, from every Bible story I have ever read, God has used broken people who no one would ever expect to be used to win souls to the kingdom of heaven. Imperfect people. God has given me another chance at life. He has given me a family and opportunities others could only dream about. I have work to do for Him. It is me vs. the former me.

Final lesson from the year: Those who check on you when you get quiet, those are your people. You should cherish that and keep them close. This is not meant to make anyone feel any certain way. This is something I learned after April 25, 2022. Those people who check on you, take care of you, reach out to you, stay in touch with you, those are the people who have taken time to do so. This means you meant enough to them for them to reach out and check on you, if not more. These are your people. These are the people whom God has placed in your life to be your circle. Cherish this.

A List Incomplete

There are so many people who helped me to get back to at least my normal, ambitious self. To those people, you know who you are. I have learned valuable lessons from you I will cherish forever. Those closest to me in my time of need and those who cared for me and even took care of my family, words will never be enough to say thank you for all you have done in our lives and for being such a blessing to me. I am so blessed every day to be able to still have opportunities to help others because others helped me.

If I am not dead, God is not done with me.

The First Great Ride: The Comeback

On 06/30/23, which was our youngest daughter's twelfth birthday, my wife and I took off work with her and met some friends at King's Island in Ohio. We got up there in the heat of the day, and it was definitely hot outside. It was our daughter's first time there, and we met up with our friends. The famous Eiffel Tower replica greets you with the fountain pool as you enter the park. The majority of my day was spent in Snoopyland (or whatever you call it).

However, that was not all that I did. I wanted...no, I *needed* to get on a real roller coaster and ride. My wife and I discussed it. We both share a love for a certain roller coaster at Kings Island. This coaster is one of reputation. It is one with fantastic extremes. The cars look like a snake.

The Diamondback Roller Coaster has ranked one of the top roller coasters in the world since it opened in 2009. The coaster ride is only two minutes long, does not go upside down, and is an overall smooth ride. However, it stands 230 feet in height at its peak and drops at a 74-degree angle with speeds up to 80 mph. It has over 5000 feet of track and around ten drops with a tail that drags the water to slow it to a stop at the final drop! This roller coaster is legit, and it is one of our favorites.

After the stroke and seizures, I was determined to live life and fly high again. We did. My wife, her friend, and I rode Diamondback, and we all made faces in the camera as we came around the corner and posed. I didn't really ride much else in regards to roller coasters that day, but I rode Diamondback. I was previously told—after the stroke—I couldn't ride roller coasters anymore. I had sat out at Disney World on some great rides. Not this day.

To some, this might not be a big deal since it is just a roller coaster, but if you have ridden Diamondback, you know what I am talking about. Ride a roller coaster after being told I couldn't ever do it again and then being cleared by the doctors to do it. Check! Diamondback...beaten. The comeback...It felt great!

—∞—

Learning When to Keep Your Mouth Shut

(Walking the Line of Duty and Being a Member of a Prominent Community Church)

I have worked a lot of cases. Or, I have been a Supervisor over a lot of cases when they were worked and know a lot about the details of cases. That, in itself, is a big thing to have to process and to have to know when you can or can't say anything. The first question anyone ever asked when they saw me out in public most of the time wasn't "How is your family?" or "How are you?" It was "What happened over on such and such street the other night?" You get the picture anyway. It drove me crazy sometimes. It was always asked out of innocence, but more times than not, I can't answer anything about the case.

Here is the problem. I worked in the schools, was heavily involved in community relations, spoke to thousands of kids and members of the community, and I am a member of a prominent community church. Not that all churches are not prominent and important, but this is a big church with lots of people. Lots of people have lots of chances to have questions. Sometimes, the world of the church collides with the world of policing.

When we respond to a call, it is often the worst situation in people's lives. I have worked murders, hostage stand-offs, suicides, robberies, sexual assaults, the list goes on and on. The church is supposed to welcome all people without judgment. We do a terrible job at that, by the way, overall in society. Sometimes, the people who ask questions are only curious about what happened or "knew" the people and thought they were good people. What if they weren't good people? I can't say anything.

Sometimes, it is the victims who go to the church whom I recognize, and they are in shame and are trying to hide their situation from everyone. It could have been a domestic violence incident or a sexual assault, or maybe I just saw them at a death scene of their loved one. Either way, I usually get eye contact with a quick look-away motion, as if I didn't just recognize them. I understand, though.

Or perhaps, sometimes, it is the suspect themselves. Yesterday, I had them in a police station interview room for two hours, trying to get a confession for a crime I *know* they committed, and I am just waiting for the evidence to come back from the lab. Then, they lawyer up and refuse to speak to me anymore when I make them uncomfortable and sweat. Today, they are lighting the candles for the Easter service and see me, wishing they hadn't. They know, and I know, but neither of us can say anything.

Knowing the dark secrets of someone's life and not being able to say anything about it is a heavy burden to bear. We are all imperfect people, sure, but having to listen to someone talk about how great a suspect is as a person when you know they would harm children or beat their wife is too much. I have gone to funerals when people talk about how great someone was, knowing in my heart they were not a good person or had a lot of secrets that should not come to light. It would change the trajectory of people's mindset of those people forever. I stay silent.

It is a fine line to walk as a Christian and very difficult not to be judgmental or have a jaded view of society when you know so much about so many people. As a church, we are supposed to love one another. How do you show love to someone you have to send to prison? Just a thought. Just a question I pose to you.

When One Door Closes…Retirement

When I was recruited to the Kentucky Police Corps, the way I was recruited was based upon a scholarship, a full-time job in policing with a four-year contract straight out of college, and a promise my family (even though I didn't have a wife and children at the time) would be taken care of regarding health insurance. Regarding my wife and I, it was promised it would be for life. We received no benefits during the academy other than the scholarship and a wage during the academy, and it would not be applied to our pensions. This was fine at the time of the contract. The problem came later.

When the financial crisis hit the United States around 2008, the legislation in the Commonwealth of Kentucky changed the pension laws and rules regarding the insurance and tier systems for retirement. I don't fault the politicians for trying to fix issues, but we all know there are funds allocated for stupid reasons at every level of government. Now, instead of receiving benefits for my family like I was promised, it would now have cost me somewhere in the realm of $1,500 per month. This was a major hit needed to be overcome and was not what we were promised by the Kentucky Police Corps. To put this in perspective, there were only about twenty Officers out of the entire Commonwealth of Kentucky this affected.

To my fellow Police Corps people, you all are the ones who helped pull off the changes. For several years, there was much work to do at the Capitol in order to get the benefits we were promised. During this time, since around 2009, we continued to work our careers. Work was done in Frankfort with the retirement people, politicians, and the financial powers-that-be.

On April 25, 2022, when I had the stroke and was put off medically, the real challenge and clock tick came to me. My comrades still worked, and I still talked to people I knew in Frankfort. Now, I had to start considering disability, which would have only been around 66 percent of my income. That was not going to cut it for my family! We talked to everyone we could about the situation, and thankfully, my Police Corps friends found the right people to talk to. After several years of working on the retirement benefits, we were grandfathered into the old system as we were promised.

While this was all going on, I had been stuck at home being taken care of by my wife and our LifeGroup at church. I was receiving rides for grocery trips and any little things we had to get done. My wife took the brunt of all the driving while I felt helpless. When they finally let me go back to work on modified duty to keep the income going, my Detectives picked me up and took me places, then even brought me home. For that, I am eternally grateful.

Also, during the time I was off work, I had some really major and depressing conversations with God about my future because all I could focus on was the now. I made God and my wife a promise during that time. I promised them if I could get back to full duty, get the benefits for my girls, and the health insurance covered, I would walk away from the career of policing.

God honored His part of my request. I honored my promise to Him and my wife. After all my colleagues worked so hard to accomplish the task, we *finally* got word from the retirement people. Our families would be taken care of with health insurance! Praise God! Once it was official and I had documentation on my account for the retirement system, and it was backed up by more than just promises, I typed the memorandum.

I closed the door to my office and got to work on the memo, and I didn't tell anyone what I was doing. That night, I showed the letter to my wife to make sure it was okay. I really needed that support, and she gave it so willingly. The following day, I turned in my memorandum to both the Chief and the Assistant Chief since they were the only Supervisors I had now throughout the entire agency. We had our conversations, and they were very gracious, saying they and the city hated to lose me. After that, I went back to my office, closed the door, and waited for the flood of emotions. I didn't have to wait long.

I let them know months in advance before I retired, and it was business as usual for a long time. After coming back to full duty, I was getting hit with more and more work and stress every single day. The longer this went on and the closer I got to retirement, the more I felt strongly about my decision.

Eventually, we all need to do it. I didn't know what God had planned for me, but I knew I needed to trust Him. My realization of just how real it was about to be for me came on July 12, 2023, at 07:49 in the morning while making a deposit at the ATM. I waited as the machine whirred inside, and I saw my reflection on the screen and in the mirror. I was wearing my Class A uniform, and it hit me. I would not be wearing it for much longer. I would have to turn it all back in, and I wouldn't be the police anymore. It made me sad at the time, in all honesty. This was all I had known for twenty years. It wasn't when I started receiving the retirement benefits notices and letters in the mail. It was that exact moment at the ATM when the weight of realization dropped on me.

Not surprisingly, God interceded for me. On the roof, as I was walking away, I heard a bird flapping and making sounds. I looked back over my shoulder to see it briefly, and it was a dove, just looking down on me. The bird of peace. A few seconds later, I heard the sounds of my people and all the sirens in an area nearby. No matter, my sadness was gone. I had the answer I needed.

The closer the date got to July 31, 2023, the more I had to pass off duties to my successor. I didn't want to. I had to for the good of the team so we didn't miss a stride. In policing, the machine keeps moving no matter what happens. I turned my office over to him on Friday, July 28, 2023. A lot of stuff had happened the week before I retired, and the Chief and Assistant Chief told me not to get into anything else major so I wouldn't have to deal with the court later on.

This is after we started the week with two separate search warrants in one morning on two separate suspects for different cases in two different locations. Coordinated planning and OPS plans were drawn up, and we hit the apartments one after another. Then, once the scenes were safe, Detectives worked the search warrants for each separate location. This was one morning.

During the week prior to giving up my office, we had the two search warrants, and my Detectives responded to all of the following: a rape of a juvenile, a kidnapping of a juvenile, a shooting, and a suicide. This was all before Friday. On Friday afternoon, I drove my cruiser home for the last time and, over the weekend, collected the remainder of my gear to turn in on Monday for my last day. My retirement would officially start on Tuesday, August 1, 2023.

On that Saturday night, just a little after 10 p.m., I started getting texts on my phone. The first text was an alert requesting a drone pilot, which, up until the day before, I had been in charge of the unit. The request was for a homicide suspect. The next text came a minute or two later and was from the group text of the Command Staff, which included the Chief and Assistant Chief, the other two Majors, and me, the Major of Support Services. Support Services Division included the Detectives. I got a text right after those from the group chat of the Detectives. There had been a double homicide.

My wife looked at me and saw I had a concerned facial expression and asked me what was going on. I told her we had a double homicide, and it was going to be a full Criminal Investigations Unit callout. Apparently, I had the look on my face next that said I was about to suit up and go out.

My wife looked at me and said, "Oh no, you are not going out to look for a murder suspect the weekend before you retire. You turned in most of your stuff and turned your office over yesterday, and you are done with policing on Monday."

I looked at her with puppy dog eyes and said, "But my team may need me." She was unphased by this. She responded with, "You built the team, and they are a great team, but you are going to have to let this go now. Besides, you were told not to go out and get into anything. Now lay down, watch TV like you were, and then go to sleep."

I chuckled a little bit but agreed. I did what I needed to. I wanted to go, but she was right. This could have gone on and on. The Assistant Chief and the Chief who ordered me not to go out on anything big were right. I would *always* want to go out to the next big call or scene. I would always want to be there for my people, even if I was just standing there holding a clipboard and taking notes. I would be there in body and spirit for them. That was the important part of being a leader in this unit. As it turns out, the suspect was caught before the next morning. They didn't need me at all, which is the way it should be. My agency is awesome!

My wife was also right about the fact that we had finally put together a great team under the Support Services Division. Two very strong Sergeants who didn't need me other than to support them and their people, good Detectives, Street Crimes/Bike Patrol Officers, Narcotics Detectives, Federal Task Force Officers, Evidence Technicians, Licensed Drone Pilots, and Firearms Instructors; it was a lot under this one umbrella. Most of them were involved in specialized units like the Emergency Response Unit (our name for SWAT Team), firearms instructors, or the Collision Reconstruction Unit.

It truly was one of the best jobs (and definitely *the* most stressful) of my career. Every single one of them has a different personality and different specialty in their fields. They drove me insane, it seemed, at times, but at the end of my career, they were definitely the team I had been trying to put together for several years. One of my favorite things we did was argue over the law when there were cases or when we had to charge someone with a crime. This seems frivolous, but I love the law. It changed over the years, and when we argued about it, we made sure someone was charged with the right charge or crime as a group effort. We argued with anyone who came into the conversation about it: Officers, Supervisors, Lieutenants, Majors, the Assistant Chief, and the Chief. The point of it was to do what was right by the laws, not what we *thought* was right. It is one of the things I miss the most.

They were *rockstars* at what they did! After several years of trying to get the team the way I envisioned it, working with multiple personnel changes, and restructuring the agency to fit the Support Services Division, the team was finally assembled. Now, it was time to pass it on to my successor. That was the hard part. We had worked so hard to get the team to be what it was. Now, I needed to move on. I figured out at the end of my career that you cannot have success as a leader unless you have a successor.

July 31, 2023, was my last day as a Police Officer. I came into work early and sat in the silence in the office for a bit before everyone got there. Then, I left the room to go start gathering my gear to turn in. When I returned later on, the Detective Sergeant was going over the good, the bad, and what needed to be done next for the double homicide over the weekend. There was a lot to do still. When I walked into the room as he was talking, he yelled at me for not being there. I looked at him and smiled knowingly. After I listened to what had occurred over the weekend and took an earful from my Detective Sergeant about how I should have been there (he knew I couldn't be but wanted to give me a hard time anyway), I took the remainder of the morning and turned in all my gear. My wife picked me up around lunchtime, and we had already had a small going-away lunch on the previous Friday. There was nothing left to do. I was sitting on the back bench waiting for my wife with one small box of items left out of an entire twenty years.

I walked out to the car when she picked me up, and I was good at that point mentally. Then, my wife and I saw almost the entire unit following me out to the car to say goodbye. They all hugged me, wished me well (some of them in their own weird ways), and my Sergeant said, "This is not goodbye. It is 'See you later.'" I got in the car, and the emotion fell on me, knowing that was it. She was so supportive and told me how proud she was of me that I had accomplished this feat.

Since retirement, I have been learning to operate at a new level of life. Vacations and doing what I want. Life has less stress on me overall, or at least different stress from policing. Life has slowed down, and overall, I can do things a bit slower. This was a good change for me since all I did was run 1000 mph in my life. I have enjoyed the quiet, the still, the rest.

I had a meeting at our church with a good friend of mine who is a youth pastor within the first month of retirement. He is someone we have worked with closely through the church with the middle and high-school-age kids. He was checking in on me in this new season of life. We always have such great conversations.

He asked me a question, as he often does. He asked me in the conversation if I was grieving my job. I didn't really understand at first what he meant. I knew about my retirement, and my wife and I planned it together regarding the finances and the timing. I told him "no" at first regarding the grieving the job.

Now, as I finish this chapter, I guess I am grieving. I am not grieving the job, per se. I have played my role, and God has something else for me. I guess I am grieving all the victims I have seen, both alive and in death, for the last twenty years.

So, to be completely transparent, I am grieving. It is just different from the way someone would normally grieve for their loved one.

You Will Never Find That Perfect Bottle of Root Beer Again

Don't Stop Looking

This chapter is for all those characters along the way (and I have been taking notes) who have helped me to taste the nectar of what life can really be and how I can be a blessing to others. It is for those people who don't even know me, who let me hear their stories, laughed with me, and taught me how to turn off the world of policing and the save-the-world mentality, even if only for a little while. This chapter is for all of those individuals who were nice to my family and my friends as we were just the "next group of tourists" and how you kept contact with me and taught me how to slow down in life... we are on Island Time now.

There have been so many books written about pirates, the ocean, and times long forgotten on the sea. Whether it has been Ernest Hemingway's *The Old Man and the Sea* or even Jimmy Buffett's *A Salty Piece of Land*, there is without question some magic that is held in the ever-changing waters.

Sunken treasure, soggy-dollar beach bars, Caribbean rum, and riding out the hurricanes are set to the rhythm of islands and long-lost places. To this day, I still stop long enough to listen to the ocean inside a conch shell at a department store somewhere, even if I am thousands of miles away from it. There is just something unexplainable about it.

It's the warm sand between your toes on a cool day. It's the waves crashing over you and taking you into the arms of the deep. It's the sound of seagulls on a deserted beach and seashells coming in with the tide. It's the sudden change in mood when you find that the ocean becomes a part of you.

This chapter goes out to anyone who has ever smelled the salt air, played in crystal blue waters, danced with a dolphin, or played in the sand. This is for anyone who has loved someone at sunset or let them go with the outgoing tide. This is for my wife, my children, my family, and friends who have watched the sunrises with me and swam in the deep waters. This is my spiritual healing. This is the memoir of my salt life.

The Healing Waters

As I sit here in silence, listening to the deafening sound of nothing but the clicking of the typing on the keyboard, I take a glance at my wall calendar and think back. The picture shows a palm tree hovering over the crystal blue waters of some faraway place as those waters kiss dove-white sands. That image alone is enough to take me back to those many, many times that I have splashed in waters up to my neck and then swam under the water as far as I could go to see the world below my feet. I have been so blessed in my life to be able to do that, and I want to recognize God's goodness to allow me to do so. The hundreds of fish that surrounded me, the jellyfish that were all around me, the spiny sea urchins below me. Something about all that mystery and danger has healing powers like you've never known unless you have experienced it. If you have been there like I have, you know that it can completely overwhelm you and then consume you, or it can melt away your heartache like a thief in the night.

The sounds of the crashing waves on the rocks and the taste of the saltwater on your tongue are enough to make you want to stay forevermore. I have gone to the ocean on a honeymoon. I have gone to the ocean with friends on random trips. I have slipped away from reality to heal from heartbreak. I have swam in the waters with crashing waves so cold my lips turned blue, and I couldn't even see my feet. I have swam and walked in the waters so clear they must be something from what I hope heaven will look like.

I have to admit it to you: I have been candid so far in this book, I might as well continue in the same manner now. I have not always been good to myself, and like most people, I have not always taken care of myself. I am certain stress had a major factor in that, but that is no excuse. As I have taken a lot of time reflecting on my life in writing this book, I have discovered I have never really appreciated the little things God gave me or the ways in which I have been so blessed.

I have passed by on valuable lessons I could have learned and missed the metaphorical big flashing sign God put right in front of my face. I have traveled a lot in comparison to some people but very little in comparison to others. Lately, as I have gotten older, I have tried to just take it all in. I have had the desire to learn from others and take in the experience.

I know it drives my girls crazy when we travel places because I will be talking to just about anyone about their life and learning and listening to what they have been through. It is innate in me, and I have found it is just who I am. If I cannot live the experience for myself, I have learned the lessons vicariously through others at times. It has created a respect for others and their situations that I brought home with me and used in policing or in my own life. I am so blessed. It has been a manner of perspective I never saw this entire time.

I have had the opportunity to hang out with billionaires on a ranch in Texas and Las Vegas through network marketing—thought they hung the moon and then realized they are people and humans, too. Once I got over the celebrity star-struck mentality, I learned a few things. Not only with the rich have I spoken, I have also sat and talked with the homeless in a park. I have told war stories with drunks in a bar, and I have met dozens of characters along the way who made a simple yet profound impact on my life.

In my policing career, as I am sure most Officers are like this, it is difficult to "turn it off." You can't. No matter how hard you try. Well, at least I couldn't. It led to stress, depression, health issues, arguments in my marriage and with my children that I started, and avoidance from others. I have finally figured out that I never really turned off the switch.

I know Officers who have worked, gone home, and stayed in their uniform, played "Call of Duty" until they fell asleep, then gotten up to do it all over again. I figured out this was not the way I wanted to live. This is not a dig at those Officers. I just found it was unhealthy for me. It was also the time when I was the furthest from God.

Over the years, I found it is better to just relax when you can. If you know me, you know that is easier said than done. There is no secret way to do it that I could reveal. You have to find that for yourself. For me, it has been spending time with my girls at home or on vacation. It has been taking my wife on dates. It has been fishing or spending time in God's creation. It is speaking in front of a thousand people and giving a message God has given me for teens to help save lives. It has been riding horses with the wind and sun on your face (that is another chapter in itself). It has been traveling as far throughout the world as I can go and meeting as many people as I can just to hear their stories. These are those times when I truly feel free.

For all the Officers I worked with over the years, you have been my family, too. But for my escape, it is not the bar scene for me anymore. It is not at work. It is finding peace in what God has called me to do: help people. Meet people. Witness to people.

We have been so blessed as a family and with our friends a few times to have the opportunity to spend time in the Caribbean. It is my happy place. The United States Virgin Islands is my go-to spot when someone says, "Where do you want to go?"

We drive on the wrong side of the road, and our ears pop from the height of the mountains and elevation in the islands. We take pictures like tourists, but we know our way around just a bit. We eat great seafood. We try our best to fit in with the locals (while still acting like tourists) in this melting pot of society that is a territory of the United States. If you ask me, given the vast history and richness in value of it, it should be considered a state in itself and a national treasure.

We have snorkeled coral reefs, swam with sea turtles, and drank from a coconut. We have also learned about the dark time in our history of pirates and slavery, and we have seen the poverty in a place considered part of our country in a sense. Hundreds of years have passed since that time, and yet our society has not learned much. The rich are still rich, the poor are still poor, and governments are corrupt.

We have eaten at fancy restaurants no longer there because they were destroyed by hurricanes, and we have eaten in restaurants while homeless men slept on the ground less than fifty yards from us. It has been eye-opening, to say the least, and there are stories upon stories that could be a book in themselves. It even led me to witness and work with the homeless in my own community.

It has been an opportunity to teach my children to experience life. It has been an opportunity to teach my children to help others as my wife handed money to a homeless man as we walked into a McDonald's after going to the beach. Our lives have been so blessed, as many others have, and yet we take the little things for granted. I have taken things for granted. With all the work I have put in to make my family successful, it has felt like a hamster wheel at times. And yet, it has been my wife and children who have reminded me sometimes it is okay to give to others. God will give it back to us.

Over the years, as we have been to the islands, we have been on a boat called *Snorkel Cat* numerous times. Our friends have been with us when we went on a day snorkeling adventure. We have snorkeled next to Epstein Island (Little St. James), and we had gotten caught in a storm while on the boat when my friend had to wear a trash bag like it was a poncho (Sorry, Jared. I couldn't resist telling that). We have been stung by jellyfish and fire coral, stabbed by sea urchins, and seen the most beautiful waters.

My wife and I have taken sunset cruises over as a couple and even with our kids. There is nothing like being out on the water when they bring up the sails while playing the music from "Pirates of the Caribbean" to make you want to live that life all the time. And although the crews have changed over the years, I am so thankful to Captain Dave, Captain Danny-Boy, Dawn, Jessie, and the rest of their crew for taking care of us and letting us feel the wind in our faces and experience the sunsets of a lifetime.

To all of our friends and family who have traveled over the years with us, our salt and sea trips hold a place in my heart like nowhere else. To the laughs, the sunburns, and the adventures, you helped me to find the escape and rest I needed to discover who I am. For the Kenny Chesney concerts where the skies opened up and we sang in the rain, man, do we have some stories to tell!

Here's to all the characters and pirates we met along the way:

Thank you to the woman who took our family's picture at one of the gorgeous beaches on St. John just after my retirement in 2023. I don't know your name, but you told me you moved to the island fifty-four years ago against your father's wishes. You told your parents you would move back in two years if it didn't work out. You told me they ended up following you to the islands, and you even met your husband there. You even stayed after your husband passed away, and you felt like you had nothing left. Thank you for helping me to learn that sometimes we have to make a decision and make a leap of faith. That is where the trust is built. That is where our legacy is. Your laugh lines in your eyes and your life story in your move to paradise is definitely one to bring inspiration to anyone. I hope you continue to love those walks on the beach in the surf.

To the old drunk who I never knew your name in Charlotte Amalie, thank you for telling me your story and letting me listen as you gave your life advice. It may have taken some years for me to listen, but I think I am finally there now.

To Jelani, the lifeguard at Magens Bay on St. Thomas in 2023, your energy and hilarious nature are contagious. You spoke to my family so well, and I wish you well. I know you were joking, but you probably shouldn't tell tourists you can't swim if you are a lifeguard at the busiest beach on the island. Be blessed, my friend.

Deandre, thank you for sharing your story about your life in the British Virgin Islands on our long flight back to your home and our favorite vacation spot. I know you will do well in all that you do, and you will be successful. Keep up the marketing and the YouTube channel. You have a bright future.

To Jeremy "the Coconut Guy" next to Coki Beach, thank you for chopping up the coconuts for my family and me so we could experience just what it was like to drink from a coconut on the islands for real. I can't think of a better business model than what you had with coconuts in a cooler full of ice on the side of the road, selling to tourists like us right next to the beach. I'm still not sure about the chickens in cages in the trees over Water Bay. But hey, you helped teach me you can live simply yet feel so alive. Don't hurt yourself with that machete and keep on making people smile.

Finally, to my wife, thank you, my travel companion, for life and for being there for me to find that perfect bottle of Root Beer at St. John Brewers when we landed at Cruz Bay. We always go back and get it when we go there, and we have never found its replacement. We may never find that perfect bottle of root beer, but we won't stop looking...together. I don't want to do this adventure called life without you.

I guess, to be honest, this chapter doesn't have a lot to do with policing at all. It is not about the calls I have been on or the craziness I have dealt with. It is not about the emotions I have felt or the blood and gore we see all the time.

I think this chapter is meant just for me to tell you this has been my way of learning how to turn off the switch.

So, whether you are a person who goes all over the place to travel, stays at home to read alone in your house, or someone who goes out into the wilderness to find solitude, you have to be able to turn it all off. Turn off the noise, turn off the stress, turn off the pressure cooker you are in. In the world we live in today, we have become so focused on getting ahead or on what others are doing. Because of social media flooding our brains, we forget the little things.

Stop what you are doing, take a moment, and just breathe in the blessings God has put in your life. Find your happy place and don't forget to take lessons from the characters you meet along the way. Maybe they came into your path for a reason. And if you ever need a little bit of guidance or a roadmap, open up a Bible. It is the bestselling book of all time for a reason. This book can't even come close to that.

Safe travels, my friends.

Epilogue

How do you end a book about your life when your life isn't over yet? I kept praying when I retired, asking God what He wanted me to do. The only thing I got out of all that so far is "*Finish the book*." So, here we are. The end of the book. But this is not the end of my story or my family's or the end of your story.

As a matter of fact, there are a lot of other stories within the stories of my life I never told. It would be a never-ending story. I guess I still have unresolved issues within my own heart and family that should probably still be worked out. I still have unresolved trauma I am still dealing with and emotions I live with and struggle with every single day. Reality is struggle.

As long as God wakes me up every single day, He has given me the tools to face the day in His holy word. I decided I wanted to be someone who took a chance. I wrote the book. Maybe people made it this far to the end. Maybe they didn't. That doesn't mean I should not try to be a good person for them, no matter what.

My family deserves the best I can give them. They deserve to know they have someone who tried his hardest to be a good man who was worth reading about and, at the very least, had some great adventures. Nobody really wants to read the story about anyone who was given everything.

If you want to do something great, buckle up, get to work. Learn to listen and execute the directions people are giving you. Create good habits for the good of yourself and other people. Quite complaining about life, suck it up, and get tough. Get to work. That is the one-way ticket to your dreams.

God has given me the opportunity to finish this book when He didn't have to. It started over fifteen years ago. And, even though I am retired from policing, God is not through with me, and He has kept me protected all these years for a purpose I still do not fully understand. I am so blessed in the life I have, and I hope this book has blessed you in some way and drawn your heart closer to Jesus.

As for me, this has been a giant mirror turned on me and staring at my own reflection for the good and the bad. God kept giving me chance after chance. Epilogue? No, I don't believe so. God is just getting started with me! I am *Protected*.

"For he will command his angels concerning you to guard you in all your ways"

(Psalm 91:11)